PENGUIN BOOKS
SACRED SPACES

Yoginder Sikand did his M.Phil in sociology from the Jawaharlal Nehru University, New Delhi and his Ph.D in history from the University of London. Presently he is doing post-doctoral work on 'Islamic Perspectives on Inter-Faith Relations in Contemporary India' at the International Institute for the Study of Islam in the Modern World, Leiden, the Netherlands. He has written several articles on Islam and Muslims in contemporary India and his book on the Tablighi Jama'at was published earlier this year.

SACRED SPACES
Exploring Traditions of Shared Faith in India

YOGINDER SIKAND

PENGUIN BOOKS

An imprint of Penguin Random House

PENGUIN BOOKS

USA | Canada | UK | Ireland | Australia
New Zealand | India | South Africa | China | Singapore

Penguin Books is part of the Penguin Random House group of companies
whose addresses can be found at global.penguinrandomhouse.com

Published by Penguin Random House India Pvt. Ltd
4th Floor, Capital Tower 1, MG Road,
Gurugram 122 002, Haryana, India

First published by Penguin Books India 2003

Copyright © Yoginder Sikand 2003

10 9 8 7 6 5 4 3 2

ISBN 9780143029311

Typeset in Aldine401 BT by InoSoft Systems, New Delhi
Printed at Repro India Limited

www.penguin.co.in

This is a legitimate digitally printed version of the book and therefore might not
have certain extra finishing on the cover.

To
Mummy, for always being there,
and
Francis Robinson, for all that he has taught me
and
In the memory of all victims of theological terror in my
part of the world.

CONTENTS

ACKNOWLEDGEMENTS

I would never have embarked on this series of journeys had it not been for Dilip Simeon, who saddled me with the onerous responsibility of managing a research project on shared religious traditions as part of the ongoing Violence Mitigation and Amelioration Programme (VMAP) of Oxfam (India). This book is also a partial repayment of a great debt I owe to Francis Robinson. No one could have hoped for a more warm and understanding guide and mentor. Aparna Rao provided her critical comments, 'aunties' Shanta and Regina, and 'sisters' Nirmala and Surya, their bubbling presence, Mummy, her sage advice, cheerfully, at least most of the time, while putting up with long spells of absence and silence. To all of them, a big 'Thanks'. Sufis and sadhus and devotees at shrines, too numerous to be mentioned here, were generous with their time and patience. This book would hardly have been possible without their help. Finally, Kamini Mahadevan proved to be a wonderful editor, combing through email after email and gently coaxing me to finish on time.

Note on Transliteration

I have employed non-English words without following any rule of transliteration, and have spelt them as they are generally spelt in South Asia. The only exception is the Urdu/Persian/Arabic letter *ayn*, which I have indicated with an open single quotation mark (').

'Hinduism', 'Islam', 'Christianity' and 'Sikhism' or 'Hindu', 'Muslim', 'Christian' and 'Sikh', are, to my mind, constructed and contested labels, not monolithic and well-defined terms. They thus deserve to be put into inverted commas, although, barring in some places, I have resisted the temptation to do so in order to make for smoother reading.

INTRODUCTION

He shook his head in incomprehension, his topknot bobbing up and down like a yo-yo.

'You must be something . . . your name sounds Hindu, so Hindu you must be,' said the exasperated census-wala.

'It is meant to sound Sikh,' I said, clenching my teeth in barely suppressed fury.

'You must be Sikh then,' he declared, like an imperious judge.

'No, no,' I protested. 'Just write "Humanism" in the box.'

'There's no such religion in the census form,' he answered smugly, scanning through the list of officially recognized creeds on the paper that he brandished before me like a summons. 'If you are not anything, then you must be Hindu,' he decided for me. 'Your parents must follow some religion and that should be yours too.'

'I'd rather be an atheist than be called a Hindu or any such thing,' I insisted.

There was no religion called 'Atheism' in the list either. He reluctantly placed me in the box meant for sundry 'Others' placed at the bottom of the list.

Resisting the tyranny of labels is a constant struggle, a daily battle. No sooner does a child come into the world than it is branded, for no fault of his or hers, with a label that generally stays until the grave, that boxes it into a specific caste or religion. The State, driven to policing its citizens, demands to know the caste and religion of the child, who is perfectly innocent of such choices, and these are duly entered in the birth certificate, its passport to the world. Shortly after, the child is officially brought into a religious community that will hereafter expect unflinching loyalty from it, brooking no dissent or questioning. Thus, the child is dipped into a pool of water and baptized as a Christian, or made to don a thread as a Brahmin, or circumcised by a barber as a Muslim. Gradually, the child is made to identify itself as a member of a given religious or national collectivity, its identity based more on what sets the collectivity apart from other groups than on what actually unites its members. Inevitably, the formation of collectivities based on identities that are not freely chosen but inherited, leads to inter-group conflict, often overt strife, as each group seeks to define itself in contradistinction to seemingly menacing 'Others'. In times of social crises, groups carefully patrol their cultural borders and forcibly silence recalcitrant members who threaten to trespass into 'alien' territory. Overlapping identities are seen as traitorous and seditious, threatening to weaken or sabotage the community, and must therefore be dealt with firmly. Neat boundaries are drawn that set groups not just apart from each other, but, and more so, against each other. This explains the rapid spread of ethnic paranoia about identity today, at a time when communities, based on religion, race or ethnicity, live in closer proximity than ever before.

This book, in a sense, partly reflects my personal struggle to come to terms with my multiple and seemingly conflicting identities. I was born in a family only very nominally religious. My father was a turbanless Sikh of sorts, who knew more about the rules of golf than the teachings of the gurus. My mother, born in a Punjabi-Hindu family, remains blissfully ignorant of religious niceties, although she has an emotional attachment to a saint who some say was a Muslim Sufi while others insist was a Hindu mystic. I was sent to a Christian school as a child, where I learnt to sing such curiously titled hymns as *Onward Christian soldiers!* and *We'll plant the cross in every heart*, mercifully without comprehending their meaning. Daily mass at the chapel was compulsory, although many of us invented ways to escape it. Jesus became more of a friend to me than the fear-inspiring dictator, promising fire and brimstone to the heathen, that our red-cheeked Irish pastor had made him out to be. At college I experimented with Buddhism for a while, after a journey to Ladakh and Lahaul in the Himalayan borderlands. Later, while at university, I managed to wangle a scholarship to go abroad for a doctorate in Islamic studies.

And so, I now find myself straddling the border between belief and scepticism, refusing to define myself as a member of any particular collectivity. Yet, to assert this claim is not easy. I am constantly badgered with anxious queries about my religion or community, and an honest reply, 'I am as I am,' is considered a joke or plain silliness, or even, on occasion, a ploy to conceal a 'low' caste identity.

My predicament is by no means a novel one. For millions of others in India, religion is a free-flowing river that meanders wherever it pleases, in search of peace and solace, or, more often, in a desperate quest for divine intervention to solve worldly woes. Scores of communities scattered across this vast subcontinent still refuse to be neatly categorized as 'Hindu' or 'Muslim' or whatever, freely borrowing from diverse traditions to create their own way of understanding the world.

Historians—and by this I mean serious impartial scholars, not the 'saffron' and 'green' pen-pushers that today stake their dubious claims to that status—have remarked on the absence of the notion of 'Hindus' and 'Muslims' as two clearly demarcated religious communities in pre-modern times. What, for want of a better term, is today referred to as 'Hinduism' is said to be a recent construct, the product of the combined labours of British colonialists, Christian missionaries, European orientalists and native pundits, engaged in a collaborative exercise to provide some sense of order and legitimation to a bewildering range of castes, creeds and sects. The early Turkish and Arab conquerors, inventors of the term 'Hindu', had used the label in a similar way. All non-Muslim inhabitants of the land east of the Indus or Sindhu were indiscriminately banded together under this catch-all phrase.

These 'Hindu' communities shared but little with each other. In fact, as even a cursory examination of the Brahminical religious texts reveals, the defining feature of these communities was their fierce opposition and hostility to each other, with the Brahmins outshining the rest in their scorn for all those who lay outside their charmed circle. The Brahmins carefully guarded their privileged access to their religious texts, laying down stern punishments for 'lower' caste transgressors. The *Manusmriti*, the Bible of Brahminism, suggested that molten glass be poured down a Shudra's ears if he should so much as dare to listen to the Vedas. The punishment for a Shudra for the crime of reciting the Vedas was even more gruesome: his tongue was to be promptly lopped off. In the Ramayana, the hapless Shudra Shambuk was killed in cold blood by Rama for transgressing the iron law of caste. Entire communities were treated as untouchable outcastes, placed outside the pale of the Hindu caste system. In some parts of India, as in Kerala, groups of 'low' castes were even branded as 'unseeables'. Not only did these various communities worship different gods and goddesses, their dharmas, understood as a bundle of caste duties, were entirely different as well. Thus, the dharma of a Brahmin was to recite the Vedas, receive vast amounts of offerings, and lord over everyone else. At the bottom of the social heap, the Dalits' dharma was to slave for their 'upper' caste masters with no hope or desire for recompense. Clearly, in no sense of the term could this motley collection of mutually antagonistic castes be considered a single community.

The early Muslim arrivals seem to have unwittingly played a central role in the creation of the notion of a single Hindu community. For the 'ulama, scholars of Islamic jurisprudence, the various castes and sects among the non-Muslims of India, though divided among themselves, were equally guilty of rank polytheism and idolatry. They were thus treated as a single collectivity, as unrepentant unbelievers consigned to everlasting doom in hell. What was originally intended as a term to describe the people of a certain geographical region was now gradually transformed to name an imagined, unified religious community.

Not surprisingly, the 'upper' castes, particularly the Brahmins, forming little more than a tenth of the so-called 'Hindu' population, played a central role in promoting the notion of 'Hinduism' as a unified, well-defined religion, for it guaranteed their own status. The Brahminical texts, now accorded the status of the defining holy texts of 'Hinduism', discussed in intricate detail their various privileges. A pervasive sense of inferiority stemming from centuries of political subordination drove nineteenth-century 'upper' caste ideologues to construct a vision of a supposed Golden Age of pure Hindudom unsullied by a 'polluting' Muslim and Christian presence. This utopian construct was lodged in the mists of the remote past, in the so-called dharam raj or 'religious rule' of the Vedas. The Vedic Hindus, ancestors of the present-day Brahmins, were considered as the fountainhead of all wisdom, the torchbearers of civilization to the benighted world. They had, it was now rumoured, made great advancements in science and technology—from steam engines and the telegraph to rocket launchers and atom bombs—which made India the envy of the gods themselves. The four Vedas were now considered as the central texts of 'Hinduism', and the Brahminical caste system the Vedas' own unique and perfect answer to the perennial problem of the division of labour.

British colonial administrators, orientalist scholars and Christian missionaries reinforced these efforts of the 'upper' caste intelligentsia. Colonial officers needed to make some sense of the baffling diversity of castes and sects among the non-Muslim population of the subcontinent that they presided over. They followed the earlier Muslim fashion of indiscriminately putting them all together as one religious community. Orientalist scholars, driven by a wistful nostalgia for an age of rusticity that had long since disappeared in Europe, saw in the Brahminical texts the roots of their own ancestry, and afforded them the status of classics. Missionaries of Christ, followers of a scripture-based religion, saw the Vedas and other Brahminical texts as representing the counterparts of their own Bible. These texts were seen as defining what 'Hinduism' was, or better still, should be. The missionaries played a major role, one that modern-day 'Hindus' would sooner like to forget, in the invention of 'Hinduism', rescuing many long-forgotten texts from oblivion, translating and publishing them and making them available to the general public.

For the 'upper' castes, 'Hinduism', as it came to be constructed, fitted in neatly with their own vested interests. It enabled a small and threatened minority to employ the logic of majoritarianism to perpetuate its own hegemony, constructed on the oppression of the non-Brahmins, by claiming to be the 'natural representatives' of the imagined 'Hindu community'. It guaranteed the supremacy of the Brahmins, for all the Brahminical texts, from the earliest Vedas to the mediaeval Puranas and the Mahabharata and Ramayana, provided divine sanction to the caste system and to the supremacy of the priests who presided over it. It also placed the vast 'lower' caste majority firmly under 'upper' caste control, for the 'Hindu' texts had declared, in no uncertain terms, that Brahma, in his wisdom had created them as menials in the service of the 'twice-born'.

Talk of 'Hindu' unity transcending the caste divide was, for many of its proponents, merely a tactical ploy to stave off increasingly visible 'lower' caste assertiveness, to subsume the Dalits and Shudras under 'Hindus' and to turn them against the 'Muslims', now cleverly projected as the great, menacing 'Other'. For these 'upper' caste propagandists, the 'Hindus' were to be considered as a single community only insofar as it suited them, particularly when it came to warding off Muslim threats to their interests, or appealing to the 'lower' castes to kill or be killed for the greater glory of 'Hinduism'. When 'upper' caste privilege was seen as threatened by 'lower' castes clamouring for social equality—demanding reservations in government jobs and even such simple human rights as drinking water from the village well or walking on common village paths—sympathy for their supposedly Hindu 'low' caste 'co-religionists' was rare.

As for the Muslims, they seem to have been only slightly less divided than the 'Hindus' themselves. Although they shared a common holy text, the Qur'an, and revered the same Arabian Prophet, they were far from being the homogeneous community that might be imagined in modern-day Islamist and Hindu discourse. Differences of caste, sect, race and regional origins were strong enough to resist the appeal of a well-defined religion that strongly exhorted the unity and radical equality of the faithful. Muslims of foreign extraction, the self-styled ashraf or 'noble-born', saw themselves as vastly superior to the great mass of the ajlaf or the 'base-born', descendants of largely 'low' caste Hindu converts. For many ashrafs, the ajlaf were not genuine Muslims at all. The fourteenth-century chronicler, Ziauddin Barani, attached to the court of Muhammad-bin-Tughlaq, Sultan of Delhi, advised Muslim rulers not to allow the ajlaf access to higher education or to high posts in the state bureaucracy on the specious grounds that 'the promotion of the low born is [. . .] against the wisdom of Creation'. He twisted the Qur'an to say, 'in the low-born there can be no piety' (Mohammad Habib and Afsar Salim Khan, . . .). Shias and Sunnis, and from the nineteenth-century onwards, new groups such as the Barelwis, the Deobandis, the Ahl-e-Hadith, the Ahl-e-Qur'an and the Ahmadis, fiercely disputed each other's claims of representing 'true' Islam, indiscriminately hurling charges of kufr or infidelity against each other. The typical nineteenth-century 'Muslim' saw himself not simply as a member of a global religious community, the pan-Islamic *ummah*, but rather, as a Muslim of a particular school of thought, caste or biraderi, and of a particular locale or region. And as in the case of the 'upper' caste Hindus, for the ashraf Muslims appeals in the name of 'Islam' and 'Muslim unity' were often little more than a thin guise for preserving their own privileges.

It was primarily at the level of the non-Brahmin 'Hindus' and the ajlaf 'Muslims'—victims of a reified 'Hinduism' and an abstract 'Islam'—that the greatest blurring of boundaries took place. 'Lower' castes converted en masse to Islam in revolt against the tyranny of the 'upper' castes and in search of social justice and self-respect. Yet they carried along with them many of their pre-Islamic beliefs and customs which gave birth to deeply rooted liminal religious traditions. These were a reflection of a process that could be called 'incomplete conversion', the strictures of the Islamic law, the shari'at, being hardly observed among the mass of the newly converted. The lingering presence of pre-Islamic customs and traditions among the 'neo-Muslims' was also evidence of a pragmatic missionary strategy adopted by the Sufis, the principal agents for the spread of Islam in the region. Too deeply rooted to be completely effaced, these customs were grudgingly accepted or else given a thin 'Islamic' veneer by the Sufis, who were content with the formal, nominal acceptance of Islam by their neophytes.

Even among the unconverted, numerous sects and communities that are today considered as 'Hindu' were actually closer to popular Islam than to the rigid Brahminical religion. Scores of 'Hindus', and not only from the lower castes, flocked to the graves or dargahs of Sufi saints, seeking peace and solace, or a miraculous cure to their worldly woes. For many of these 'lower' castes, dargahs were the only places of worship that welcomed them. As non-Muslims they could not worship in mosques; as Dalits and Shudras they were banned from Hindu temples. Not surprisingly, the cults of the Sufi saints flourished particularly among the downtrodden.

Many mediaeval Sufi and Bhakti saints supported the 'lower' caste challenge to the tyranny of the 'Hindu' and 'Muslim' priests, who thrived on pitting 'Hindus' against 'Muslims'. These men of God bitterly critiqued the Brahmins and the 'ulama attached to Muslim courts for their soulless ritualism, irrepressible avarice and ignorance of true spirituality. Nanak and Kabir, who insisted that they were neither Hindu nor Muslim, along with other similar iconoclasts, defied the might of the Brahmins and Mullahs. Appealing for a new vision for humankind that transcended man-made differences of caste and community, they challenged the thesis of 'Hindu'-'Muslim' rivalry and ushered in a new cultural synthesis. By refusing to acknowledge narrowly inscribed boundaries, they pointed to a universal humanism grounded in a simple faith in God and good works, which, they insisted, were all one needed for salvation.

By the late nineteenth century, however, shared popular religious traditions increasingly came under attack. As always, religion was employed as a powerful tool to serve the interests of elite politics. The British had firmly established themselves as rulers of virtually all of India. Due to the demands of a new breed of western educated Indians, the British gradually began opening up the lower levels of the administration to the natives. Jobs for members of each religious group were to be allocated on the basis of its share in the population in each province. The British saw middle-class Indians—as the latter saw themselves—as the 'natural leaders' of their communities (although there is little evidence to suggest that the vast majority of their co-religionists shared that opinion), and grudgingly provided them access to a piece of the colonial pie. Middle-class Hindus and Muslims, now acutely concious of the politics of numbers, began frantic efforts to inflate the numbers of their co-religionists, since their own privileges had now been linked to the numerical strength of their respective religious communities. By the first decade of the twenty-first century, this had set off a frantic race for numbers. Hindu, Muslim, Sikh and Christian missionaries began to flock to villages in droves seeking to court Dalits and tribals whom they saw as neither Hindu nor Muslim but somewhat in between, in the hope of herding them into their own respective folds. Mass conversions followed, sometimes a consequence of promises of improvement in the worldly fortunes of their converts, and of eternal salvation in the after-life.

The first step towards this competitive scramble for numbers seems to have been taken by the Arya Samaj, a Hindu revivalist organization set up in 1875 by the Gujarati Brahmin Dayanand Saraswati. Dayanand believed that the Vedas alone represented the true Word of God. All other scriptures were either man-made or divine revelations that had been distorted over time. Contrary to the Sanatanis or orthodox Hindus, he passionately argued for taking back into the Hindu fold Hindus who had earlier converted to Islam and Christianity and their descendants. Accordingly, he developed a formal conversion procedure—the shuddhikaran or 'purification' ritual—which he sought to bestow with appropriate Vedic sanction. In Dayanand's time the Aryas made little headway in their *shuddhi* drive, although they did successfully combat the efforts of Christian missionaries in some areas. The Samaj managed to recover only a handful of Hindus who had converted to Islam after being excommunicated from the Sanatani fold for transgressing the rules of caste.

It was only in the early 1920s that shuddhi finally emerged as a mass movement, with entire neo-Muslim castes being targeted by Arya missionaries. The shuddhi drive was led by the redoubtable Lala Munshi Ram—popularly known as Swami Shraddhanand—a former Congress stalwart. Under him, the Aryas joined hands with their former Sanatani foes and launched an ambitious drive to bring into the Hindu fold vast numbers of people who straddled the unclear border between popular 'Hinduism' and 'Islam'. They first targeted the Malkana Rajputs—a community several hundred thousand strong— living in the western districts of the then United Provinces. Although they registered themselves in the census as Muslims, the Malkanas claimed to be of Rajput, Brahmin and Jat descent, and had retained many of their pre-Islamic customs. Hence they were also known as Adhbariyas or 'half and half'.

Arya shuddhi work among the Malkanas began in early 1923. The enthusiastic propaganda of Hindu missionaries, exhorting the Malkanas to revive the 'lost' glory of their supposed valiant Rajput ancestors, and, as some Muslim were to argue, the lure of money and other petty worldly blandishments, drove large numbers of Malkanas into the Hindu fold. However, little attention seemed to have been given to the spiritual instruction of the converts. It seemed to suffice for the Hindu missionaries that the fresh converts simply gave up practising 'Islamic' customs of burying their dead or circumcising their male children. Four years later, when the campaign had reached its peak, a leading newspaper reported that, 'The shuddhi propaganda [. . .] is no longer the exclusive concern of the Arya Samaj. An overwhelming majority of the Hindus are now identified [with it]' (*Tribune*, 4 May 1927).

With over a hundred thousand Malkanas converted to 'Hinduism', the joint forces of the Aryas and the Sanatanis now began training their eyes on other similar neo-Muslim groups, carefully drawing up plans to take the shuddhi campaign to them as well. Hindu leaders issued shrill appeals to target virtually all the Muslims of India for shuddhi. At a public rally in Lahore, Shraddhanand exhorted the 'Hindus' to 'bring back' to 'Hinduism' some 65 million Indian Muslims (Sayyed Ghulam Bhik Nairang, 1925, p. 4a). The Sanatani leader Swami Bhaskartirth, deputy to the Shankaracharya of the Sharada Peeth, announced that barring a few hundred thousand Indian Muslims whose forefathers had arrived from Central Asia and Arabia and settled in India, the rest were descendants of Hindu converts and that, therefore, they were all to be made Hindu once again (Nairang, 1925, p. 58). The Aryas are said to have publicly sworn that they would not rest till they had unfurled the sacred flag of Hindudom over Mecca and Medina (Muhammad Shafi Aslam, 1924). Thrilled by its missionary success among the Malkanas, the All-India Shuddhi Conference, an outfit sponsored largely by the Aryas, declared that since, allegedly, 'the founders of all the religions of the world were either Hindus or their descendants', their present-day followers must join the Hindu fold 'in the interests of the future of mankind' (J.H. Hutton, 1933).

Arya activists now spread across the north Indian countryside in search of liminal neo-Muslim communities. The Meos of Mewat, the Gupti Momins of Punjab, the Mula Jats and Gujjars of Haryana, the Imamshahis and Satpanthis of Gujarat, the Maiwaris of Sind, the Cheeta-Merats of Rajasthan, the Maul-e-Salam Girasiyas of Kutch, and scores of such little communities for whom neither 'Hindu' nor 'Muslim' elites had displayed any particular concern for centuries, were now actively courted by saffron-clad missionaries, who exhorted them to abandon their Muslim customs and 'purify' themselves by embracing unadulterated 'Hinduism'.

Predictably, the depredations of the Aryas put Muslim leaders on the defensive as the prospect of a large number of neo-Muslims going over to the 'Hindu' fold loomed large on the horizon. It was as if the death-knell had been sounded for the very existence of Islam in the country. As a leading activist of the Jami'at-ul 'Ulama-e-Hind ('The Union of the 'Ulama of India') put it, 'If the rapidly spreading movement of apostasy were not checked at once, the Indian Muslims would be certain to meet the same tragic fate as their co-religionists in mediaeval Spain' ('Abdul Halim Siddiqui, 1923). A top Muslim leader, Maulana 'Abdul Bari, the rector of Lucknow's famous Firanghi Mahal Islamic seminary, calling on Muslims to rise to the Arya challenge, declared, 'While protecting the Ka'aba made of bricks is a solemn duty, if the spiritual Ka'aba and the real house of God, the heart of the true believer, were to be emptied of faith, a very big Ka'aba would indeed be destroyed' (Abdul Bari, 1923).

Accordingly, Muslim leaders hurriedly cobbled together their activists and followers and established small tablighi or Islamic missionary outfits. Tablighi activists travelled through neo-Muslim dominated villages, preaching the basics of Islam and warning the villagers of the threats of the Aryas. Hindu and Muslim missionaries often worked in the same areas. Although they thundered against each other, they both railed against the popular practices of the communities among whom they preached: the Hindus declaring that their 'Muslim' customs were a blot on Hindudom, a sign of abominable slavery, the Muslims insisting that their 'Hindu' practices were unpardonable in Allah's eyes, effectively closing the gates of paradise to them if they did not reform themselves immediately.

By the end of the 1930s, many of these communities that once sat comfortably on the fence between 'Hinduism' and 'Islam' were now sharply divided into mutually hostile 'Hindu' and 'Muslim' camps. Consequently, the missionary wars fought between the Hindus and the Muslims led to widespread inter-community violence, resulting in the total collapse of the short-lived effort at Hindu-Muslim unity during the Non-Cooperation and Khilafat Movements. In the early mid-1920s, precisely at the peak of the shuddhi and tabligh movements, Hindu–Muslim hostilities touched new heights. As the years passed by things got only worse. 'Hindu-Muhammadan relations,' remarked a colonial intelligence officer in 1924, 'have seldom, if ever, been so strained as at the present time,' adding that the furore over shuddhi and tabligh had been 'the most important contributory factor leading to this situation' (Letter from Colonel Kaye, Intelligence Bureau, to Sir Alexander Muddiman, Home Department, Government of India, Delhi, 12 October, 1924, in 'Notes on the Tanzim and Tabligh Movements', *Home Political*, 6/ix, 1924, National Archives of India, New Delhi). As the *Indian Daily Telegraph* succinctly put it: as a consequence of the shuddhi campaign,

The Hindus and Muslims are systematically pulling against one another. Anyone who now talks of Hindu-Muslim unity must be insane. Here is a deliberate proclamation of war. (Notes from the Press [United Provinces of Agra and Oudh], 1923.)

The bloodletting of the missionary campaigns of the 1920s was to finally culminate in the blood-soaked Partition of India two decades later.

In addition to the machinations of middle-class Hindus and Muslims, and the shuddhi and tabligh movements they led, other forces at work led to a gradual disintegration of shared or liminal identities. With the introduction of the census by the British colonial administrators in 1871 many groups were now called upon to rethink their identities. For the census officials, communities that seemed to defy the simple logic of clearly defined religious identities were difficult to deal with. They were thus forced to declare themselves as clearly 'Hindu' or 'Muslim' or 'Other'. Moreover, urbanization, growing literacy and dwindling importance of caste disabilities opened up new avenues of upward social mobility for the hitherto marginalized communities. Typically, the quest for social ascension translated into assertions of a more orthodox 'Hindu' or 'Muslim' pedigree. Consequently, upwardly mobile sections within these communities fiercely attacked the shared religious traditions that had once characterized them. Thus, for instance, the sweepers of Punjab—followers of Bala Shah, probably a Muslim figure—stopped visiting Sufi shrines and observing the 'Muslim' Moharrum rituals. Bala Shah was transformed into Valmiki, who is believed to be the author of the Ramayana. Likewise, the Meghwal leather workers of Rajasthan—followers of Ram Dev or Rama Pir, in all likelihood an Ismaili Shi'a saint—transformed their clan deity into an orthodox Hindu Rajput warrior, probably to assert their own claims to a higher status—of full-blooded Hindus—in the local caste hierarchy.

Today, shared religious traditions are clearly under siege. The government has emerged as the most effective missionary agent by transforming vast numbers of liminal communities into unambiguous 'Hindus' with the stroke of a pen through the agency of the census. 'Hindu' and 'Muslim' revivalist groups thunder against what they see as violations of communal boundaries by communities and religious traditions that do not obey their tyrannical logic. In many parts of India, Sufi dargahs, where 'Hindus' and 'Muslims' would earlier worship together, have been converted into Hindu temples through force or fraud, or because local Muslims have abandoned them. The properties that some of them possess and the regular stream of donations that they receive make them a lucrative target. New stories about buried saints have been invented to explain their clearly Islamic traits. Champions of communal harmony or even missionaries of Islam whose shrines now boast of a new set of Hindu—generally Brahmin or another 'upper' caste Hindu—owners have been blessed with invented hagiographies that would surely make the saints turn in their graves.

Classical Brahminism had little place for historiography. Fanciful tales filled up the pages of the 'Hindu' epics and Puranas. Priests anxious to court royal favour and patronage promoted petty princes to the status of powerful gods. Dalit and Shudra opponents of the 'upper' castes were, likewise, transformed into monstrous, fang-spouting asuras in the 'Hindu' imagination. The line between fact and fiction in

'Hindu' tradition has thus always been very thin, and holy legends can be manufactured almost at will or on demand. A pundit with an acute business sense might proclaim that the little patch of land on which his hut stands was actually the birthplace of some obscure goddess. Soon, the mud shrine that he has built on the spot may be turned into a sprawling temple of the Devi, bringing in a steady flow of pilgrims and donations. The transformation of many Sufi shrines into Hindu temples today is thus part of a more general phenomenon.

On the 'Muslim' side, too, shared religious traditions have come in for severe criticism. In West Bengal, ecstatic *fakirs* who sing of the love of God have been physically attacked by irate mullahs, and many of these folk mystics have been driven underground. In Kashmir, Sufism has raised the hackles of hard-core champions of the shari'at, the Islamic law. All over India, the Tablighi Jama'at—the largest Islamic movement in the world—has been actively engaged in countering cults centred on the shrines of the saints, branding these as *bida'at*, 'wrongful innovations from the path of Muhammad', and even worse, as undistilled kufr or infidelity.

I do not wish to romanticize religious liminality or syncretism, nor am I unaware of its limits. While acknowledging that shared religious traditions and shrines, where people from different communities worship together, do provide a space for friendships and relations to develop across confessional barriers, I would go as far as to suggest that in many cases, as the reader will discover in this book, religious liminality is itself often a cause of inter-communal strife. This happens all the more when such shrines own vast estates or possess great wealth, or have a large following. Such has also been the fate of the traditions associated with some of the most radical opponents of communalism—Nanak and Kabir. Readers will recall that soon after their death, their Hindu and Muslim followers came to blows with each other on what was to be done with their dead bodies. (It is another matter, however, that, their bodies are believed to have turned into heaps of rose petals, which were then equally divided among the two contending parties, thus amicably resolving the dispute.) Neither Nanak nor Kabir seemed to have had any intention of forming a new community of his own. On the contrary, both spent their lives crusading against the notion of one 'chosen' religious community above the rest. And yet, as has been the tragic fate of most religious reformers, not long after their death both Nanak and Kabir emerged as holy icons. Those who claimed their mantle spawned new communities named after them, adding to the already bewildering number of squabbling confessional groups. And so it happened that far from effectively challenging the division of humanity into mutually opposed communities as Nanak and Kabir had attempted to, their followers only exacerbated the problem that they had set out to resolve.

When assessing the possible potential of shared religious traditions in countering the politics of communal strife it is important to bear in mind that a religious tradition that borrows freely from various sources need not necessarily make those who claim to follow it tolerant of other religions and their followers. Thus, the fact that Nanak's chief disciple, Mardana, was a Muslim or that the Granth Sahib contains verses composed by leading Sufis or even that the foundation stone of the Golden Temple of the Sikhs at Amritsar, their holiest of holies, was laid by a Muslim divine, Hazrat Mian Mir, did not prevent Sikh mobs from slaughtering Muslims in the eastern Punjab during the Partition riots. Nor does it help in any way counter widespread anti-Muslim prejudices among many present-day Sikhs.

The mere fact of people from different communities worshipping at a common shrine need not necessarily promote inter-community understanding or a deeper awareness of the faith of others. Thus, for instance, for many Hindus who visit

Sufi dargahs, Muslim saints are revered in a purely functional sense—powerful beings endowed with considerable shakti or power, capable of granting their wishes, of providing sons to barren women or a cure to a deadly disease. Hence, they may be willingly accepted as a welcome addition to the populous pantheon of Hindu deities. As pious, Allah-fearing followers of the Prophet's faith, Muslims who visit the same shrines might see the saints in a very different way. In such a case, there is no real sharing between the Hindu and the Muslim.

Then again, religious syncretism can sometimes be a cover for religious proselytism rather than a means to bring people of different faiths together despite their differences. Crucial to the spread of Brahminism from its heartland in the Indo-Gangetic belt to the rest of India was the process of the incorporation of indigenous 'low' castes and tribal deities. This gave birth to the many varieties of popular 'Hinduism' as they exist today—a syncretic mix of Aryan gods and goddesses and Dravidian heroes. The destruction of Buddhism in the land of its birth can also be put down to a deliberate policy of syncretism adopted by Brahminical elites who deciphered in the Buddha's message of egalitarianism a radical challenge to their privileges. Thus, certain aspects of Buddhism that had popular appeal—such as the stress on non-violence and vegetarianism—were now adopted by the Brahmins. The Buddha was converted into a harmless incarnation of Vishnu, which paved the way for the absorption of Buddhists into the Hindu caste system.

Similar instances abound in the Muslim, and, to a lesser extent, in the Christian tradition as well. The success of the Ismai'ili Nizari Shi'a or Aga Khani faith in Gujarat owes almost entirely to what appears to be a deliberate strategy of syncretism developed by its missionaries—the da'is. The poetical compositions of the da'is—the ginans—are replete with references to Hindu deities. One of the most sacred of the Nizari texts, the *Das Avatar*, goes as far as to accept the nine incarnations of Vishnu, then declaring Imam 'Ali, son-in-law of the Prophet Muhammad, as the tenth and last herald of the true faith—the Sat Panth. Likewise, in the Christian case Roberto de Nobili, a sixteenth century Italian Jesuit who worked among the Tamils, donned the garb of a Brahmin, wore a holy thread and observed the strict rules of pollution vis-à-vis the untouchables, in the hope of winning the Brahmins over to the Catholic faith. Needless to say, while the Brahmins saw through his guise, they saw no need to give up their privileges for a religion that promised them little in return.

And yet, despite these caveats, I believe that exploring the rich legacy of shared religious traditions in India is a valuable exercise. For one, shared religious traditions boldly defy the logic of religious communities as sharply divided from each other, homogeneous and neatly defined—the very basis of communal discourse. They point to ways in which people and groups can come to terms with multiple identities. They also suggest the possibility of finding truth in a multiplicity of religious settings. Finally, many of these traditions represent a sharp critique of established religions, their hierarchies and orthodoxies, and could be called nascent liberation theologies— protests articulated in religious terms against the oppression of the pundit and the Mullah alike, and of the ruling secular elite.

As ethnic strife conquers fresh ground in India, leading some observers to liken it to Nazi Germany, it is necessary to build bridges between different ethnic groups, particularly different religious communities. Bred on the idea of religion being the 'opium of the masses', secularists in India are averse to engage in a serious debate on religion, thus leaving the entire domain of religion to trident- and AK-47-wielding fundamentalists and blood-thirsty theocratic terrorists. While hard-core secularists might wish it away, religion in India is still too deeply rooted in the consciousness of the people to be ignored. If religious terror and fascism are to be countered, we must seek to uncover positive, humanistic and liberal understandings of religion, in order to challenge the merchants of theological terror. India's rich heritage of shared religious traditions, of religious liminality that refuses to buckle under the logic of mutually opposed religious communities, is, I believe, a valuable resource that must be made use of in the struggle for a new humanity. It is with this in mind that I decided to undertake the journeys I have recounted in this book.

THE GOD OF THE MOUNTAIN

With its roughly equal population of Christians, Muslims, caste Hindus, backward castes and Dalits, Kerala is truly a melting pot of religions, cultures and ethnicities. The original inhabitants of Kerala are today's Dalits, tribals and fisher folk, of Dravidian or Proto-Australoid stock. Centuries ago migrants and conquerors from the north reduced these people to virtual slavery, driving many of them into dense forests and mountain fastnesses, where they live till date in abject poverty. Many others were incorporated into the caste hierarchy as shudras and untouchables. The caste system in Kerala was so rigidly enforced that some castes were considered as 'unseeables'. It was believed that the mere sight of those belonging to such castes was enough to render the 'upper' castes 'impure'.

The steady trickle of migrants from the north was accompanied by the spread of the Brahminical religion in the area. Brahmin priests were granted vast tracts of land, and temples were endowed with sprawling estates of their own in return for the legitimacy that they bestowed on the local chieftains. That is how Kerala came to be known as 'The Land of the Gods'.

As elsewhere in India, religion was employed as a convenient means to buttress 'upper' caste hegemony and keep the 'lower' castes firmly in their place. Legends were woven that told of how Vishnu himself had granted Kerala to the Brahmins as their own personal fiefdom. According to one story, Parasurama, the Kshatriya-slaying incarnation of Vishnu, had thrown his axe from Gokarna towards the south. The axe fell at Kanya Kumari, the southernmost tip of India, and the ocean retreated, lifting a narrow strip of land along the coast—the present-day Kerala—out of the sea. Parasurama is then said to have divided the new land into sixty-four parts which he gifted to the Brahmins whom he had brought with him from the land to the north of the Vindhyas.

With the spread of the Brahminical religion in Kerala, local Dravidian gods and goddesses whom the indigenous inhabitants of the land deeply revered were given a suitably invented Aryan pedigree. Many of their shrines were taken over by Brahmin priests. Later, scores of Buddhist temples met with the same fate, and the Buddha, whose message of social equality had come as a call for the deliverance of the downtrodden, was conveniently absorbed into the Brahminical pantheon as one of the numerous incarnations of Vishnu. This served to neutralize any resistance that the Dravidian religion could have offered to Brahminical hegemony. Yet, despite the unrelenting Brahminical assault on popular religion, traces of the original Dravidian faith can still be found in Kerala today, intertwined with Brahminical, and, in many cases, Muslim and Christian influences.

The shrine of Ayyappa at Sabari Mala is to Kerala what the Golden Temple is to Punjab or the Tirupati temple to Andhra Pradesh. A visible symbol of Keralite identity, today it attracts an estimated thirty million pilgrims every year from all parts of South India. The origins of Ayyappa remain obscure. Perhaps of pre-Aryan, Dravidian stock, Ayyappa, like many other local deities of Kerala, has been gradually incorporated into the Brahminical pantheon. In his study of the Ayyappa tradition, P.T. Thomas notes that even today the name Ayyappa is common among all castes of the Hindus in Kerala except the Brahmins, citing this, and the fact that in no Brahmin temple in the region is Ayyappa worshipped as the chief deity, as evidence of the cult's pre-Aryan roots. Referring to Ayyappa and other local gods, he writes, 'Later, the Brahmins, in order to please the natives, accepted these deities into their systems and gave them a secondary place' (P.T. Thomas, 1973).

Yet, despite centuries of careful efforts to Brahminize the tradition, the pre-Aryan, local tribal, Dravidian, and, most interestingly, Muslim influences on the cult of Ayyappa are clearly visible. So inclusive is the cult that some Christians claim him as their own, for Ayyappa is also said to be a brother of St. John [J.J. Roy Burman and A.F. Mathews, January–March 2001]. But as the Ayyappa tradition has, in recent times, been transformed from a local cult to a pan-South Indian phenomenon, attracting an ever-increasing number of devotees and a steady flow of money, the fascinating liminal nature of the cult seems to be suppressed, denied or suitably reinterpreted in the process of being further Brahmanized.

Little is known about the historical origins of the Ayyappa cult. According to a story given in the *Bhutanathaopakhyanam*, Ayyappa was the offspring of Vishnu and Shiva, the product of the union of two male deities who, in earlier times, are said to have been bitterly opposed to each other. This itself suggests a rather late development of the Ayyappa tradition.

Brahma, Vishnu and Shiva, so the story goes, manifested themselves together in the form of Dattatreya, the son of Athri Rishi and his wife Anasuya. The consorts of Vishnu and Shiva combined in the form of Leela, the daughter of another rishi, who later went on to marry Dattatreya. Not long after his marriage, Dattatreya decided to renounce the world, but Leela protested. Thereupon, the adamant Dattatreya cursed his wife to be reborn as Mahishi, a dreaded she-buffalo. Not to be outdone, the intrepid Leela condemned her husband to be reborn as a male buffalo to satisfy her desires in her next life. In course of time, Leela died and was reborn as Mahishi. She devoted herself to stern penance and austerities. So pleased was Brahma with her piety that he granted her the boon that she had asked for, that she would be killed only by an offspring of the union of the two male gods Vishnu and Shiva—something she thought to be an impossibility.

Having been blessed by Brahma, Mahishi set about striking terror in devalok, the abode of the gods. Indra, the king of the gods, fled his kingdom while Mahishi placed herself on his throne. The panic-stricken devas flocked to Brahma's court, begging him for help. Brahma then arranged for Dattatreya to take the form of a handsome buffalo, Sundara Mahisha, thus fulfilling Leela's curse on Dattatreya in her previous birth. Consequently, Mahishi fell insensibly in love with Sundara Mahisha, who succeeded in charming her out of the heavens down to the forests on earth, thus enabling the hapless devas to return to their heavenly abode.

No sooner had the devas resettled in heaven than tragedy struck again. The hot-headed Rishi Durvasa, offended by Indra for not showing him the respect that he commanded as a Brahmin, cursed him and his fellow devas, causing them all to turn old, ugly, bent and infirm. The distraught devas learnt that the only way they could have their eternal youth restored was by drinking the nectar obtained by churning the Ocean of Milk. The devas did this along with their arch enemies, the demonic asuras, using a massive mountain to churn the milk. Finally, a pot of ambrosia emerged from the bosom of the ocean, but just as the devas were about to reach out for it, it was snatched away by the greedy asuras.

Witnessing the plight of the devas, Vishnu rushed to their rescue, and, assuming the form of the dazzling temptress Mohini, approached the asuras. Struck by her beauty, the asuras began quarrelling among themselves, each hoping to win her

as his wife. To settle matters, Mohini told the asuras to close
their eyes, promising to marry the one who would open his
eyes last. While the asuras did as they were told, the crafty
Mohini grabbed the pot of nectar and fled with it to devalok,
where she appeared before Shiva. No sooner had he set his eyes
on Mohini than Shiva fell desperately in love with her. From
their union a son was born in the form of Ayyappa, the Hari-
Hara Putra, or 'the son of Vishnu and Shiva'—the designated
slayer of the evil Mahishi. The she-buffalo had wrongly
imagined that two male gods could never produce an offspring.

The child Ayyappa was then sent down to earth, placed on the
banks of the Pampa river in the dense forest where Mahishi lived
with her husband Sundara Mahisha. One day, the chieftain of
Pandalam was passing through the forest on a hunting expedition.
Finding the abandoned child, he picked him up and took him
to his palace, adopting him as his son, for he himself was childless.
Some years later, the chieftain's queen gave birth to a son of her
own. She, along with the prime minister of Pandalam, set about
plotting the death of Ayyappa, hoping to have her own son
installed as the heir. Accordingly, the queen feigned a dreaded
illness, and the royal physician was suitably bribed to announce
that the only remedy for the unknown disease was a special
mountain herb and a bowl of tiger's milk.

The crafty queen knew that besides Ayyappa, no one else
would dare venture into the forest to procure the medicine that
she needed, for the boy was both brave and devoted to her. As
the queen had hoped, Ayyappa volunteered to bring her the
bowl of tiger's milk. The queen was secretly pleased, confident
that he would be killed by a wild animal and the way for her
own son's ascension to her husband's throne would be cleared.

At the same time, Mahishi, who happened to be living in
the same forest, set about plotting revenge with the asuras. She
rushed to devalok, producing thousands of creatures like herself
from each follicle of her hair, and together they lay to waste the
heavenly kingdom of Indra. The distraught devas fled to earth

to seek the help of Ayyappa, who was roaming in the forests in search of tiger's milk. Hearing of their plight, he accompanied them to the heavens where he caught Mahishi by the horns and hurled her down to earth, to die there, according to one version of the story, to miraculously transform herself into the goddess Malikappurathamma, according to another.

Having defeated Mahishi, Ayyappa subdued a tiger with his divine powers and then astride the animal, rode into Pandalam, accompanied by an army of fierce beasts. Realizing that he was the lord of the evil age of Kali Yug, the king and his plotting queen fell at his feet. Ayyappa then instructed the king to construct a temple in his honour in the forest. This is how the Sabari Mala shrine came into being.

This legend, based on Puranic myth and Brahminical interpolations, conceals much more than it actually seems to reveal, and is particularly silent about the association between Ayyappa and the figure of the Muslim warrior Wavar who is a central figure in the popular oral traditions of Ayyappa. It is clear from the rituals associated with the shrine that it has a history deeply rooted in Kerala's pre-Aryan past. It is probable that the story of the contestation between the devas and the asuras, and between Ayyappa and Mahishi, are actually metaphors for the enmity between the indigenous forest-dwelling Dravidians and the invading, conquering 'upper' caste Aryans. The refrain 'Sharanam' of the pilgrims making their way to the temple is a possible remnant of a Buddhist tradition that has still survived centuries of Brahminical onslaught. The other name by which Ayyappa is also known—Shasta—is said to be that of a Buddhist deity. The Petta Thullal war dance that takes place at the mosque of Wavar at Erumeli, with pilgrims dressing up like forest-dwelling tribals and prancing like wild animals, is suggestive of a possible ancient tribal origin of the cult, which was only later Brahminized as Hinduism gradually spread to the tribal areas, incorporating the forest people as serfs and slaves into the caste hierarchy.

Other historical explanations of the Ayyappa cult argue to the contrary, suggesting that Ayyappa and Wavar represent urban 'upper' caste Hindus and Muslims who joined forces to vanquish the forest-dwelling tribals, represented by Mahishi, and reduced them to slavery by conquering their lands. In their study of the Ayyappa tradition, Srikant and C.V. Manoj (1998) write that the kingdom of Pandalam was established in the tenth century AD, when a scion of the declining Pandya kingdom of Madurai fled to Kerala in the face of an attack by the rival Cholas. Around this time a brigand named Udayanan had established himself in the forests of the Manimala range, pillaging the trade caravans that passed through on their way to Pandalam and beyond, not sparing even the ancient temple at Sabari Mala, which is said, according to this story, to have existed long before Ayyappa himself. Udayanan is said to have looted the temple and killed its priest, causing the priest's son to flee for his life. Then, he is reported to have marched on to Pandalam itself, attacking the palace and abducting the Raja's daughter. On his way back to the forests, Udayanan and his fellow bandits were attacked by the priest's son, who set the princess free, then married her and settled with her in the forest near the present-day settlement of Ponnambalamedu. The couple prayed to the gods to provide them with a son to destroy Udayanan and to liberate the Sabari Mala temple from his clutches. Their prayers were soon answered and the princess gave birth to a boy. One day, Rajashekar, the king of Pandalam, ventured into the forest where he discovered the priest's son along with the child. The child's father handed the boy to the king, who took him home and gave him the name of Ayyappa.

When Ayyappa entered his teens, he left home on a divine mission to kill Udayanan. He set about gathering followers, appointing the Muslim Wavar, a pious Sufi or a medicine man according to some, as his lieutenant. For Wavar and his fellow

Muslim soldiers, Ayyappa arranged for the construction of a mosque at Erumeli. Wavar is credited with having led the army of warriors that stormed Udayanan's fortress and finally slayed him. Thus, it is suggested, Hindus and Muslims joined hands to defeat the army of wicked 'dacoits', who may actually have been, for all we know, hapless tribals resisting the encroaching might of urban civilization.

The traditional pilgrimage trail to Sabari Mala starts from the town of Chengannur, a two-hour train journey from Kottayam, and I decided to follow the route at least part of the way. Many pilgrims undertake the long journey on foot. I boarded a rattling Kerala Roadways bus instead. After all, I wasn't there on a pilgrimage myself.

As the bus rolled out of Chengannur, it made its way through an endless carpet of paddy fields, and over vast sheets of water and numerous little palm-fringed rivers. White herons, their wings tucked under their stomachs, waited patiently in little pools for fish and prawns to swim their way. Clumps of slender rubber trees dotted the landscape, the little coconut shells wound around their trunks overflowing with thick, milky-white sap trickling out of deep gashes. Large dug-out canoes with thatched straw roofs, painted in florid colours, gently made their way down swollen streams.

The road then began a steady, measured ascent up the hunched hills, passing through Mar Thoma country, the bastion of Orthodox Christianity in Kerala. Grand mansions of rich Christian landlords, painted strawberry-pink, parrot-green and electric yellow like fancy birthday cakes, rolled past—signs of prosperity recently acquired from the Gulf. An hour later, as the ascent grew steeper, the steeples of the churches gradually gave way to the slender, austere minarets of mosques and the imposing gopurams of temples, teeming with gods, both fierce and benign.

The bus huffed into Erumeli late in the afternoon. The sun was gently slipping behind the thickly forested hills of the Manimala range, turning the sky into a vast sheet of pale turmeric yellow. From the makeshift bus-stand a long knot of pilgrims wound their way through the narrow streets. Almost all of them were men, for women from puberty till menopause are strictly forbidden from entering Ayyappa's chambers. Bare-chested, streams of sweat running down their black skin, black cotton lungis draped around their waists and strings of beads wound around their necks—they seemed indistinguishable from each other. In the course of the pilgrimage, all social hierarchies had been overturned. In one loud voice they boomed, 'Swamiye Sharanam Ayyappa', imploring the 'god of the jungles' for his protection.

I joined this vast sea of humanitiy, conspicuous by my distinctly North Indian looks and the T-shirt and jeans that I was wearing. I was uncomfortably over-dressed for the occasion. The crowd moved up the road through a welcome arch made from bamboos strung together with ropes and festooned with banners depicting Ayyappa astride a fierce tiger. The pilgrims congregated at the steps of a little temple, then, one after another, flung coconuts on a stone as a ritual offering to the deity, the colourless milk flowing through a channel into a festering pool underground. The ceremony over, the men set about preparing for the next stage of the pilgrimage—smearing their black bodies with coloured powders to represent the bloodstains of the injuries sustained by Wavar and his army in their battle against Udayanan. Stuffing feathers into their matted hair caked with dust and grime, bearing cardboard crowns with pictures of a benign child-like Ayyappa on their heads, daubing their foreheads with sandalwood paste and carrying wooden swords, paper maces and bunches of leaves in their hands, their bodies streaked a violent red, orange, yellow and green, they marched out of the temple, heading towards the mosque—the Wavar Masjid—on the other side of the road.

The Wavar Masjid is an ancient structure, and no one seems to remember when it was built. Recently renovated, it has a massive white stone central dome, surrounded by several small arches and minarets, like a miniature Taj Mahal.

'It has been here ever since people started going to Sabari Mala,' said Yusuf, a young Muslim college student, whom I met after the evening prayers. 'The Hindus believe that before going up to Sabari mountain, they must first come here to the mosque to pay their respects to Wavar who built it.'

The crowd of pilgrims, now dressed and armed like a battalion of troops, swept into the mosque compound, brandishing their paper maces and dagger-shaped sticks, crying out Ayyappa's name in chorus to the throbbing of drums, celebrating Wavar's killing of the wicked Udayanan. The Muslim faithful, dressed in simple white lungis and white skullcaps, stepped out of the mosque after the prayers gave over, bemused at the sight. Having circumambulated the mosque, the devotees of Ayyappa bowed at the entrance, while a heavily bearded Muslim maulvi patted them with a bunch of peacock feathers and gave them each a pinch of sacred ash that they smeared on their foreheads. In return, the pilgrims dropped coins into an offering box, and placed at the foot of the mosque little plates of leaves laden with balls of black pepper, thick thumb-like cheroots, fresh green coconuts and lumps of sugar.

A group of Tamils implored the maulvi for a tin of water from the pool inside the mosque where the Muslims performed their ablutions.

'Nectar,' explained Velu, an elderly peasant from Tanjore.

Blessed by the maulvi, the pilgrims walked backwards with folded hands till they returned to the street, then danced their way to another Ayyappa temple located near the bus-stand, to take a bath there in a dirt-laden pool of stagnant water.

I spent that night at Yusuf's home, a small thatched hut built in a niche cut into the face of the hill, and surrounded by a small carefully tended plantation of banana and jackfruit trees and coffee bushes. It was impossible to sleep amidst the din of pilgrims singing and dancing to the beating of drums and the plaintive wail of reed pipes that carried on well into the early hours of morning. After a bath at the well, and a breakfast of vegetables cooked in sweet coconut milk and paper-thin *appam*s, I boarded the bus to Pampa, the next leg of the pilgrimage to Sabari Mala—a journey of some four hours.

Many pilgrims still make the journey to Pampa from Erumeli on foot, walking through dense monsoon forests that are home to a variety of wild animals. During the pilgrim season, which lasts a brief period of three months from November to January, the government arranges for special bus services to haul thousands of people to Pampa.

When I got to Pampa—otherwise a little settlement of just a few dozen houses—a sprawling makeshift township had been set up under thousands of little tarpaulin tents and plastic sheets stretched across bamboo poles driven into the ground. Hundreds of stalls selling all manner of pilgrim accessories seemed to be doing brisk business, for, I was told, some one hundred thousand people had arrived in Pampa that day. In a week—during the peak of the pilgrim season—the number would more than double. For the pilgrims, mostly poor peasants and labourers, the pilgrimage was also a vacation, a relief from the drudgery of daily labour, and a time to make purchases for their homes—pictures of gods and goddesses riding various animals, metal lockets, plastic beads and round, rough-edged *rudraksha mala*s, shiny glass bangles and cheap plastic flower vases, *murku*s wound up in knots, and large, round laddus made of fresh ghee. Poor tribal women squatted with worn-out rags in front of them, on which were placed little bunches of roots and fruits of the forest—medicines for a range of illnesses. On the banks of the Pampa river that wound its way from the hills beyond, rows of corpulent Brahmins, their holy threads prominently displayed across their bare chests, had set up their stalls, promising instant salvation or predicting the future, and offering the ancestors a place in heaven, all for a handsome fee.

The metalled road stopped abruptly at Pampa. From here a narrow path led to the temple atop the hill of Sabari Mala some eight kilometres ahead, an arduous walk in the glaring sun. On either side of the path that led beyond the hills draped in a thick blanket of mist, were dense tropical forests of sal and teak cradling a variety of orchids, massive banyans with their aerial roots dangling like paralyzed limbs, and clumps of tall bamboos creaking in the wind. In earlier times this was a life-threatening journey, undertaken only by the most devout, for the area is still home to tigers, leopards and wild elephants, and is now part of the sprawling Periyar Tiger Reserve. Notices with pictures of tigers, warning pilgrims of feline predators were put up on trees, but all I saw was a large jungle rat scurrying into a hole and a pack of black-faced langurs swinging on a *jamun* tree munching on its ripe purple fruit, flinging the seeds below on the heads of unsuspecting pilgrims.

A young lad bent down to pick up a stone to shoo the pests away. A middle-aged man, his hair wound into a blob like a bale of matted jute—presumably the father—grabbed the young lad's hand just as he was about to fling his missile.

'Arrey Muthoo!' he scolded him angrily in Tamil English. 'No doing that. Monkey is Hanuman God.'

The child was clearly not amused. Nor, it seemed, were the animals flattered. They snarled angrily at father and son, baring their fangs and sticking out their purple-stained tongues.

Half an hour after I had set off from Pampa, trudging up the steep slope under the relentless glare of the sun, I stopped in my tracks, too exhausted to move any further. I sat on a mossy bank, drinking from my flask and watching a family of yellow-beaked mynahs twittering to themselves and playing hopscotch. Meanwhile the stream of pilgrims had turned into a flood. A thousand men or more must have passed me by in the quarter of an hour that I sat transfixed, wondering at the irrepressible faith that drove this vast sea of humanity to a little shrine atop the mountain, now faintly visible in the distance. Carrying little, carefully wrapped bundles of coconut shells filled with ghee on their heads—humble offerings to their forest god— their bare feet trampling thorns and wading through slush, these men pushed their way ahead, surging towards the temple.

Almost five hours later I finally reached the shrine complex at Sabari Mala—a number of green Stalinist-style drab box-like structures built around a temple in a sprawling clearing in the forest. Passing through a massive, ugly concrete shed built to accommodate several thousand people, I made my way to the entrance of the temple.

'Vie you veering shaart-pant—aah?' asked a stout man with big purple blotches on his face, a foul smell emanating from the bush growing in his armpits. He wanted to know why I had not come to the temple scantily dressed like the others.

He was the seventh person to ask me that question, and by now I knew what to say.

'I am here on a holiday, not on a pilgrimage,' I said.

He scratched his head, perplexed.

'People going Baambay or Dilli for aaliday, yes. No one coming here aaliday. Only for pilgrim,' he said, curling his lips into a pout.

'You no possible to climbing golden entrance,' he added quickly, for only genuine pilgrims had the privilege of entering the temple by climbing a series of nineteen especially holy steps. For lesser beings like me, there was a separate entrance from the rear end.

The temple itself was small and unimpressive, built in the traditional Kerala style with a sloped, tiled, gilded roof, surrounded with massive ornate lamps and a carved metal flag post. I barely managed to get to the entrance of the temple when I was rudely pushed aside by a tide of pilgrims eager to have a darshan of the idol of Ayyappa in the dark sanctum, carefully guarded by a group of Brahmin priests. I caught a brief glimpse of the idol made of gold, some two feet tall, weighed down with precious stones and ornaments and surrounded by an array of oil lamps. Two rows of Brahmins standing on either side of the idol washed it with bowls of milk and pitchers of ghee, while throngs of pilgrims outside cried out to Ayyappa in a frenzy and invoked his name, throwing coins around and smashing coconuts.

Pushing my way down the steps through the crowd, I spotted a Muslim man, dressed in a starched white lungi and black fur cap, sitting at a grubby tea-stall.

'You from Dilli-aah?' he asked, as I passed by.

'Come, come, you having tea now,' he insisted, making it clear that I could not disobey his orders.

The man's name was Hussain and he hailed, he told me, from the family of Muslim custodians of the shrine of Wavar that was located in a corner of the Ayyappa temple complex. He took me to the shrine—a long structure shaped like a grave built under a tin roof, draped with a green cloth embossed with the Islamic insignia of the crescent and star, and a rusted sword placed across it. Outside, a board in Malayalam and English announced the shrine of 'Wavar Swamy'. Crowds of Ayyappa devotees, streaming out of the temple, wound their way to the shrine, bowing before the mock grave and making offerings of little bags of black pepper and bits of camphor. An ageing maulvi, the seventy-two-year-old Haji Abdur Rahman Musaliar, smeared holy ash on their foreheads, then recited the fatiha, the opening verse of the Qur'an, beseeching God to grant His blessings to Wavar and to the faithful in general.

It was dark by the time I finally made my way down to Pampa. The sky had turned a deep purple, splashed with blotches of fiery orange and pink. The fires outside the tents were being lit, and the pilgrims were setting about cooking their dinner on kerosene stoves outside their tents.

The last bus for Erumeli was just about to depart as I reached the bus-stand. It was overflowing with pilgrims, so I scrambled aboard the roof, braving the icy winds as the bus wound its way down through the forests to the sultry plains below.

3

THE STAR OF THE SEAS
OUR LADY OF HEALTH OF VAILANKANNI

A thunderous squall accompanied by howling winds rampaged through the paddy fields, blowing off thatches, scooping a flock of squawking hens up into the air and sending packs of pedestrians scurrying into the bus-stand for shelter. A sari rushed past, gesticulating wildly, while a distraught bald woman ran after it helplessly. The angry clouds burst forth, sending down torrents of rain, and in no time the carpets of parrot-green paddy were turned into vast silvery lakes. An hour later, the rains stopped, as suddenly as they had begun. The sun crept out stealthily, and the towers of the basilica drew into view in the distance as the curtain of clouds began to lift.

Across the bus-stand stood a large arch built across the main road. At the foot of the arch squatted a grim, almost comic, statue of Indira Gandhi mounted on a pedestal and shaded by a painted stone umbrella. From a row of cement pillars washed-out flags of various political parties hung languidly. A drunken man snatched a flag and draped himself with it. The supporters of the party to which the flag belonged bellowed out in violent protest, rushing to its rescue and giving the man a sound thrashing. 'Insulting our leader, you!' they screamed, pelting the hapless man with their fists and reducing his face to a fine red-blotched mess.

'Till the sun and the moon shall last, our great leader X shall last,' screamed a slogan painted on the wall of a roadside tea-stall nearby, where the army that had just scored such a stunning victory over its enemy had descended to celebrate the occasion. Above the slogan, a peeling poster displayed a picture of an enormous man with a moustache shaped like a bow, and a pair of square dark-glasses stuck on his nose. He might well have been a local dacoit or a failed film star, but a slogan crowning his face exclaimed, 'How should our leader be? Like Mr Y, Like Mr Y.' As if mediating between these two political heavyweights, a woman, provocatively thrust her melon-shaped breasts forward, her hair carelessly scattered over her face, from a poster advertising a new Tamil movie.

Perched at the top of the welcome-arch Our Lady of Good Health, the Blessed Virgin Mary of Vailankanni stood in all her imperious splendour. Armed with an orb topped with a cross in one hand, and cradling a sleeping pink-cheeked Jesus in the other, she was clearly not amused, and had raised an eyebrow at the vulgar display of political intrigue and primitive passion that engulfed her feet like Noah's great flood. Her pale cream face, thin crimson lips, wavy blonde tresses and soft blue eyes pointed to remote foreign origins, for in Tamil country almost everyone was a rich chocolate brown or a burnt ebony, and only ghosts and ghouls had eyes and hair any other colour than black. As if to make her feel more at home in her new environment, she had been draped in a silk sari, while fading Indian tricolours fluttered on either side of the ledge on which she was perched. Relentlessly reviled by Hindu extremists for allegedly being a carefully concealed guise for Western imperialism, Christianity was now being given an Indian garb. 'Be Greek with the Greeks and Jew with the Jews,' a wise Christian sage had once said, perceptively noting that it was only by being all things to all men that at least some could be won to the Lord-God Jesus.

At an hour's drive from the town of Nagapattinam in coastal southern Tamil Nadu, Vailankanni is one of the most popular Catholic places of pilgrimage in all of Asia, drawing every year hundreds of thousands of pilgrims, and not just Catholics. Christianity made its presence felt in this part of India several centuries ago. Legend has it that St. Thomas, one of the twelve apostles, arrived on the Coromandel coast shortly after Jesus's death. Numerous conversions are attributed to him, but his success proved to be his own undoing, for enraged Brahmins are said to have speared him to death in AD 72. He now lies buried under a rock in a village just outside Madras. Thereafter, sporadic efforts were made by enthusiastic evangelists to win over fresh converts, particularly after European traders and adventurers began visiting the Tamil coast from the late fifteenth century onwards. The converts were few and far between, however, because for the Tamils, Christianity was the religion of the white man. In 1605, an Italian Jesuit, Roberto de Nobili was dispatched by the Holy See to Tamil country. The task before him was to guide the heathens of the Coromandel coast to the True Faith.

De Nobili seems to have been a volatile, yet colourful character, with a flair for languages and a characteristically Jesuitical dedication to the holy cause of expanding the frontiers of the Church of Rome. He settled at the temple town of Madurai, where he spent forty years doing missionary work. Discovering to his dismay the indifference of the Tamils to the True Faith—because they found it outlandish and alien—he launched an ambitious programme of what is today fashionably called in missionary circles as the 'indigenization' or 'inculturation' of Christianity, seeking to present it in terms that were familiar to the Tamils, convinced that this was the only way in which the Word of the Lord could gain entry to Tamil soil. Accordingly, he set himself up as a learned Brahmin, donning the Brahminical thread and wearing the robes of a Hindu sadhu. He mastered Sanskrit, the language of the

Brahminical texts, and even wrote a number of essays on Christianity in highly Sanskritized Tamil. Emulating his Brahmin rivals, he rigidly adhered to their practices of purity and pollution in his treatment of the 'low' castes, thus seeking to out-Brahmin even the Brahmins themselves.

Shortly after his arrival in India, de Nobili formulated a new strategy of preaching the gospel. He suggested to his fellow Jesuit missionaries working in India that in order to win over the Brahmins to the True Faith they declare that they were not 'low' caste foreigners or firanghis but actually of noble birth; that they abandon all European customs the Brahmins found abhorrent; and that they cut off ties with the disreputable wine-guzzling and meat-eating Portuguese and other European *mleccha*s or with 'low' caste Tamil Christians. 'High' caste Christians were to pray in separate churches and they were to be assured that they would not lose any of their caste privileges after conversion.

De Nobili hoped that by thus accommodating itself to the cultural mores of the Brahmins, Christianity would be able to make great headway among them. If the Brahmins were to turn Christian, he believed, the 'lower' castes would follow them en masse. Despite considerable opposition from within sections of the Catholic Church to what were seen as his unwarranted concessions to undistilled paganism, in 1623 de Nobili's programme received official sanction from Rome. The papal Bull *Romanae Sedis Antistes* approved of de Nobili's methods for acquiring fresh converts through the creation of a Brahminical Catholicism.

Very few Brahmins actually converted to Catholicism, however, for, their status, power and privileges were all too closely bound up with Hinduism. Rather, from the eighteenth century onwards, much to the dismay of many Christians of 'upper' caste origin, a vast number of Dalits and Shudras began flocking to the Church, and soon came to form an overwhelming majority of the Tamil Christian population.

Many of them were 'rice-bowl' Christians, who had lined up outside European missions, to be baptized in exchange of a bowl of gruel during long spells of drought and famine. Free education and medical facilities for Christians at Christian schools and hospitals attracted others to the new religion. For many more, conversion to Christianity represented a rebellion against the tyranny of the Brahmins and the caste system that they had invented.

With an ever-increasing number of Dalit and Shudra converts, the Church itself underwent a gradual transformation. Catholic places of popular pilgrimage sprung up, promising miraculous cures to mysterious illnesses. Great visual displays and theatrical performances such as chariot processions and demon exorcisms, festivals of fiery lights and throbbing devotional music, all these readily appealed to the 'low' castes, for whom the sombre, staid ritualism of both the Brahmins and the Church of Rome were equally alien. By the 1980s, Dalits in the Church were up in arms against what they saw as their continued oppression by 'upper' castes within the Church and outside it. There was now talk of 'Dalit Christianity' and of 'Jesus, the Black Man'. The lingering presence of 'Brahminical Christianity' was repeatedly denounced. Clearly the followers of de Nobili were now outliving their usefulness to the Church.

While de Nobili and his fellow Brahminical Christians represent one aspect of the Catholic Church in India, the great basilica of Vailankanni represents another, a Christianity that has sought to be rooted in the culture of the 'low' caste Tamils, although, so it appears, somewhat nervously and half-heartedly. The shrine dedicated to Our Lady of Good Health, also called Our Lady of Vailankanni, a pilgrim guidebook says, 'is built on the place chosen by the Blessed Virgin to dispense her healing miracles to all humankind'.

Local legend has it that sometime in the sixteenth century, Mary appeared along with the baby Jesus to a Hindu cowherd as he rested in the cool shade of a banyan tree on the banks of a pond in the village of Vailankanni. She woke him up and asked him for some milk for her child. No sooner had the boy given her the milk than the divine apparition suddenly vanished with a blinding flash of light. When the boy picked up the pail he discovered to his surprise that it was still full. Soon, news of this supernatural event spread like wildfire. Christians and Hindus alike were convinced that she had been none other than the Blessed Virgin herself.

Not long after, the Blessed Virgin is said to have appeared in the village again, this time to a crippled buttermilk seller. She asked the boy to travel to the neighbouring town of Nagapattinam and inform a certain wealthy Catholic merchant of her miraculous appearance. When the boy stood up, overawed at the apparition, he discovered to his utter amazement that his crippled leg had been miraculously cured. Meanwhile, the Blessed Virgin also appeared in a vision to the merchant from Nagapattinam, commanding him to build a chapel for her at the site of her second appearance. The Blessed Virgin's fame as healer of afflictions now began to draw large crowds to the shrine of Arokia Matha, the Mother of Good Health. And, for the Church, ever increasing hordes of pilgrims held out promises of fresh converts.

The first available documentary reference to the shrine of Vailankanni dates back to 1630, when the Portuguese friar Paulo de Trindade mentioned in his chronicles the existence of a Christian settlement in the area, which he described as being 'under the patronage of Our Lady of Good Health'. Portuguese sailors and traders seemed to have played a central role in popularizing the tradition of the Blessed Virgin of Vailankanni. 'The Star of the Sea', as she was known, Mary was looked upon with particular devotion as the protector of sailors. Sometime in the early seventeenth century, a Portuguese ship on its way to Macao was caught in a fierce storm off the Tamil coast. The sailors turned to Mary for help, and, according to the legend, she guided them to safety—to the beach at Vailankanni. As a mark of their gratitude, they built a small chapel in her honour on the spot where a small mud shrine dedicated to her had previously stood. Over the years, thanks to Portuguese munificence, it gradually grew into a fine, imposing shrine, owning vast stretches of land and attracting a steady stream of pilgrims. By the turn of the nineteenth century, Vailankanni had etched itself on the global Catholic pilgrimage map, receiving the title of 'The Lourdes of the East'. In 1962, in a rare display of papal generosity towards the Third World, John XXIII bestowed the shrine the status of a 'minor basilica'.

The basilica lumbered like a beached whale at the end of the road which turned off the main highway, and dipping under the grand welcome-arch, ran along lush green palm-fringed paddy fields, dotted with ancient Hindu temples and Christian shrines and cemeteries standing cheek by jowl. Stalls at the bus-stand did brisk business, crowds milling around them, inspecting goods and bargaining angrily. Bunches of red, cone-shaped bananas hung from log-like stems in shop windows, and ropes of sweet-smelling *malligey* and cream-yellow *sampangi* flowers lay in coils in cane baskets on the pavements. Mountains of puffed rice spilled out of giant jute sacks. Wooden trays on wheeled trolleys displayed bits of sandalwood, pyramids of red kumkum powder, bottles of holy oil and balls of sacred yellow thread. An army of Malayali customers, their neatly starched lungis lifted up to their knees in the Keralite fashion, haggled with a shopkeeper over a plastic Jesus with a halo of coloured lights. Tamil devotional music exuded from hidden loudspeakers and ownerless cows munched on piles of garbage. This could well have been just another South Indian Hindu centre of pilgrimage.

The annual chariot festival, celebrated on 8 September every year to mark the feast of the Nativity, first established by the Portuguese sailors to commemorate their miraculous survival was a fortnight away, and already buses and trucks were disgorging ever-increasing hordes of pilgrims.

'This is very big function,' the owner of the roadside food-stall assured me, serving yet another soft idli in my plate. 'Hindus, Muslims, Christians all coming to see divine grace of Matha.'

More than a million people were expected to participate in the nine-day festival. The chapparam—the giant chariot of the Virgin—would be driven through the streets of the town, accompanied by throngs of the devout shouting her praises like enthusiastic activists at a political rally. Votive flags would be unfurled and special prayers offered to cure the sick.

I walked towards the shrine, its tall, imposing, towers culminating in crosses dominating the skyline. An aged Christian priest in a stained, frayed habit leant on a stick and hobbled along the path. His toothless gums broke into a friendly smile.

'I was going strong all these years,' he said, 'but now I'm here to ask Mother for her blessings. I had a nasty fall a month ago and the doctors have almost given up on me.'

'Mother is sure to cure me,' he added, nodding his head and fingering the wooden cross that dangled on his neck. 'She's the world's greatest doctor.'

A team of officious-looking nuns dressed in crisp grey cowls passed by. A Muslim couple—a man with a tangled beard like a vulture's nest hopping on his only foot and a woman draped in a black burka—followed after me. I slowed down and turned to the man.

'Salaam,' I said, raising my hand in salutation.

'Waleikum Salaam,' he murmured somewhat reluctantly.

A furtive look of embarrassment clouded his face, like a child caught stealing from a tin of sweets. Probably he had taken me for a fellow-Muslim. He opened up somewhat, however, when I set his fears at rest.

'As long as I get my foot cured, what does it matter?' he asked, as if seeking my approval. 'After all,' he added, stopping to light a cigarette, 'no sensible person asks a doctor what his caste or religion is before deciding to go to him. So, what's wrong in a Muslim coming to a Christian shrine?'

Hindus seemed to outnumber Christians at the shrine. A pack of sadhus in saffron robes squatted on the road, begging for alms. A busload of Hindu girls merrily chatted away, pointing at me and laughing. A wizened Brahmin, his holy thread coiled around his ears and his head smeared with caste marks, emerged from behind a bush, followed by a train of children. A team of aged Hindu women lumbered along, huddling under their floral parasols.

A young man dressed nattily in jeans and a crisp cotton shirt walked up to me grinning.

'You taking fautoo of me and my Mrs,' he said, more of an order than a request.

He introduced himself. 'By the way, I Mr Venkat G. from Tirunelveli. Pleased to meeting you. She be my new Mrs, Sita.'

The newly wed Hindu couple were here on a pilgrimage-cum-honeymoon. Venkat placed his arm around Sita, posing like a villain in a Tamil movie, his fingers clutching at her slender waist. Sita smiled embarrassedly and Venkat beamed in child-like glee, as I clicked.

'We sending you one momento copy pucca. Praamis,' Venkat vowed. Why had the couple decided to come to Vailankanni for their honeymoon, I asked. Wouldn't the beaches along the Coromandel coast or, better still, the rolling hills of Ooty, where juvenile Hindi film stars danced behind trees and plotted elopements or murders, have been a more suitable destination?

'You see, Maatha is Maatha,' Venkat said.

'Well, she sure must be,' I answered, trying to be cheeky, 'just as Venkat is Venkat.'

'Ayayo, you naat understanding,' Venkat protested. 'She being great gaad-ess. Just like power gaad-ess Shakti, gaad-ess of wealth Lakshmi, gaad-es of wisdom Saraswati. She be big, big gaad-ess. She doing whatever she waant-ing.'

'We starting new life, me and my Mrs. So we start on auspicious note with gaad-ess blessing.'

We walked together, the newly wed couple and I, to the market that spilled into the streets at the entrance of the shrine. A neatly painted board announced 'Tonsure Hall for Pilgrims'. Venkat went inside and I followed him, while Sita sat in a coffee-shop waiting. The hall was packed with pilgrims, holding plastic tokens in their hands and shuffling their feet noisily in their rubber chappals. A harried watchman directed them to the barbers who leant against the walls, menacingly brandishing their weapons. Venkat squatted on a block of stone, and the barber reached out at his thick, black mane with a vengeance. Piles of hair fell to the ground, as he ran an evil-looking knife over his scalp with brisk precision. Venkat winced as the blade cut into the side of his head and blood trickled down his neck. Five minutes later the operation gave over. Venkat got up and peered at himself in a stained mirror.

'Ayooo! Not a hair left on my head!' he exclaimed, twisting his mouth and scowling. 'What my Mrs now saying to me?'

The barber rubbed a ball of sandalwood and a dash of turmeric past on Venkat's bald head.

'That will keep you cool up there,' he said with a flourish. 'And forget about your Mrs. If Matha is happy with you, why bother about what your Mrs says?' he chuckled.

That evening I joined Venkat and Sita for the mass at the shrine. The sun, gently slipping into a blanket of grey, rain-laden clouds, had turned the sky a mottled orange. Shafts of soft light fell upon the basilica, bouncing off its white-washed stone walls, now a mellow, gentle cream in the gathering dusk. The grand structure appeared like the creation of some logic-defying post-modern artist—a mediaeval Latin castle with its giant steeples, here in the heart of Dravidian country.

Tamil temples were a riot of colours and shapes, peopled with entire tribes of gods and demons and packs of half-human animals that peered down from invisible ledges. Fumes from pots of incense mingled with the stench from the mounds of cow-dung and the smell of flowers, sweat and the refuse outside.

The basilica made no concessions for human ingenuity or local taste, however. The firmly straight lines of its doors and windows, its monochromatic white walls and its near-perfect cleanliness suggested a different understanding of order and control, religion and devotion.

Inside the dark chamber, however, the Tamil spirit seemed to have reasserted itself. A crowd of pilgrims, men with shaven heads and women with the *pallu*s of their saris neatly draped around them, loudly sang Tamil odes to the sari-clad Blessed Virgin, who sat in a special chamber, surrounded by a bower of plastic roses in golden vases. An old woman sobbed into her sari, tears filling the hollows of her sunken cheeks. A young man fell to his knees, knocking his head on the floor. Another man crossed himself nervously as he stared at the statue of the Blessed Virgin, suitably hypnotized. An old woman sat on the floor cross-legged in the lotus-pose like a yogi and recited the Lord's prayer. A party of school children counted the tiles on the floor, blue and white slabs brought from Macao over three hundred years ago, depicting European sailing ships and Portuguese men in tall hats and curled boots against the background of sloping Chinese pagodas.

From the window I observed a family of Hindus circumambulating the model of a seventeenth-century Portuguese sailing ship docked in the courtyard. They tied little locks on the iron fence that surrounded it ('in order to remind Matha to fulfil their request' I was told), then knelt down in silent prayer.

Amidst the sonorous chorus of 'Amens' and 'Hallelujahs', I strode down the nave and headed for a well-deserved dinner.

I spent the night in the run-down 'Mutthu Hotel'. The strains of Tamil hymns shook me out of my slumber just before dawn.

Mutthu thumped on the door and asked, 'Saar, you vaanting tea or caafee?'

'Coffee,' I said.

'Vee no having caafee saar. You better having tea instead,' he replied unapologetically.

I strolled down to the beach, a hundred metres away, with a plastic cup of sticky-sweet tea in my hand. Shutters—jute matting tied to bamboo sticks—were being rolled up at stalls getting ready to sell balloons, plastic toys and ubiquitous pilgrim paraphernalia. Two bare-chested men dressed in lungis and sports shoes jogged down the oil-stained stretch of sand. A catamaran bobbed up and down in the distance. Waves lapped the shore gently, cleansing it of great quantities of pilgrim refuse.

Breakfast that morning consisted of a paper-thin dosa and an onion pancake, washed down with a glass of sweet coconut water. It was ten and the sun had climbed high up in the cloudless sky by the time I left the restaurant. I headed towards the Mother's Well—a pool of water said to have been especially blessed by the Virgin—a kilometre north of the shrine.

The path was brimming with the devout crowding around statues of the Blessed Virgin and her child placed in glass boxes like museum exhibits. The entire life of Christ, from the manger to the cross, was up on display. Mournful maidens and swooning saints provided a sombre background to a tale of relentless sorrow and suffering. Pilgrims gazed glassy-eyed upon the idols, folding their hands and mumbling their prayers.

An elderly man, his ebony-black face gnarled with age, dragged himself on his knees along the burning sand. Beads of perspiration ran down his face, drenching his shirt. I drew up to him as he rested for a while in the sparse shade of a coconut tree.

'Myself Ramakrishna, 57, retired head-master,' he introduced himself to me. 'I walking on knee in sand to praise the great Matha.'

He was a Hindu of the Naidu caste from Andhra Pradesh, and had been making an annual pilgrimage to Vailankanni for the last three years. 'I had accident, terrible accident,' he said, shaking his head from side to side. 'I losing my tongue but Mary Matha curing me.'

With his now functional tongue he licked off the beads of sweat that sparkled on his chin like pearls.

'Mary Matha always staying with me in heart,' he beamed, holding his hand to his chest.

To show his gratitude to the Blessed Virgin for having cured him of his speech ailment, he had recently spent a thousand rupees, almost half his monthly salary, on placing a little advertisement in a local daily to say, 'Thank you Mother Mary of Vailankanni for favours received,' below a passport-sized picture of the Blessed Virgin. Alongside were several other similar pictures and messages sponsored by yet other beneficiaries of the Blessed Virgin's supposedly miraculous curative powers.

No pilgrimage to Vailankanni is complete without a visit to the shrine's museum, possibly the only medical museum in India. Its holdings are said to be valued at over Rs 50 crore making it one of the richest private museums in the country (A Church Where All Religions Come Together,' *Indian Express*, 16 August 1994). It occupies an entire floor of a building just in front of the basilica. A narrow flight of stairs leads to a many-roomed hall, full of long glass cases mounted on wooden legs. The cases contain specimens of various offerings provided by pilgrims returning to Vailankanni to thank the Blessed Virgin for what they believe to be favours granted to them by her. Each specimen is different, and is related to the particular blessing that the donor is said to have received. The most common ones are little bits of silver designed as the part of the pilgrim's body said to have been cured by the Blessed Virgin: lungs, hearts, ears, noses, feet, hands and, indeed, almost every conceivable part of the human anatomy, carved out of beaten sheets of silver and sold in small stalls around the shrine for anything from between Rs 20 to Rs 2000 apiece.

A middle-aged woman pointed excitedly to a silver snout-like nose in a glass case. A band of giggling children stood on their toes to take a look.

'See, James and Hilda!' the woman cried out. 'Remember when I got cured after that operation, when I slipped down the stairs and broke my nose? The doctors had almost given up but Mary Matha cured me.'

'Yes Mumma,' wailed pigtailed Hilda. 'It was really bad, na?'

'Praised be the Lord,' said Hilda's father, who plucked at the woman's nose to make sure it was still intact.

A fading note that the woman had written many years ago after her recovery was tied to the silver nose. 'Thanks be to Mary Matha for the successful operation,' it read.

Each exhibit had its own particular history, testifying to the awesome powers of the Blessed Virgin who could cure ailments for which even modern science had no remedy. The Virgin seemed to be general fixit for all sorts of problems, and she was available to all who approached her in humble devotion. A certain Lakshmi C. from Coimbatore, probably a Hindu, had offered the Blessed Virgin a set of four fountain pens for having helped her successfully clear her higher secondary examinations. The obviously Hindu proprietor of Sri Rama Transport Service had donated to the Virgin a silver model of a truck. Another thankful Hindu pilgrim was the anonymous donor of a silver statuette of a frolicking Krishna. The director of Saravana

Industries, Salem, in gratitude for a year of successful business, had provided the museum with a tiny model of an old-fangled industrial machine. A small silver milk can was probably the gift of some grateful cowherd. The Muslim Dr S.Z. Zahir Hussain had offered a pair of stethoscopes for having been miraculously granted a medical degree. A certain C. William, a policeman from Bangalore, peeped out from a fading photograph—a grim-looking officer with an enormous moustache—stuck on to a board along with little silver stars and a silver model of a police control room. A note scribbled on the board revealed:

I suffered a lot for promotion. I had been for training (twice), but couldn't get my promotion for past two years. After that I made up my mind and prayed to Our Lady Annai Vailankanni for promotion that I will come with my family and offer you thanksgiving mass. At last my ambition was fulfilled and I got success. I got my promotion as ASI PF/BNC. Now I am offering you thanksgiving mass as a small contribution from me and our family.

The Virgin performed hundreds and thousands of such miracles every day, and would continue to do so till the end of the world, amen, the toothless museum guard assured me as I made my way out.

'You having any problem, she helping you,' he said, quickly adding, 'she only doing if you having faith in her.'

That evening I strolled down to the beach again and settled under a shack perched on a mound to watch the sun gently slip behind the horizon and drown into the sea. A family of seagulls squawked past and tiny crabs raced into crannies of giant weather-beaten rocks. A cloud of flies feasted on a pile of seaweed freshly washed up from the deep. A gang of fishermen squatted in the sand, sorting their catch by weight and species, while hungry dogs looked on expectantly. Here, perhaps on the spot where I was sitting, I thought to myself, four hundred years ago, a treasure-laden Portuguese ship had run aground, washing its crew ashore. I pictured them in my mind—murderous white-skinned, blue-eyed buccaneers, driven by an irrepressible zeal for the Church and the Holy Empire, scouring the seas for the untold riches of the Orient. Marooned in a land of abundant polytheism and superstition, they had sought to recreate a slice of their own lost world. Four centuries later hundreds of thousands of people still flocked to the shrine that they had built, making it the largest, and one of the richest Catholic pilgrimage centres in Asia. But for the numerous fisher-folk who lived at the foot of its walls, the emaciated peasants who laboured in the fields of the village landlords and the countless limbless beggars who scoured the streets for scraps of food, life continued as miserably as before, or seemed to have got even worse.

A poodle-shaped cloud drifted past slowly. My eyes gazed in studied silence upon the Madonna. If the Blessed Virgin could cure fractured noses and help dull-headed college girls pass their examinations, why, I wondered, as I let my thoughts drift, did she seem so oblivious of the misery immediately around her?

My musings on the strange ways of the gods proved to be all too brief, however. A young man in his early thirties, his black face silhouetted against his bright orange T-shirt, walked up to me, holding a bunch of leaflets in his hand.

'Can I join you?' he asked.

Before I could answer he dragged a stool and sat down opposite me.

He spoke Tamil English in a curious American drawl. Bold pink letters on his shirt announced, 'Jesus, the ONLY Saviour,' and a cross and a sword spiked into a shield decorated his back. He introduced himself as James Kennedy.

'You know Kennedy,' he said, as if the late lamented American President happened to have been some dear personal friend.

He handed me a leaflet, a glossy sheet of paper filled with colourful cartoons. A bearded Jesus carried a flaming cross in one hand and the Bible in the other, mounted on a white charger.

Under the forelegs of the animal a dreadful serpent bearing a crown of nettles spewed a steady stream of fire and smoke.

'The Lord God trampling to dust the devil,' Kennedy explained.

'The end of the world is near, brother,' he said gravely, like a doomsday prophet. 'Repent for your sins for the Hour is coming.'

Kennedy was convinced that he would be soon gathered into the bosom of Christ and miraculously transported to the City of Heaven.

'Seven doors of gold and precious jewels the City of the Lord has,' he exclaimed, his stern, raven-like eyes suddenly mellowing and sparkling with delight.

Kennedy had been out of work for the past three years. Before that he had worked as a poorly paid accountant in a factory in Madras.

'Four kids and a wife to support, man. Impossible to survive. Really, these are the last days,' he prophesied, clicking his tongue at the way the world was heading.

Then, as his luck would have it, he had met an American Bible-thumping missionary couple travelling around the world on a ship belonging to a certain American Protestant evangelical group, preaching the Word of the Lord to the benighted. Impressed with his dedication to the holy cause, they took him in their employment on a monthly stipend of four thousand rupees. His job consisted of pestering unsuspecting victims with tales of eternal damnation.

'But I won't be doing this for much longer,' he confessed with an audible sigh of relief. 'My sponsors are getting me a job in America and I'll soon be working there. Probably in a pizza parlour or a petrol pump,' he said.

Our conversation turned to the shrine of Vailankanni and the conditions of the Christians in India.

'Many problems now,' he said gravely. 'Hindu fascists on a killing spree. Burning down churches and setting alight priests and nuns. The wrath of the Lord shall soon be upon them,' he declared.

I asked him what he thought of Vailankanni and its basilica.

'These Catholics have turned Christianity into a pagan cult,' he thundered, biting into the tail of a particularly sinister-looking fish. 'I mean,' he growled, as he stretched out for an oil-soaked prawn, 'this place looks like a Hindu temple, with all these idols and offerings and head shaving and stuff. Where's Christ the Lord in all of this, man?'

Kennedy was convinced that the Catholics had abandoned the True Faith, pandering to paganism in order to win a steady flow of converts and money. And so he went on, haranguing the Church of Rome and exulting in the glory of the United States—'God's very own country' as he put it. Then, finishing his speech and the plate of fish that I had ordered for myself, he trumpeted a hearty burp and got up to leave, realizing that his words had fallen on barren soil.

4

SRI GURU DATTATREYA BABA BUDHAN
DARGAH

It was in the winter of 1998 that I first heard of the Sri Guru
Dattatreya Baba Budhan dargah. Reports of the five rath yatras
organized by the self-styled Datta Peetha Samrakshana Samiti
('Committee for the Liberation of Datta Peetha'), an outfit floated
by the Vishwa Hindu Parishad (VHP) to 'liberate' the shrine
from Muslim control, were splashed prominently across the
front pages of the local newspapers. I was in Bangalore at the
time visiting my mother, and itching to get back on the road. So
I decided to head off to the shrine to find things out for myself.

The nine-hour bus ride to the town of Chikamagalur was
largely uneventful. I tried to grab whatever sleep was possible
amidst annoyingly boisterous Kannada disco music and the
shrieks of a buxom woman bouncing on a flower-strewn bed
on the television screen above me. The bus-stand was desolate
and silent when we arrived early next morning. Cows munched
on discarded temple garlands and a mad man squatted on a
banana leaf, admiring a ring of human refuse. The van heading
for the dargah was waiting on the street outside, and pilgrims
with their bedding and cooking utensils balanced on their
heads were jostling with each other to grab the best seats.

An hour later, the van purred gently up the road and out of
Chikamagalur town. It began a gradual haul up the hills,

passing by endless stretches of coffee gardens, their dark bushes groaning under the weight of their red, ripening beans. Cubes of light filtered in through thin wisps of mist, and it became colder as we turned at each hairpin bend. Further up, coffee estates gradually gave way to vast swathes of forest stretching into the horizon. The red and grey tops of the Baba Budhan hills remained shrouded in thick clumps of fog, towering defiantly against the clear blue sky.

A mild drizzle had set in when we finally arrived at Dada ka Pahad, the hill of Dada the Sufi, at a height of 6214 feet above sea level, the highest peak in Karnataka. The bus stopped abruptly in a small clearing and the last remaining passengers got out. A couple of huts, a long dormitory-like building and a paan shop lay ahead, while a green tin board, with fading letters, announced in Urdu, Kannada and English the 'Sri Guru Dattatreya Baba Budhan Dargah'. A heavy draught of breeze rushed in from the forest below, sending a group of pilgrims scurrying into the roadside shed that served as a makeshift bus-stand and an occasional animal pen. Women huddled in coarse woollen shawls and men peered from under their monkey caps and mufflers, waiting for the rain to subside.

'Welcome to the abode of the Baba,' a voice called out.

I looked about me, but saw no one.

'Here I am,' said the voice.

I scoured around, but still saw nobody. I was beginning to imagine that it was a ghost.

'Arrey, here!' cried the voice. 'Behind the bush with the cloth banners.'

I turned around and spotted the bush, draped with strips of red and green cloth—votive offerings left behind by some absent-minded pilgrim. Behind the bush, on a plastic packet, sat a curious apparition. His weather-beaten face suggested a venerable age, and his kohl-ringed, glassy eyes made him appear like some surreal wizard. He wore a long black robe and his messy, knotted hair was curled into a ball that sat precariously on his head. Strings of plastic beads garlanded his neck. In his hand he held a clay pipe from which rose a plume of grey smoke.

'Ganja!' he said, breaking into a laugh. 'But you seem to be a good boy so I am not going to give you any of it.'

'I'll make you some tea instead,' he offered.

He set a small tin can on a kerosene stove. The stove kept up a steady hiss and the tea bubbled noisily.

'Come, share my blanket with me,' he said.

I declined politely. 'I'm warm enough,' I replied, although the cold had got to my bones.

He introduced himself as Hussain Sharif from Andhra Pradesh. He was a Qalandar, a wandering Muslim dervish, and spent his time travelling from dargah to dargah in search of the 'Friends of God', living off the munificence of the devout.

'You must know of what's happening in the dargah these days,' he said to me grimly as I sipped syrupy tea from a clay pot.

I remained silent, not wanting to influence his response.

'This place is especially blessed by the Dada, and Hindus and Muslims all come here to worship together,' he said, puffing away at his chillum and emitting a great cloud of sweet-smelling smoke. 'Why can't the netas let us be? They want to make this another Ayodhya. Don't they have the fear of God in them?' he thundered. His eyes turned into sharp shards of stone as he hurled imprecations against the politicians in his mind's eye.

'You're not one of them?' he asked me, as he tapped the chillum with a twig and set about preparing it for another round.

'Oh no!' I protested, 'Not one of them at all! I'm just a humble reporter.'

That seemed harmless enough to him.

'Come, I'll take you to the Pir of the dargah and he'll tell you all you want to know,' he said. His eyes had now transformed themselves into little pools of soft light.

He walked up the stony path towards the Pir's house and I followed after him. He left me mid-way, pointing out the green

door where an old man sat in an ochre robe, counting his
beads. 'That's the Pir himself. Now I must go, for my chillum
beckons,' he said with a child-like laugh, and turned around to
head back to the bush where he lived.

'Be careful,' whispered a shopkeeper who called out to me
after the Qalandar had left me. 'This man is a *jalali fakir*, a
particularly angry one at that!'

'You must stay with us,' insisted the amiable, silver-haired,
middle-aged Pir Sayyed Pir Muhammad Shah Qadri Qalandar,
after I had introduced myself. 'This is a Sufi lodge,' he said, as
we warmed ourselves in front of the log-fire in the kitchen,
'and here everyone is welcome. You can stay for as long as you
like. Subramaniam Shastri is here if you need anything,' he
added, introducing me to a man in his early fifties dressed like
a sadhu in a white *veshti* and vest, a thin cotton towel draped
over his shoulders. A visitor from Mumbai was waiting outside,
said the Pir. 'We'll meet for dinner and then you can ask me
all you want,' he offered. 'Till then you can speak with Shastri.
He knows almost as much about this place as I do.'

'Come closer to the fire or else you'll freeze,' said Shastri,
stirring a pool of thick, steamy dal cooking in a massive iron
cauldron after the Pir had left. Seated on a quilt on the floor,
warming my feet in front of the pile of burning logs, I felt
refreshed. Shastri busied himself arranging large pots of grain
and oil on the shelves, as he answered my queries. He was, he
told me, a Brahmin by birth and one of the closest disciples of
the Pir. He had retired as a clerk in a bank and had then taken
diksha from a sadhu, a certain Sridharswamy of Wardahally. After
spending some years with the sadhu, he was instructed to go to
the dargah for further spiritual training, and, as he put it, 'to
serve the followers of Dada, irrespective of caste and creed'.

'My guru,' he said, as he bundled himself next to me and
adjusted the folds of his veshti, 'once visited this shrine many

years ago during Dada's annual *urs*. He distributed money among the fakirs who had gathered there. They all took the money willingly, but one of them declined, saying that he relied only on God to feed him.' 'Guruji,' he added, shaking his head approvingly, 'was so overwhelmed by the fakir's total dependence on God that when he returned he ordered me to shift here, thinking that this was the ideal place for me. And that's how I'm here. It's been almost four years now,' he said with a chuckle that lit up his otherwise stern, wrinkled face.

What did he think of the recent events at the dargah, I asked him hesitatingly, not knowing how he would react.

'Don't talk about it, my son,' he answered, curling his eyebrows into a worried knot. 'It's all politics. Do you think these VHP leaders are really religious? Doesn't Dada belong to all? Doesn't God lie in every heart?'

Dinner at the *khanqah* was a simple fare—thick, spicy dal and mountains of boiled rice flavoured with freshly prepared coconut chutney. We seated ourselves in two rows along a long plastic sheet, with the Pir at the head. His disciple from Bombay, a Roman Catholic, sat opposite me, and the Qalandar from the bush sat at the far end, next to Shastri. The meal ended with a prayer by the Pir. 'Oh Allah!' he said, his palms stretched out, 'Thank you for whatever you have given us today,' followed by an incantation in Arabic that no one but he seemed to understand. 'Ameen,' intoned all of us after him, cupping our hands over our faces in gratitude.

That evening I walked down with the Pir to the dargah. A comet raced through the star-littered sky, and packs of jackals howled in the distance. We passed through an ancient burial ground. 'Generations of my ancestors rest here,' said the Pir, pointing out each grave and identifying its occupant. A band of fakirs huddled together under a tree smoking their chillums. A bearded man bent with age wobbled out of an ancient white-washed mosque. Trailing the thin stream of light from a torch I followed the Pir down a flight of steps into a narrow-mouthed cave. It was dark and cool inside, like some primeval womb. The torch cast tall eerie shadows, and the Pir's soft whispers echoed loudly as they bounced off the walls.

Inside, on an elevated mud pedestal stood four raised stone structures covered with swathes of embroidered silk and great heaps of jasmine flowers. 'The seats of four of the Baba's closest disciples—Jan Pak Shahid, Malik Tijar Faruqi, Malik Wazir Isfahani and Abu Turab Shirazi,' the Pir explained. A grilled door stood at the far end of the cave, behind which a rock opened out into a narrow tunnel. 'Dada Hayat is said to have left the cave through this opening and travelled all the way to Medina,' explained the Pir. On the other side, a little mud plinth marked the place where Mama Jigni, said to be a princess of the royal family of Tiruchirapalli, meditated for many years while training on the Sufi path under the Dada.

It was this unassuming little structure that had now hit the headlines, as the VHP went ahead with its plans to 'liberate' it from Muslim control.

As dawn broke, the next morning, I walked up a stony goat trail into the wooded hills beyond the shrine. The sun remained veiled behind a stationary army of clouds, filtering though in soft, warm shafts. A cool breeze rose from the valley below. I stopped for a light breakfast at Palang Talab, the Pond of the Bed, a little lake ringed by gently rounded knolls. Pilgrims—Hindus outnumbering Muslims—were performing their early morning ablutions in its green, algae-rich waters. A boisterous young woman filled a tin from the pond and drank it greedily. 'Holy water,' explained a passer-by. A queue of worshippers stood with folded hands and bated breath outside the

anthill-shaped shrine of Biru—a Hindu devotee of the Dada—
at the edge of the pond. A Dalit priest, bathed in a river of
sweat, cracked a pile of coconuts and distributed the fruit to the
starry-eyed devout.

After a two-hour trek I arrived at Manak Dhara. A noisy
waterfall tumbled through thickets of ferns, sending up tall jets
of spray. Men and women stood around in two separate pools
in various states of undress, lathering themselves and beating
soap bubbles out of their clothes. Piles of decorated underwear,
torn blouses and shreds of dhotis and lungis lay about carelessly.
'If you want to make your wish come true you must discard
at least one piece of clothing here,' a young man called out to
me from inside the water.

I sat on a rock, shamelessly watching the half-naked men
frolicking in the water. A middle-aged man approached me, a
thin, flimsy sheet tied around his loins, his belly shaking like
a pot of jelly. A thin chord snaked its way around his stomach,
marking him out as a Brahmin.

'Myself named Jagadeshwar Bhat, native of Mangalore,' he
said, introducing himself.

'Why you not taking bath here?' he demanded to know.

'I don't have any spare clothes to donate to the Dada,' I
answered.

'What Dada?' he asked angrily, as if I had taken the name of
the devil himself. His face was now contorted with rage, and
had assumed the terrifying appearance of an evil-eyed asura on
the gopuram of a South Indian temple.

'There's no Dada-Wada here,' he insisted. 'It's Swamy
Dattatreya. And we must liberate him from the wretched
Muslims.'

Little is known about the life of Dada Hayat Qalandar, also
known as Swamy Dattatreya. Like most other wandering
dervishes, his story is wrapped up in layers of myth. He is said

to have been one of the three-and-a-half Qalandar masters—
members of a Sufi order of considerable influence in South
Asia. The principal shrine of the Qalandars is that of Lal
Shahbaz, 'the Red Falcon', located in Sehwan in Sind. Next in
importance is the dargah of Bu 'Ali Shah in Panipat, in present-
day Haryana. And then comes Dada Hayat's dargah. The half
Qalandar is Rab'ia of Basra who was denied full membership
in the Qalandar order because of her gender.

Local legend has it that the Dada's real name was Shaikh
'Abdul 'Aziz Makki, and that he was born in the town of Ta'if
in Arabia, sometime in the sixth century BC. He is said to have
been a companion of the Prophet Muhammad. Originally a
Christian, he later converted to Islam and was blessed by the
Prophet with a long life and the accompanying title of Hayat-
ul Bahr-e-Zinda—'The Living One of the Life of the Seas'. He
is claimed to have been the first of the Qalandars, although this
must certainly be disputed by the followers of his two-and-a-
half colleagues.

The Dada's hagiographers believe that he was especially
commissioned by the Prophet to travel to Chandradrona hill,
as Dada ka Pahad was then known, to put an end to the
oppression of the poor by the local *palegar* landlords. The
palegars, write 'Abdul Wasi 'Asri and 'Abdul Jabbar in their
Tazkira-e-Hazrat Dada Hayat Mir Qalandar, 'had turned this
natural heaven into a veritable hell with their oppression and
cruelty', 'playing holi with the blood of innocents every day',
sacrificing them to appease blood-thirsty goddesses. Moved to
pity by the plight of the people, Muhammad had dispatched
the Dada to rescue them.

After a long and uncomfortable journey across the Arabian
Sea on the back of a giant fish, Dada Hayat and a band of his
followers finally reached Chandradrona hill. Night had already
fallen when they arrived, and while his disciples went off to
sleep, the Dada entered a cave on the top of the mountain and
began making preparations for the night prayer. Just then, so

the story goes, he saw a group of palegars dragging along with them a man bound in chains. The man was to be slaughtered for having intruded into their territory. No sooner had the palegars unsheathed their swords that, all of a sudden, the Dada caused their weapons to fall from their hands, and the chains binding their captive to snap open.

Realizing that the Dada was no ordinary mortal, the palegars fell at his feet, begging him for mercy. To express his gratitude to the Dada for having saved his life, their captive became his disciple and converted to Islam. Soon, the news of the Dada's miraculous powers spread like a forest fire, and large crowds began flocking to his cave to seek his blessings. It appeared to them that Swami Dattatreya, the much-awaited incarnation of the Hindu Trinity of Brahma, Vishnu and Shiva, had appeared to them in the form of the Sufi. Some of them converted to Islam at his hands, while many others, without abandoning their ancestral faith, accepted him as the Datta Avatar.

The equation between Dada Hayat and Dattatreya in popular lore should not be seen as particularly strange or unusual, given the fact that numerous other popular Sufis in the area have been associated with Dattatreya, himself a late Puranic figure and designed, it appears, to reconcile what were, till then, the conflicting Shaivite and Vaishnavite traditions. As the *Gazetteer of Belgaum* notes, 'Dattatreya represents not only the synthesis of Shaivism and Vaishnavism but also of the Sufi cult' (Government of Karnataka, 1987, p. 187). Among the several Muslim saints of the Deccan who have been equated by Hindus with Dattatreya are Shah Fakir, Chand Bhole, the Sufi spiritual preceptor of the Brahmin Janardhana Swami, and, closer to our own times, the Sai Baba of Shirdi.

The early Dattatreya tradition seems beyond doubt to have been an anti-Brahminical one, part of the broader Awadhut tradition that upholds a formless god and sternly condemns the caste system and the sacrifices so central to classical Brahminism. In the *Siva Purana* Dattatreya is said to have developed the *sanyasa* mode of a world-renouncing mystic. In the *Markandeya Purana*, Dattatreya appears as an antinomian yogi. We are told that although he wanted to be alone, the sons of the sages always surrounded him. In order to drive them away, he submerged himself in a lake and emerged from it accompanied by a lissome maiden, with whom he set about sharing a glass of wine, in the hope that witnessing the amorous couple the young men would leave him alone. The *Markandeya Purana* tells us that once, when the gods were defeated by the demons in a battle, they approached Brihaspati for help. Brihaspati sent them to Dattatreya. When the gods approached Dattatreya, they found him drinking wine in the company of Lakshmi. The gods prayed to him for help, but he pointed out his own faults: 'Drinking, attachment, affection and sexual enjoyment of women.' This clearly points to a strong anti-Brahminical Tantric strand in the original Dattatreya tradition.

To come back to the story linking Dada Hayat with Dattatreya, it is interesting to note that belief in the coming of a messiah in the form of Dattatreya to deliver the world from strife and oppression was central to the early Dattatreya cult as it had evolved in the Deccan. Dada Hayat's battles with the oppressive palegars seem to have been a confirmation of this belief. It is thus hardly surprising that many Hindus, particularly from the 'low' castes, saw him as their awaited messiah who would deliver them from servitude. Consequently, Dada Hayat was regarded as none other than Dattatreya himself, the word 'Dattatreya' being, in this context, perhaps a corruption of the word 'Dada'.

As to the location of Dada Hayat's grave, different stories circulate. The Pir and his followers insist that he is still alive, although hidden from the public gaze, tirelessly engaged in guiding the faithful. The custodians of at least two other Sufi shrines in South India—the dargah of Mardan-e-Gha'ib at Shivasamudra, not far from Bangalore, and the dargah of Hazrat

Tabal-e-'Alam at Tiruchirapalli, in Tamil Nadu—claim that Dada Hayat died a natural death and is buried in their respective shrine complexes.

Although Dada Hayat is believed to have remained unmarried throughout his life, he is said to have appointed   a native of Yemen, a certain Sayyed Shah Jamaluddin Maghribi— popularly known as Baba Budhan—to manage the affairs of the shrine after him. Baba Budhan is best remembered for having introduced the cultivation of coffee into the area. He divided his followers into groups and dispatched them to places as far as the Nilgiris, Coorg and the hilly regions of north Kerala, where they preached Islam and special Yemeni techniques of growing the intoxicating bean. Before his death, Baba Budhan appointed his nephew, Sayyed Musa Hussain Shah Qadri, as his successor. The custodianship of the shrine is still retained by this family, the present sajjada nashin—custodian of the shrine—being the sixteenth in line from Sayyed Musa.

Over the centuries, various Muslim as well as Hindu rulers patronized the dargah, endowing it with considerable wealth and land. Thus, during the time of the second sajjada nashin, Channamaji, the Hindu queen of Nagar, contributed lavishly for the repair of the dargah's aslah khana, the storage house for weapons for the protection of the fakirs. Haider 'Ali, the ruler of Mysore, donated several villages to the dargah for its upkeep, as did his son, Tipu Sultan. Another great patron of the shrine was Sri Krishnaraja Wodeyar III, the Hindu ruler of Mysore. He is said to have held the shrine in particular reverence, and to have received regular spiritual instruction from the then sajjada nashin, Pir Sayyed Murtaza Shah Qadri Qalandar. Besides the patronage extended by various Hindu and Muslim rulers, the dargah also emerged, over time, as a popular pilgrimage centre for large numbers of ordinary Muslims and Hindus from all over the Deccan and the far south.

It is interesting to note that the custodianship of the shrine being vested in the family of Muslim sajjada nashins was never challenged by any Hindu ruler or by the local Hindus. Indeed, in the royal documents detailing the grants given to them by various Hindu kings, the sajjada nashins were recognized as the mathadipathis or 'heads of the matha (shrine)'. They were also known, according to the *Gazetteer of Mysore*, by the honorific title of 'Sri Dattatreya Swami Baba Budhan Swami Jagadguru', 'The Teacher of the Entire World'. Accordingly, they were granted certain privileges that were on par with those granted to the heads of some leading Hindu shrines. Thus, under the Hindu Wodeyars of Mysore, the Sajjade Sri Guru Dattathreya Bababudanswami, as he was officially known, was among the seventeen 'gurus' to be exempted from personal appearance in the civil courts of the state, and also the only Muslim 'guru' to have enjoyed that honour.

It was only in the mid-1960s that a dispute arose over the control of the shrine, and even then, curiously enough, it was not between Hindus and Muslims but, rather, between two government-controlled administrative bodies—the Karnataka Waqf Board, in charge of Muslim endowed properties, and the Muzrai Department, the general overseer of Hindu religious and charitable endowments in the state. Interestingly, the Muslim custodians of the dargah supported the Muzrai Department's stand, arguing against the Waqf Board's claims on the grounds that the dargah was not exclusively a Muslim shrine as it was venerated by both Muslims and Hindus. It is likely that the sajjada nashin feared that a Waqf Board take-over would sharply curtail his privileges and his control over the considerable donations offered by the devout. The matter went to the courts, and several cases and counter-cases were registered. As matters stand today, the courts have ruled that the dargah is under the jurisdiction of the Muzrai Department and not the Waqf Board; that the Muslim sajjada nashin is the sole administrator of the dargah, and that the rituals that have traditionally been conducted at the shrine be continued and not tampered with.

Concerted efforts to project the controversy as a Hindu-Muslim dispute can be traced to the early 1980s, when militant Hindu supremacist organizations succeeded in establishing a strong foothold in parts of Karnataka. In 1989, the VHP floated an organization for the 'liberation' of the shrine, organizing in December that year a three-day so-called *Datta Jayanti* at the dargah, amidst Muslim protests and tight police security. After the destruction of the Babri Masjid in Ayodhya in 1992, the campaign to take over the dargah got fresh impetus. With the state seeming to turn a blind eye to Hindu militant provocation, or, even as some saw it, actually being complicit in the affair, what was once a unique centre of pilgrimage bringing people from different communities and walks of life together in common worship, was now transformed into a centre of furious communal contestation.

As Hindutva leaders sped on their raths of wrath through Karnataka that early December, Hindus clashed with Muslims. Despite pleas that the rath yatras be stopped, the state administration refused to act. The five raths reached Chikamagalur on 30 November, and the dargah on 1 December, amidst unprecedented police protection. Although the district administration had clamped prohibitory orders on a ten-kilometre radius around the dargah, banning the assembly of four or more persons, no restriction was placed on the assembly of Hindutva activists at the shrine itself. By 3 December, their number had swelled to more than 10,000. Senior leaders of the Bharatiya Janata Party (BJP) had also been roped in. Prominent among them was Ananth Kumar Hegde, BJP member of Parliament from neighbouring Karwar, who, six years earlier, had personally participated in tearing down the Babri Masjid at Ayodhya. Hegde had publicly announced that he would dispatch 'suicide squads' to ensure the success of the campaign (Parvathi Menon, 1999). A massive rally was then held outside the dargah, in which fiery speeches were delivered against the Muslims. Addressing the rally, a certain Swamy Sadanandji, head of the little-known Ajjampura Math, declared, much to the mirth of the mob, 'The shrine will be liberated or a bloodbath is certain' (B.R. Srikanth, 1998). Impassioned cries of 'We will shed blood to save the Datta Peetha' rent the air (*Communalism Combat*, December 1998), and it was falsely alleged that the Muslim sajjada nashin was obstructing Hindus from worshipping at the shrine.

Emboldened by this fiery rhetoric, activists of the fascist Bajrang Dal tore down the green flags fluttering near the dargah and, in their place, hoisted saffron Hindutva flags. The police and the local administration remained mute spectators to this vandalism. The deputy commissioner of Chikamagalur, K.S. Manjunath, and the inspector general of police (Western Range), B.N. Bhonsale, claimed that this could not be stopped as this would lead to a confrontation (*Indian Express*, 4 December 1998). The police and the administration had reportedly been warned that if they attempted to remove the saffron flags, their hands would be 'cut off' (*Communalism Combat*, December 1998). Sensing that the police were in no mood to stop them, Hindutva activists carried a three-headed idol purported to be that of Dattatreya inside the cave and worshipped it. The Muslims protested, arguing that this was a clear violation of the court's orders, but their plea was turned down on the flimsy grounds that removing the idol then could result in communal violence. As a result, for the first time an idol was worshipped at the dargah. This continued for three days, till 3 December. A group of Brahmin priests associated with the VHP also tried to take a two-foot idol of Ganesha inside the shrine, fully aware of the tradition that once an idol of the elephant-headed god is installed at a particular spot it cannot be removed. The administration did not allow them to carry the idol inside, although they were allowed to worship it at the entrance of the cave. After this, the idol was taken by the deputy commissioner of the district, who told visiting newspersons that at an earlier meeting with VHP leaders, he had agreed that any 'offering' that they made to the shrine 'would be accepted' (*Asian Age*, 4 December 1998).

After the so-called puja gave over, a dharma sabha (religious council) was organized outside the dargah, which was addressed by senior VHP and Bajrang Dal leaders. They announced that they were giving the government a year's ultimatum to hand the shrine over to them, failing which they would be forced to 'choose the path of confrontation', promising a 'bloodbath' (*Asian Age*, 20 December 1998). They also demanded the removal of the Muslim sajjada nashin and the appointment of a Hindu priest in his place, and the offering of Hindu-style puja at the dargah every day. The state convener of the Bajrang Dal, Pramod Mutalik, demanded that the annual Sufi 'urs festival, which has been held for several centuries at the shrine, be discontinued forthwith (*Asian Age*, 3 December 1998). Not to be outdone, the all-India general secretary of the Bajrang Dal, Prakash Sharma, demanded that only Hindu puja be allowed at the shrine. At a rally organized later at Chikamagalur, he thundered, 'If Allah and Christ do not accept *Saraswati Vandana*, why should our *Dattapeetha* accept Muslims?' (Parvathi Menon, 1999).

From 1998 onwards the VHP and its associated outfits have been regularly holding a so-called puja at the dargah every December and organizing large, slogan-shouting rallies for the 'liberation' of Dattatreya. The state, true to its traditions, has done little, if anything at all, to hold in check this fast-spreading campaign of terror. And so, steadily but surely, this little shrine tucked away in a remote cave up in the thickly wooded hills of Chikamagalur is probably on its way to becoming a second Ayodhya.

'Hey you, newspaper-wala,' someone shouted out as I he ded down the next morning to catch the bus back to Chikamagalur. I turned back to find the ganja-puffing fakir, clutching at the hem of his robe and strolling towards the bus-stand, waving out to me. He seemed somehow less intimidating, in fact somewhat jovial, with his matted hair now covered with a black turban, and an enormous turquoise pendant dancing from a string around his neck.

'So, you're off, are you?' he asked me.

'I don't know what you're going to write about the dargah,' he said, as he struck a match and lit his chillum. 'But always remember son,' he mused, closing his eyes and blowing a cloud of smoke out of his hairy nostril, 'Come what may, God is always with those who are faithful to Him.' And, clearing his throat, he recited in a voice that seemed full of pain, a couplet which he said he had picked up from some wandering *qawwal:*

Allah ko dhundo Allah ke pyaron mein
Allah samaya hai in ishq ke maro main
(Search for God among God's loved ones
For God is to be found among those smitten by love.)

'Allah be with you, son,' he said, and drew me to his cloak. His heart pounded heavily against my chest. I looked up and saw a stream of kohl trickling down his wet eyes.

5

THE SUFI-SADHUS OF
NORTHERN KARNATAKA

Living together for centuries in isolated hamlets and small
towns, several communities in the dry, inhospitable districts of
northern Karnataka developed over time their own unique
shared religious traditions that had borrowed freely from a
variety of sources. At local shrines of holy men or warrior
saints, or even downright charlatans, Hindus, Muslims, Dalits
and Lingayats often gathered in common worship and
celebration. Certain shrines were reputed for their powers to
heal and grant requests, and were visited by people across what
we would today call the Hindu-Muslim divide. As elsewhere
in India, wandering Sufi masters and mendicants had a large
following in the area. Their message of equality and
brotherhood seemed to have particularly appealed to the 'lower'
castes, many of who thus converted to Islam. Denied access
to Hindu temples, they were welcomed in the dargahs of
the Sufis.

Sufi ideas also seemed to have deeply influenced other
communities that did not convert to Islam. For instance, the
Lingayats of the Deccan, one of the most populous religious
groups in the region, seem to share much with the Sufis in
terms of belief and practice. The eleventh century founder of
the Lingayat faith, Basava, is said to have been born in a royal

family, and to have later been appointed a minister at the court of the king of Kalyan, in north-eastern Karnataka. A restless seeker of truth, he abandoned the religion of his ancestors, threw off his 'holy' thread and spent the rest of his life crusading against caste, idolatry, polytheism and untouchability. In short, like Sufism, the Lingayat faith emerged as a powerful challenge to Brahminical hegemony in the Deccan. Not surprisingly, like the Sufis, the Lingayats were particularly successful among the 'lower' castes. And it is primarily among the 'lower' castes of the region that the shared religious shrines were particularly popular. But things are beginning to change today, and many shared shrines in northern Karnataka are now emerging as centres of contestation, in some cases transformed beyond all recognition.

For some time now Elamma of Sauditti has suffered a rather bad press. Located in a small settlement in the impoverished Belgaum district near the contentious border between Maharashtra and Karnataka, her temple has for centuries been the centre of the flourishing Devadasi cult, the cult of the 'female slaves of the gods'. Every year scores of 'low' caste women flock to the shrine, dressed in nothing but strings of leaves covering their private parts. After an elaborate ritual, they are believed to be blessed by the goddess and admitted into her large retinue of servants. Strictly debarred from marrying, sooner or later most of these women are forced by circumstances and tradition into prostitution. The government of Karnataka is said to be trying to abolish the practice, but old practices die hard, as does bureaucratic inertia. Even threats of imprisonment and hefty fines have done little to do away with such practices.

A cloud of dust rose from the mound of garbage at the bus-stand as I got off at Sauditti. The summer sun was high up in the cloudless sky, and had transformed the grasslands beyond into a vast cracked plain—like a shattered windscreen. A team of wiry women sat in the shade of a neem tree, banging an old tin and clanging little brass cymbals in a haunting rhythm. In the centre of the group sat a girl, probably in her late teens, her coal-dark face smeared with streaks of vermilion, a giant red blob placed in the centre of her forehead. She balanced a series of copper pots, decorated with shrubs on her head. A toothless crone shrieked an ode to the goddess. All of a sudden, the girl began swaying violently. Froth collected at her mouth and trickled down her chin. 'Hayya, hayya,' she cried, furiously beating her breast, and the women around her bent low to touch her feet with their hands folded in awe.

'The devi has come upon her,' they told me. 'You better go from here.'

I walked down to the temple of Elamma, a short distance away. Blisters covered my bare feet as I tiptoed through piles of rubble, discarded garlands of marigold and little cakes of human excrement.

The enormous shrine is a new stone structure, of little architectural interest in itself. Inside the gloomy sanctum, the goddess sits perched on a throne, weighed down by layers of necklaces and flowers. The overpowering smell of incense and ghee drove me out in an instant.

A bare-chested priest waddled up to me as I unloaded the reel from my camera.

'Why you no doing puja?' he asked, as he drummed his ponderous, hairless belly. 'You no Hindu or what?'

I fluttered my eyelashes and forced on a smile, pretending not to follow his broken English.

The origins of the cult of Elamma and of her temple at Sauditti have remained largely unexplored by scholars of popular religion in the Deccan. Some believe that the temple once belonged to the Jains. Jainism, in its origins a distinctly anti-Brahminical religion, found warm support in Karnataka and other parts of South India, particularly among the 'lower' castes. However, as elsewhere in India, by the ninth century AD, Brahminism was once again on the rise in Karnataka. The Brahminical revival was accompanied by large-scale slaughter of Jain monks and the destruction or, more commonly, the appropriation of their temples. The shrine at Sauditti, so some say, was among the numerous Jain temples that were taken over by the Hindus at the time.

Traditionally, Dalits and other so-called lower castes formed the bulk of the devotees of Elamma. That her cult is almost certainly of 'low' caste origin is suggested by the *Gazetteer of India*, which notes that it is a blend of Mahayana Buddhist and Nath Shaivite traditions, both of which started off as powerful anti-Brahminical movements (Government of Karnataka, 1987 p. 186). Elmore, one of the few scholars to have studied the Elamma tradition, maintains that Elamma is actually 'the original form' of Mathamma, the patron goddess of the Madiga Dalits, considered to be one of the lowest communities in the local caste hierarchy (Wilber Theodore Elmore, 1925).

Although the Madigas and other Dalits claim Elamma as one of their own, she has now been transformed into an incarnation of the Goddess Durga and incorporated into the Brahminical pantheon of 'respectable' deities. The cult has been Brahminized to such an extent that the 'upper' caste priest I spoke to denied vehemently 'low' caste origins of the goddess.

'Elamma is a form of the Shakti herself,' he insisted, offering me a booklet penned by an unknown Brahmin scholar, as if the published word itself was enough to silence all rival claims.

'The goddess appeared in the form of Renuka in the sat yug, the age of truth; as Draupadi, the wife of the five Pandavas in the dvapar or second era; as Janaki in the treta, the third era; and in this evil age of kali yug she has assumed the form of Elamma to redeem the world,' the booklet announced.

It was obvious that with the swelling numbers of pilgrims at the shrine, Elamma's 'low' caste origins were hurriedly being swept under the carpet, and she was now to be accorded a more 'honorable' pedigree. A 'low' caste goddess was a poor business proposition.

If Elamma's Dalit ancestry is today vehemently denied, so, too, are the stories of her links with a Sufi who lies buried on top of a knoll some hundred metres from her shrine. The priest of the temple said he knew nothing about the Pir Baba, but a group of Banjara tribals whom I met outside insisted I accompany them to the dargah.

'Bhaure Shah Wali is the spiritual brother of Elamma,' they said. 'How can you expect to get the full blessings of the sister if you don't meet the brother?' they asked, amazed at my stupidity.

An old Muslim woman sat at the foot of a small grave, which was draped in a green sheet of shiny silk decorated with silver tassels. An array of copper horses stood on the edge of the grave.

'The Baba's mounts,' she pointed out proudly, quite oblivious of the Islamic horror of idols.

'Baba Bhaure Shah was a wandering Madari Sufi,' she told me, as I settled on a frayed reed mat, while the Banjara women circumambulated the grave, in their brilliantly coloured ghagras.

The woman coughed up a ball of phlegm, spat it out violently into a rusting tin, and said, 'At the time when the Baba arrived here, this area was a dense forest. He settled here on this hillock where he spent many years in deep meditation. One day, Elamma, a poor woman who had been afflicted by leprosy, took refuge in the forest, for no one would give her shelter. The Baba, taking pity on her, accepted her as his disciple, and with his miraculous powers, cured her of her illness. Then, the Baba gave a seat for her to meditate on the spot where her temple stands today.'

There had apparently been much give-and-take between Elamma's temple and the Baba's dargah in the past. It is said that on the day of the full moon, when Elamma is believed to have lost her husband, special food would be cooked by her followers and sent to the Baba's shrine. It was once a common practice for pilgrims travelling to Elamma's temple to visit the dargah as well. But as Elamma was transformed into an orthodox Brahminical goddess, this practice has now almost completely stopped.

'Let people think what they want to and let the world go to hell,' said the woman as she returned my parting salaam. 'But I can never abandon Elu-bai, sister Elamma.'

Ilkal, in the Bagalkot district, is a dry, dusty town criss-crossed winding, dirt-clogged lanes lined with decrepit houses and dark, gloomy workshops where teenaged workers crouch over ancient looms that churn out the delicately woven saris for which the town is so famous. At the far end of the town, behind the great row of huts that garland a fetid pond, is the towering dome of the dargah of Sayyed Shah Murtaza Qadri, a descendant, as all genuine Sayyeds are, of the Prophet Muhammad.

A giant vat stood on a heap of logs, coughing up huge clouds of smoke as I entered the shrine. A large crowd had assembled here for a special feast. Muslim women, dressed in black burkas and Hindu women in flimsy chiffon saris (none in the fine Ilkal handlooms, I noticed) sat in a pavilion grinding spices and chopping vegetables. A Hindu sadhu, his hair matted like a bird's nest, perched on a rock, counting his rudraksh beads. A number of elderly Muslim men, their full beards hennaed a pale orange, sat at the foot of a gnarled tree, reading from the Qur'an, moving forward and backward in unison. It was the 131st death anniversary of Sayyed Murtaza, and an occasion of great joy for the pilgrims who had gathered there to celebrate the 'urs or 'marriage' of the saint—his final union, after his death, with God. Now infinitely closer to God than when he was alive, he was believed to be in a particularly propitious position to intercede with God to grant humble petitioners their various requests: a cure for a painful illness, a job for the unemployed, milk to a woman whose breasts had gone dry or a change of government for a politician belonging to a party in the opposition. His clients that day included a motley crowd of Hindus and Muslims, men and women, and even a foul-mouthed and richly painted eunuch.

Sayyed Murtaza was the son of Sayyed Shah Pir Pasha Qadri, a noted Sufi from a little village in neighbouring Raichur. He was educated by his father and in keeping with the customs, of well-established Sufi families of his times, he was taught the Qur'an and the Hadith—the traditions of the Prophet—besides Arabic, Persian and Sanskrit, by his father. His uncle, Dada Pir, initiated him to the Sufi path, and taught him about the great Muslim mystics of the past. Dada Pir also instructed him in the Bhagwad Gita and the Bible. By the time he succeeded his father as the the head of the monastery that the latter had established, his fame as a pious saint and a powerful miracle-worker had spread far and wide.

Among Sayyed Murtaza's many friends and admirers was a leading Lingayat priest of the town, a certain Shri Mahant Swamy. One day, so the story goes, the Sufi and the Lingayat were sitting together and pondering over the complexities of the world of the spirit.

'My friend,' said the Sufi. 'We have been companions for a long time, and so we must fulfil our duty towards each other. Accordingly, after I die you must bury me and I shall do the same to you after your death.'

The Lingayat priest agreed to perform what seemed to be an impossible duty. Shortly after, Sayyed Murtaza breathed his last. Remembering his promise, Shri Mahant accompanied the procession to the graveyard and buried him. A few days later, Shri Mahant, too, left the world. A furious dispute broke out between the followers of the two holy men. Sayyed Murtaza's disciples insisted that the body of Shri Mahant could not be laid to rest until Sayyed Murtaza, now long since deceased, kept his word and buried him. Swamy's disciples protested, arguing that the Sufi was dead and so could not fulfil his promise. Just as the quarrel was about to break out into a riot, a whirlwind rose from Sayyed Murtaza's grave, bringing along with it an enormous cloud of dust that settled on Shri Mahant's body, tucking it into a grave. In this way, it is said, the two friends kept their promises to each other in death, as in life.

'Because of the blessings of the two friends, Ilkal has remained free of Hindu-Muslim riots for decades now,' said a wizened Muslim man, spraying little specks of betel nut on to my face. He broke off to pat an old woman—obviously a Hindu from the enormous bindi on her heavily lined forehead—with a bunch of peacock feathers. 'Transferring energy from the dargah,' he explained. 'Hindus and Muslims come to the Baba in equal numbers, and he loves both of them.'

'You must know Nar Singh Chauhan,' he asked me.

I shook my head, embarrassed at my ignorance.

He twisted his eyebrows in surprise. He seemed to think that just about everyone had heard of this Hindu disciple of the Baba who had taken care of the Baba towards his last days and in whose lap the Baba had rested his head when he breathed his last. Nar Singh's descendants, he told me, were expected to arrive at the shrine that evening, and they had a particularly important role to play in the 'urs celebrations. They had the privilege of carrying a special green cover for the Baba's tomb and offering a crown to the Muslim sajjada nashin, the custodian of the shrine.

'You must stay till they arrive, and join us all for dinner,' said the man. I was sorry to have to rush off, however. The last train to Bangalore was leaving in less than an hour.

'If only we had more people like the Baba and Nar Singh today, Hindus and Muslims would live in peace,' the old man sighed, and handed me a bunch of petals as a parting blessing.

'Allah be with you,' he cried out, wrapping me in a tight embrace before I stepped out into the street and hopped into the waiting auto-rickshaw.

Wading through great puddles of slush, I moved up the narrow goat trail, past the tumbling huts and the enormous cow-dung mounds of Shishunala, an impoverished little village tucked away in a remote corner in the Haveri district of northern Karnataka, some fifty kilometres from the town of Hubli. A clump of ochre-robed sadhus walked ahead, carrying with them round-bottomed copper pots and strings of red and white flowers. A giant stork prodded the still waters of the paddy field with the fine tip of its chopstick beak, adroitly picking out a spotted green frog. Banana trees heaved under the weight of ripening fruit, attracting a family of noisy mynahs, their eyes ringed with giant circles like ill-fitting spectacles. Devotional music played from a loudspeaker in the distance.

A freshly white-washed building stood at the end of the path, atop which, on the four corners, lazed meek-looking terracotta bulls, with jewels carved out of stone around their necks. A rusting tin board announced, 'The Temple of Shishunala Sharif, the Kabir of South India'. Under an old neem tree in the courtyard, a raised stone plinth covered a row of graves. It was covered with flowers and little clay lamps from which emanated a soft mellow light.

'The *samadhi* of Sharif and his parents,' the friendly, handsome priest told me, as he took me around.

We settled on a stone bench after the guided tour.

'You living Karnataka but not you knowing the Kannada?' queried the priest, visibly upset at my poor linguistic skills.

His English seemed to be as good as my Kannada, so our dialogue was restricted mainly to nodding heads and exchanging smiles. Shortly after, despairing of the poor readway we were making a schoolboy was summoned to translate for us. The priest now began talking about the Muslim Sharif and what was, as far as I could see, his distinctly Hindu temple.

Sharif, or, more properly, Muhammad Sharif Nawar, was born in 1819 to Imam Sahib, a poor Muslim doctor from Shishunala, and his wife Hajjama. For twelve long years after their marriage, the couple remained childless. One day, Imam Sahib heard of a powerful Sufi called Shah Wali Qadri in the neighbouring village of Hulugur, who was rumoured to grant people their wishes. Imam Sahib and Hajjama went to meet the Sufi and spent the next few months at his monastery, sweeping it clean every morning and meeting his every need. Impressed with their devotion, the Sufi is said to have blessed them with a son who, he prophesied, would grow up to be a great saint. Some months later, Muhammad Sharif was born.

Sharif is said to have frequented the company of Sufis and sadhus as a child, and to have been indifferent to the snares of the world. He studied at the village school, after which he began teaching there. He also started instructing the village lads in the martial dances that are performed by Muslims during the month of Muharrum to commemorate the martyrdom of Imam Hussain, the grandson of the Prophet Muhammad. It was at this time that he first met Govind Bhat, a Hindu mystic from the village of Kalas in Dharwar. Impressed with the young lad's dedication, Govind Bhat accepted Sharif as his disciple. Taking a Muslim as his student is said to have earned him the wrath of the local Brahmins. Undeterred by their opposition, Govind Bhat took Sharif in his care, and the boy lived with him till the guru breathed his last several years later.

The story of Sharif's first meeting with Govind Bhat is particularly interesting, and shows a remarkable fluidity of religious identities and the interweaving of various traditions that characterizes much of popular religion in northern Karnataka.

Govind Bhat, it is said, had been in search of a true disciple. Many leading Brahmins of his village had sent their sons to him but he had turned them down. One day, he heard a voice instructing him to set off for Shishunala where he would find the student he was looking for, in a Muslim family. When he finally met Sharif he decided to test him by asking him a set of questions on the intricate points of philosophy. The boy answered these to the satisfaction of the guru, and Govind Bhat suitably impressed requested his parents to allow him to take the boy with him. Under Govind Bhat's tutelage, Sharif spent the next few years studying yoga and the teachings of the Bhakti, Lingayat and Sufi saints. This earned him the title of 'Triveni Sangam' or the 'Confluence of the Three Traditions'.

As night crept in, little fires in the courtyards of village homes began sending up plumes of purple smoke. A herd of red-horned cows plodded down a path, driven by an old man in a tattered loincloth with a weather-beaten face, crumpled like an ancient parchment. A couple of leathery bats flew out from their perches on a banyan tree searching for food and swept down on a bush of berries. A battalion of mosquitoes hovered above my head, diving down to attack my ears with their pointed pincers and their piercing war cries.

Presently, a group of men arrived, dressed in patched dhotis and coloured cotton kurtas. They sat under the neem tree and took their musical instruments out from cloth bags that were slung on their backs. A fat man with a bulbous, pimple-laden nose thumped the dholak that rested on his belly, pulling at its ropes and powdering its sides in preparation for the concert. A lean stick of a man, who, judging from his clothes, was probably the leader of the group, cleared his throat and emptied his mouth into a tin spittoon before ascending to a high-pitched hum, his long, slender fingers blithely dancing over the keys of the harmonium. Two young boys dressed in their school uniform, their moth-eaten ties hanging loose over their unbuttoned shirts, sat behind them and muttered a silent prayer.

A crowd of villagers had gathered to hear the group, apparently of considerable local repute. Women cradled bawling babies in their arms; excited old turbaned men nervously stroked the edges of their bushy moustaches into menacing curls; little girls in long skirts and half-sleeved blouses strung bunches of pink flowers into each other's hair; the village lunatic giggled to himself, furiously scratching his groin.

'Brothers and sisters,' said a young man, who stood on a makeshift dais, his topknot furiously swinging each time he nodded his head. 'We are greatly honoured to have the world-renowned Ramappa and party sing to us tonight the verses of our own beloved Sharif of Shishunala,' he announced. The crowd clapped excitedly. A sullen, crooked-mouthed man, dressed in an ill-fitting safari suit, gleaming white leather shoes and dark glasses delivered a long incomprehensible speech.

'A local politician,' indicated my neighbour, in hushed tones. 'He be big, very big man.'

The politician gesticulated wildly, waving his hands about in the air for effect, reminding his captive audience of the many promises that he had made to the people of the village the previous year, solemnly vowing to renew those promises that year as well. A young boy shot out of the crowd and shouted him down. 'We've come here to listen to Ramappa sing, not you singing your own praises,' he yelled.

After frayed tempers had cooled, and the visibly embarrassed politician forced to climb down from the dais, Ramappa and his men began their performance. They sang verse after verse from the mystical songs penned by Sharif, which had recently been put together in the form of a book, the *Shishunala Sharif Gitagolu*. My neighbour translated them for me as the performance proceeded. They sang of the sorrow of the poor, the fleetingness of the world, the love for God and the essential oneness of humankind. I scribbled a song in my notebook:

From the mud-pot the three worlds were born,
So, where is this caste and that caste?
God is one, and God's teachings are one
God's language is one, too.
People express their devotion to Him in different ways
And in different ways do they see Him.
All is one, All is one. Sing, all is indeed one.

The concert carried on till late in the night. One by one people got up and moved towards Sharif's grave, bowed before it and smeared ash on their foreheads. They offered leaves filled with bits of coconut and flowers to a Lingayat priest sitting on one side of the grave, and packets of incense sticks and balls of sugar to the Muslim squatting opposite him. Then they slowly wound their way to their hovels, wading through the waterlogged goat trail in the envelope of darkness.

The bullock cart creaked its way down the road, swinging dangerously from side to side as it climbed in and out of yawning holes, with the decaying ruins of Bidar slowly receding into the distance. The sun shone brightly, and waves of steam rose from pools of melting tar. The smell of human excrement and discarded rubber tyres filled the air. The bullock plodded along gently with streams of sweat rushing down its mottled hide and its eyes half closed to keep out the heat.

'Hurry up! I'm already an hour late for the puja,' bellowed the Brahmin seating next to me. Beads of perspiration had smudged the moon-shaped bindi on his forehead and little crimson rivulets ran down his face.

The bullock cart owner swung his whip and brought it crashing down on the bullock's back.

'Harder! Harder!' yelled the Brahmin.

The whip whooshed up in the air and came down upon on the animal's back with renewed ferocity, forcing it to break into a trot.

'Aren't Hindus meant to worship the cow?' I asked the Brahmin, making no effort to conceal my disgust.

'Yes, yes, Aaa-Ma. We worship mother cow. But not worshipping to bullocks,' he replied smugly.

Three-quarters of an hour later, the massive domes of crumbling Muslim tombs drew into view. We had arrived at the village of Ashtur, the resting place of generations of Bahmani Sultans of Bidar. The fine masonry and semi-precious stones that had once adorned the domes had all but disappeared, and brambles and peepul shafts had sprouted in the crannies of the brickwork. Pieces of Iranian-style blue and green tile on narrow ledges were the only reminder of the grandeur of an age long gone by.

An elderly Muslim woman, bent over a sickle and cutting wild grass, pointed out to me the tomb of Sultan Ahmad Shah. It stood at the end of the row of royal mausoleums, towering above the rest, and in a somewhat better condition.

'You must meet him. He's a great saint,' she said, as if the Sultan was still sitting on his throne. 'We call him Wali, or friend of God.'

Sultan Shihabuddin Ahmad Shah Wali was the son of Sultan Hasan Gangoh, the founder of the Bahmani dynasty. Hasan Gangoh's own humble origins did not seem to favour his imperial ambitions, but saints have a way about them that defy all rules of logic. He is said to have been an orphaned village lad, who was blessed by a Brahmin who found him one day in a forest, shaded from the sun by a cobra that had spread its hood over his head. The Brahmin predicted that he would go on to establish a great kingdom, and when the prophecy came true and Hasan ascended the throne of Gulbarga, he added the title 'Bahmani', a corruption of the word 'Brahmin', to his name as a mark of his gratitude to the Hindu priest.

Sultan Ahmad succeeded his father in 1422. Eight years later, he shifted his capital to Bidar, some 300 kilometres to the east, where water was in plentiful and where the defences of the fortress were stronger. Like his father, the Sultan was said to have been a pious man, and kept the company of Sufis and sadhus. His own reputation as a saint owes much to a great miracle that he is said to have performed. One year, the rains failed miserably, and the people of the town—Muslims, Hindus, Lingayats and others—all flocked to his palace beseeching him for help. The king stood at the window of his palace and lifted his hands in supplication. All at once, dark thunderous clouds gathered in the sky and it began to rain torrentially. From then onwards, he was remembered as a Wali by his Muslim subjects, and, curiously enough, as an incarnation of Allama Prabhu, the twelfth century guru of Basava, the founder of the Lingayat religion, by the Lingayats and the Hindus.

Inside the dark tomb-chamber lay the saintly Sultan in eternal repose under green and orange silk sheets and strands of sweet-smelling flowers. Delicately crafted Qur'anic calligraphy, defaced by centuries of pigeon droppings, graced the inner walls in snatches. An ostrich egg dangled over the grave, at the foot of which were a pack of metal horses, each bearing on its back an outstretched palm, representing Muhammad and his household—the panjanatan pak, the 'five holy ones'. A group of Lingayat peasants in thin, almost see-through dhotis and Congress hats, stretched out in a corner, muttering to themselves. A Muslim man sporting a tall green turban handed me a ball of sugar and offered a prayer on my behalf.

I rested in the cool darkness of the tomb, nibbling at the lump of sugar. A while later, the Lingayats called me over to join them. They were from the village of Mudiyal, they said, and had come to the shrine on foot—a five-day journey in the blistering sun. They had made the journey in order to meet the Muslim priest of the shrine to make arrangements for the forthcoming 'urs festival.

'You must come for the festival,' they insisted. 'Thousands of people come here, and you'll never see anything like this elsewhere.'

'What's so special about the festival?' I asked.

'Where else would you have a Lingayat priest leading a flock of Lingayat, Hindu and Muslim devotees who have walked five days on foot to worship at a Sultan's tomb?' they exclaimed.

I asked them to tell me more.

There was a small structure dedicated to the Sultan in Mudiyal, they said, which they regarded as the temple of Allama Prabhu. On the occasion of the 'urs, the Mutthiya—the Wodeyar caste priest of the temple—would don a long Iranian-style *choga* and a belt inscribed in Persian, which no one in the village could read, and a green and red striped Muslim cap, all of which are said to have been gifted to one of his ancestors by the Sultan himself. Then, this modern-day petty potentate would march on to Ashtur at the head of a vast army of devotees, to the accompaniment of pealing conchs and hymns sung in praise of Ahmad Shah. Once at the shrine, he would offer coconuts and flowers at the grave and the Muslim custodian would read the fatiha, the opening verse of the Qur'an, over the offerings, which would then be distributed among the pilgrims. Crackers would be burst; Kannada bhajans and Urdu qawwalis would be sung; rows of hapless animals would be sacrificed and boisterous wrestling matches would follow.

I took an early morning bus to Mudiyal, seventy kilometres from Bidar, a two-hour bus journey. Giant mounds of baked clay lay scattered on the near empty plain quivering under the heartless summer sun. Weak, thirsty stalks of jowar and thorny bushes sprouted in pools of shade cast by monstrous boulders. A string of paper flags fluttered above a broken-down temple and the grave of a long-forgotten Muslim saint built next to it. A flock of grey-blue vultures danced over the carcass of a donkey, stripping it to the bones.

The bus dropped me off at a turning on the main road, and I dragged myself up the path leading to the 'temple'. It stood behind the ruins of a mediaeval fort amidst the crumbling remains of several Muslim-style graves. Inside, a series of steps led to a three-domed structure, guarded by minarets bearing the Islamic insignia of the crescent. A long stone slab resembling a Muslim grave lay in a corner. It was covered with a green cloth. On top of it seemed to be a recently placed Shiva linga, the Lingayat phallic symbol, around which were bunches of betel leaves, white flowers and miniature copper horses. I had been told that it was not an actual grave, however. According to one version of the legend, it marks the spot where Ahmad Shah killed a man-eating devil, Maimartappa. In gratitude for being saved from the torments of the cannibal, the villagers are said to have promised to undertake a pilgrimage to Ashtur once a year that would coincide with the Sultan's 'urs. This practice is followed to date. An idol of the demon with its pointed fangs and a great, fearsome red tongue, is taken by the pilgrims every year to the court of Ahmad Shah.

The Mutthiya stepped out of his house, built inside the shrine complex, knotting his dhoti and adjusting his cap.

'This is the shrine of Allama Prabhu,' he said, as he took me around. 'He was a world-renowned saint, you know.'

I remarked that, as far as I knew, most other Lingayats had probably never even heard of the embarrassingly diminutive shrine, where, as he claimed, or so I thought he did, the teacher of their guru Basava lay buried. He mumbled a reply in garbled

Kannada which I could not follow. I asked him about the association of the shrine with Sultan Ahmad.

'No, it has nothing to do with any Sultan-Wultan,' chipped in another Lingayat man who accompanied him.

'See,' he said, pointing to a row of obviously recent pictures of a variety of multiple-limbed Hindu deities. 'How can this be a dargah if it has Hindu pictures in it?' It was clear that the obvious Muslim associations of the shrine were now being either denied or concealed.

Not all Lingayats seemed to share these views, however. I struck up a conversation with a young Lingayat student while waiting on the road for the evening bus to arrive.

'Muslims used to come to the shrine in equal numbers,' he said. 'But that was before the Police Action in 1948.'

Till then, the village had formed a part of the vast dominions of the Nizam of Hyderabad. In 1948, Indian forces took over Hyderabad in a swift operation that lasted less than a week. Scores of people, mostly Muslims, are said to have been slaughtered during the communal riots that ensued.

'Some say that the Shiva linga that is now placed at the shrine was forcibly installed then,' said the boy.

It has not, however, been possible to efface the Muslim dimensions altogether. Even today, the boy said, on the day of the 'urs of the Sultan at Ashtur, a Muslim arrives at the shrine in Mudiyal and recites the fatiha. It is only after this that the Mutthiya and his troops can set off on the five-day journey to the grave of the Sultan, or to what some of them now claim to be the samadhi of Allama Prabhu.

Similar efforts at reinterpreting the history of the Ahmad Shah tradition are underway at the other shrines located in the villages of Hunchi Hadagil, Jiroli and Halgi which are also associated with the Sultan. All these are presided over by Lingayat priests of the Wodeyar caste, and have considerable tracts of land attached to them, perhaps bestowed on them by the Sultan. With the Hindu-Muslim divide now etched in popular imagination and the Lingayats in these parts being almost completely Hinduized, these shrines are well on their way to being converted into Hindu temples. The shrine at Jiroli, near Aland in Gulbarga, is now, for all practical purposes, a Hindu mandir. All that remains of its original structure is a low brick wall with small minarets growing out of its corners. The old shrine, consisting of five dargah-like structures, referred to as the graves of the *panch pir*s, has been pulled down and a new Hindu temple, replete with idols and posters of various gods and goddesses, has taken its place, groaning under the weight of a tall gopuram, draped with orange Hindu flags. The shrine in Hunchi Hadagil has, mercifully, been spared the zeal of Hindu enthusiasts, but the Mutthiya of the shrine insists that it has nothing to do with the Sultan.

Thus, as Muslims abandon the courts of the saints, condemned as dens of a false religion by puritan preachers, and as Hindus transform Muslim shrines into temples, the Sadhu-Sufi Sultan grovels in his grave at the temerity of his upstart subjects.

Bundling myself into the back a lorry, I found myself one summer day heading for Kowthalam, a village in Andhra Pradesh's Kurnool district just across the border from Karnataka, about an hour's drive from the decrepit town of Adoni. Sitting on a massive sack of freshly harvested rice, I was sandwiched between a drunken peasant, reeking of arrack, merrily singing away at the top of his voice, and a beedi-puffing old woman who purred out a hearty burp each time she emitted a stream of smoke from her nose. The lorry was packed with pilgrims— boisterous *banjara* women, decked in bright ghagras and strapless cholis, their ears and noses crowded with chunky silver jewellery; a group of Muslim women draped in sombre black burkas; a Sufi shaikh and his band of disciples, ponderous turbans wound around their heads, and a sundry collection of peasants heading for the dargah of the 'Teacher of the Entire World', the Jagat Guru 'Abdul Qadir Linga.

We finally got to Kowthalam just as the call to prayer drifted from the village mosque. Strings of little green and yellow bulbs lined the lane leading to the shrine of the Jagat Guru. The lane passed by the intricately carved doorway of a crumbling Ram temple, an ancient Shiva temple now sinking in the soft mud, and an assortment of little shrines of various snake deities, fierce-looking hooded creatures with human bodies, painted in bright red and white stripes.

The lane ended abruptly in a large square, dominated by a massive neem tree, below which a large group of fakirs with matted hair sat cross-legged. They represented almost the entire spectrum of the tribe of wandering dervishes: fierce glassy-eyed black-robed Jalalis, displaying heavy iron chains clasped to their ankles; bearded Madaris in white lungis and green kurtas, black turbans bandaged around their heads; a team of Banavas in a state of drug-induced ecstasy, and ochre-robed Rifais, with strings of red and green beads around their necks, pounding away at broad-rimmed drums. They puffed away furiously at the clay chillums that were being passed around, and giggled and chatted away endlessly. A large crowd had gathered under a shamiana, and listened in rapt attention to the haunting strains of an ode to the Jagat Guru sung by a team of qawwals, dressed in black Aligarh-style sherwanis, who had come down from Hyderabad especially for the occasion. Makeshift stalls did brisk business, selling plastic toys, glass bangles, cattle ropes, copper bells, puffed rice, popcorn and bright pink and green candy shaped like the Taj Mahal and the Tirupati temple. At one end, a large, gaudily painted welcome thermacol arch announced in Urdu and Telugu the 296th death anniversary of 'Hazrat Jagat Guru 'Abdul Qadir Chishti al-Qadri Ling Bandh'.

There are several layers to the legend of the Muslim Jagat Guru of Kowthalam. Here, as in the legends of many Sufis and Sadhus, fact seems to be indiscriminately mixed with fiction. 'Abdul Qadir Ling Bandh is said to have been a descendant of the Prophet, hence a Sayyed, and one of the chief disciples of the sixteenth century Sufi of Bijapur, Hazrat Khwaja Aminuddin. In his time, the Khwaja was regarded as a heterodox rebel by an influential section of the Muslim scholars or the 'ulama attached to the 'Adil Shahi court. He is said to have had numerous Lingayat and Hindu disciples, in addition to his Muslim followers, and to have preached an ethical monotheism that transcended differences of caste and religion. For his radical views, he had been declared a heretic and apostate.

'Abdul Qadir, so the story goes, was born in a local noble family in the village of Bapuram, now in the Bidar district in northern Karnataka. As a young man, he entered the army of the 'Adil Shahi Sultans as an officer, but soon grew weary of a life of luxury. Setting off in search of a spiritual master, he travelled widely in the region before finally reaching the village of Darga, on the outskirts of Bijapur, where Khwaja Aminuddin had established his Sufi lodge. The Khwaja accepted him as his disciple, and under the Khwaja, he trained for twelve long years on the Sufi path. Thereafter, he was instructed to travel and make his own disciples.

Accordingly, 'Abdul Qadir set off, riding a tiger, with a linga, the sacred symbol of the Lingayats, wound around his foot. When he arrived at the village of Kowthalam, he was met with a crowd of Lingayats, led by their chief priest, a man called Narasimaiah or Narsu, enraged at what they saw as the desecration of their holy stone.

According to another version of the legend, 'Abdul Qadir's vocal opposition to people in the village being forced to wear the linga angered the Lingayats. In the fracas that followed, 'Abdul Qadir challenged the Lingayats to a spiritual duel. Narsu and he, he offered, would both throw their lingas into the village pond, and the one who was able to order the lingas to emerge from the water would be considered the victor. Narsu agreed, and the next morning, a large crowd gathered to witness the event. The Sufi and the Lingayat priest both took off their lingas and threw them into the pond. All the Lingayats of the village followed suit. 'Abdul Qadir asked Narsu and his Lingayat followers to call on their lingas to emerge from the water. This they tried for three continuous days, but to no avail. Without their lingas they could not eat a morsel. On the fourth day, driven by pangs of hunger, they beseeched 'Abdul Qadir for help. The Sufi is said to have ordered the lingas out of the pond, and, miraculously they emerged and wound themselves around his foot, testifying, so the story suggests, to his greatness. The true linga, where God resided, 'Abdul Qadir said to them, was not a mere piece of stone. Rather, it was the human heart, the throne of Ishwar or Allah. Witnessing the miracle, the Lingayats fell at his feet and accepted him as the Jagat Guru, the 'Teacher of the Entire World'. At their request, he settled down in their village where he spent the rest his life.

Another version has it that when 'Abdul Qadir arrived at Kowthalam, the cupful of ashes that his Pir, Khwaja Aminuddin, had given him suddenly burst into flames. This he took to be a secret message from his master instructing him to settle down in the village. The intrusion on his territory of the wandering dervish kindled the wrath of Narsu, described variously as an evil magician or a pious Lingayat priest. A spectacular battle of miracles ensued, in which Narsu was worsted and forced to flee the village. Before he could escape, 'Abdul Qadir grabbed him by the hair, plucking off a fistful of his matted locks, now preserved in a glass tube stuck on the ceiling of a chamber leading to 'Abdul Qadir's shrine.

'Abdul Qadir's duel with Narsu can be read in different ways. It could be seen, for instance, as a standard 'Hindu-Muslim' confrontation and an illustration of Muslim 'intolerance' and 'Hindu passivity'. A more nuanced reading suggests, however, that it may have been nothing of the sort. 'Abdul Qadir's own Pir, Khwaja Aminuddin, it must be remembered, had been branded as a heretic by the 'ulama, and he was known for his scant observance of the shari'ah. Furthermore, he is said to have had numerous Hindu disciples whom he never converted to Islam. Even more revealing is the fact that after he settled in Kowthalam, 'Abdul Qadir attracted numerous Hindu and Lingayat followers, almost all of whom remained non-Muslims. In fact, he is said to have become so popular among the peasants of the area—Lingayat, Hindu and Muslim—that the Muslim governor of Adoni, Siddi Masud Khan, fearful of his popularity, accused him of heresy and had him arrested. Legend has it that he was thrown into a fire, but when that failed to harm him, the governor ordered that he be crushed to death by a mad elephant. He, however, or so it is said, miraculously survived this ordeal as well. Realizing that he was probably an accomplished Sufi, Siddi Masud begged him for mercy, and, as a token of his devotion, gave him thirty villages in the area as a jagir, and his daughter in marriage.

A voice crackled over the microphone announcing that the qawwali session was about to start. The fakirs had seated themselves under a large cotton sheet striped like a tiger skin and pinned on to the wall. On either side, mats had been laid out for the pilgrims. The qawwals took their place at the far end. After the recitation of a verse from the Qur'an, they began a rhythmic clapping of the hands, accompanied by a throbbing dholak. The old and toothless lead qawwal rendered Amir Khusrau's qawwali, in praise of the Prophet and his son-in-law, Hazrat 'Ali, with passion and grace. Then followed a string of Khusrau's compositions in Farsi, Braj Bhasha and Arabic. A fakir suddenly stood up and started twirling like a top, while a woman began beating herself, banging her head furiously on the floor. The dholak throbbed as the woman went into a trance, scratching her breasts and imploring the saint.

'Ya Bade Pir!' she cried out, and collapsed in a heap, exhausted and motionless.

'She's got a jinn in her,' a man sitting next to me whispered, 'and it just refuses to go.'

The musical evening stretched into the wee hours of the morning, when the call to prayer marked an end to the night's revelry. After the prayers gave over, the fakirs led a long procession of pilgrims to the Pir's house, to the accompaniment of the deafening din of drums and tambourines. A group of fakirs began whipping themselves with flails, while others drove long spears into their cheeks without wincing. Another jabbed his eye with a heavy nail, while I stood watching, aghast. This carried on for almost half an hour before it suddenly stopped. The head of the shrine and a direct descendant of the Jagat Guru, Pir Sayyed Shah Hussaini Chishti Lingbandh, solemnly walked out of his house, and stepped into the crowd that had gathered at the entrance. He wore an ochre robe with a bandana wound tightly around his head. A young disciple held an embroidered parasol over him to shade him from the sun. He was followed by a long retinue of relatives, sundry followers and general hangers-on that Pirs seem to attract in plenty, all wearing yellow cone-shaped hats, the emblem of the Chishti Sufi order. The Pir's brother, dressed in a starched sherwani and a Turksih fez, carried a pot of sandalwood paste on his head. The procession wound its way to 'Abdul Qadir's grave. The Pir's brother then set about washing it, plastering it with sandal paste and covering it with a new silk sheet. The Pir then lifted his hands in prayer, and the congregation followed after.

'Oh Lord,' he prayed, in chaste Urdu, that few of the pilgrims seemed to fully follow, 'Bless all your faithful servants. Help us to love one another and live together in peace.'

'Ameen,' intoned the crowd after him.

Vast throngs began milling around the grave, which was now hidden under an ever-increasing mountain of flowers. A row of plastic bottles filled with water were laid out before the tomb, in order to absorb the dead dervish's powers and blessings, to be used for curing a range of illnesses. Pilgrims queued up patiently to drop little bits of camphor into a giant copper incense burner, exuding grey clouds of sweet-smelling smoke. Two Hindu women, the pallus of their saris demurely drawn over their heads, prostrated themselves before the shrine, and gave a Muslim man a coconut to smash on a slab of stone at the foot of the grave. In turn, the man handed them a packet of sticky white sweets, blessed especially by the Sufi, and patted their backs with a bunch of peacock feathers.

The women walked over to the Pir's chambers and queued up to seek his blessings. The Pir, an unassuming man in his early sixties and dressed like a sadhu in ochre robes, pointed them out to me and said, 'See, these women have more faith than most of my Muslim devotees.'

'Half of my disciples are Hindus,' he added, as he sipped his tea from a saucer and insisted I take a third, dangerous-looking jalebi. He waved his hand towards the entrance gate. 'Those animals there,' he said, indicating a pair of terracotta tigers—as harmless as little puppies—that graced the archway, 'were put up by another Hindu disciple of mine.'

Hindus and Muslims sat together on the floor lapping up curry and popping balls of rice into their mouths in a spirit of rare camaraderie, while the Pir expostulated on the miracles of his ancestor.

'Don't believe a word of this nonsense Pir-Wir business,' said a hefty Reddy landlord, as I waited at the stop for the bus that was to take me back to Adoni. 'It's all a lot of humbug and a clever way for priests to make money.' A Muslim maulvi nodded in agreement. 'No one outside these parts has ever heard of 'Abdul Qadir, the man with the linga, and he thinks he is the teacher of the whole world! The cheek of it!'

The sound of Telugu disco music blared from a shop, drowning the heated conversation of Hindu and Muslim discussing what they saw as the folly of their incorrigible co-religionists. Meanwhile, hordes of other Hindus and Muslims hurried up the lane, making their way to the dargah of the little-known Teacher of the Entire World.

6

THE DEENDAR CHANNABASAVESWARA OF ASIF NAGAR

Religious syncretism and inter-faith dialogue may not always be what they might appear to be—a call for an appreciation of, and respect for the faith and autonomy of the other. Often, they can simply be a pretext for a missionary agenda that, having appropriated elements from other faiths or having established parallels between one religion and the other, seeks to absorb the other into the fold of what must be imposed as the only true faith. The twin imperatives of dialogue and mission are constantly at odds with each other, with importance being given to one or the other depending on circumstances and changing fortunes. Sometimes, the thin veil covering this hidden agenda slips to reveal the use of dialogue as a means to pursue sinister, often violent ends. Such, indeed, has been the case with a hitherto little-known sect, the Hyderabad-based Deendar Anjuman ('The Pious Association') which made the headlines of Indian newspapers in 2000 for its alleged role in a series of bomb blasts in Christian, Hindu and Muslim places of worship in various towns of South India, resulting in the sect being banned by the government early the following year.

While government officials and Indian newspapers joined hands in alleging that the group was an 'Islamic terrorist' outfit with possible links with the Pakistani secret services agency—

the Inter-Services Intelligence (ISI)—Muslim groups responded by denying religious affiliations with the Deendaris. The Deendaris, however, insisted that they were perfectly innocent, and that communal harmony and inter-faith dialogue were the principal tenets of their faith.

More than a year before the Deendar Anjuman shot into prominence, I was in Hyderabad, teaching Islamic history to a group of Christian priests. An acquaintance of mine, a Sunni Muslim who insisted that the Deendaris were a dangerous bunch of heretics, had told me about them and had guided me to their headquarters in the congested locality of Asif Nagar in the Old City.

Gleaming spirals whirling out of the domes of ancient mosques, nudged against the dull, stolid cement blocks of half-built squalid houses and offices. The narrow, potholed lane, lined on either side with open drains clogged with months of refuse, wound itself in knots. Bleary-eyed maulvis in red fezzes and long coats sat in the veranda of a tea-shop, while a group of Muslim women, draped from head to toe in black, hurried into a side-lane to escape the prying male gaze. Pie-dogs growled and fought with each other over the head of a goat lying in a fresh puddle of crimson splattered on a non-existent pavement. An overpowering stench of raw leather and fermenting garbage filled the air.

The rickshaw creaked to a sudden halt outide a parrot-green metal door. A signboard in Urdu, Hindi and Telugu announced 'The Jagat Guru Ashram Sarwar-e-'Alam Khanqah'. A crudely-painted buraq—a creature with a woman's face, a horse's body, an eagle's outstretched wings, and a peacock's tail—perched precariously on the gate. Some believe that Muhammad had travelled on it during his flight to the seventh heaven. To the Deendaris, it also represents the Hindu kamadhenu—the cow whose supply of milk never runs dry.

A wizened old man bent over a stick opened his mouth to let out a stream of blood-red betel juice.

'Who are you and why have you come here?' he asked gruffly.

I explained to him the purpose of my visit. He demanded to know who had told me about the 'Ashram of the Guru of the World'. I told him about my Sunni friend, but wisely said nothing about what he thought of the community.

I was led inside by the man, who, I discovered later, had in his youth been a leading missionary of the sect. He took my hand in his bony paw, and guided me to the 'office'—a small box-like structure in the centre of a large open compound, with a wooden signboard announcing it as the community's central office. A fading, moth-eaten mat lay on the floor. The room had four massive wooden cupboards that contained bound volumes of various holy texts piled up untidily. The poster of an inter-faith dialogue meeting that was held at the 'office' two years ago hung on the wall. A low table occupied one corner of the room. Sitting on the floor before it were three bearded men, wearing long saffron robes and ponderous green turbans, pouring over a motley collection of tomes in Arabic and Hindi. They introduced themselves as missionaries and office-bearers of the Deendar Anjuman and beckoned me to sit down on a cushion.

Tea was served in stained, chipped cups from a tin kettle on a kerosene stove. Pleasantries exchanged, I was taken on a guided tour of the complex—the headquarters of the Anjuman. I was shown around the mosque, where only Deendaris prayed, for other Muslims considered them as apostates and refused to worship along with them, although both prayed in exactly the same manner. A separate mosque for ladies was shown to me from a distance. The idea in itself was radical, for in most parts of South Asia Muslim women are not allowed to pray in mosques, although the Qur'an allows for it. The short tour ended at the white marble grave of Siddiq Hussain, the founder of the sect, where the three men murmured their prayers and implored Allah to bless their master.

As we sat in the cool shade of a neem tree on a charpoy, I listened to the maulanas expounding on the principles of their faith.

'We believe in universal love, and harmony between all religions,' said one maulana, who seemed to be the senior-most.

Another one, a middle-aged pockmarked man with a mouth protruding like a duck-billed platypus, chimed in, 'Ram and Krishna were also great prophets of God, and the Vedas are, our master Hazrat Siddiq Hasan has written, a divinely revealed scripture.'

The third man, who had doffed his turban to reveal a bald head, beads of sweat decorating it like a string of Hyderabad pearls, interrupted his comrade to say, 'We teach the Ramayana and the Gita to our children in addition to the Qur'an,' fixing his eyes on me as though hoping to shock me into appreciation.

Seeing disbelief writ large on my face, he yelled out to a young boy who was building a castle in a sandpit. 'Arrey, Ahmad! Come here at once! Recite for Babuji the verse from the Ramayana that I taught you yesterday.'

The boy, hardly five, waddled up to the cot, wiping a stream of green slime flowing down his nose with the sleeve of his shirt. He stood at attention, his hands behind his back, as if in a military drill, and then burst into a long Sanskrit sloka, which, made no sense to me, and nor, I imagined, to him.

The learned maulanas looked up to me, beaming with pride, and patted the child on his back.

'That was from the Ramayana, you know,' said the head of the trio, 'when Shri Ram tells Hanuman to pray in the *ashtang* way, which is but another word for the Muslim *namaz*.'

The maulanas poured forth their wisdom with bountiful quotations from the Hindu and Muslim texts supposedly predicting the arrival of Siddiq Deendar as the Messiah. An hour later, with the sermon showing no signs of concluding, I was itching to crawl out of the charpoy and rush back into the grime and stench of the street outside the massive green gate. Qur'anic verses, Sanskrit slokas, snatches from the Bible, the Zend Avesta and even from the Analects of Confucius had been put together to reinforce the fanciful theories that the maulanas were pressing me to accept. Those who spurned the claims of the Chosen One, whom God, in His inscrutable wisdom, had sent to the slums of Asif Nagar, were warned of eternal doom in the fires of *jahannum*.

'Serpents that bite for seventy years at a stretch, gallons of boiling water poured down the throat, and nails driven into the head day after day,' would be the punishment for infidels, insisted the maulanas.

The call to the evening prayer drifted from the loudspeaker on the minaret of the mosque almost two hours later, and the sermon hurriedly drew to a close.

'We are so sorry, but we have to go now,' said the head Maulvi, picking his nose and shuffling his feet in his leather sandals.

'You need not be sorry at all,' I felt like saying. Instead, I forced on a smile, and thanking them for their time and for the carton of books that they had gifted me, I made my way out of the gate, relieved to be back in the squalour of Asif Nagar.

Sayyed Siddiq Hussain, the founder of the Deendar Anjuman, was born in 1886 at Balampet in Gulbarga, then part of the Nizam's Dominions. His family traced their descent to the Prophet Muhammad, and were known to have produced numerous leading Sufis. He received his primary education first at Gulbarga, then at Hyderabad. Later, he enrolled at the Bursen College, Lahore, for higher education. In the course of his studies he is said to have mastered eleven languages, and become an expert in medicine and the martial arts.

As a young man, Siddiq Hussain displayed a great interest in various religions, and came into contact with several noted

Islamic scholars of his time. In 1914 he joined the Qadiani branch of the heterodox Ahmadiyya community that held the belief that its founder, Mirza Ghulam Ahmad, was a prophet sent by God. Since this was contrary to the Islamic belief in the finality of the prophethood of Muhammad the Ahmadiyya community was considered outside the pale of orthodox Islam. Siddiq Hussain took the oath of allegiance at the hands of the then head of the Qadiani *jama'at*, Bashiruddin Mahmud Ahmad, son of Mirza Ghulam Ahmad. Fourteen days later, however, he renounced his membership, accusing the Qadianis of being kafirs for considering the Mirza as a prophet. It is likely that at this time he may have moved closer to the rival Lahori branch of the Ahmadis, who split from the main Ahmadi jama'at in 1914 on the issue of the status of the Mirza. Unlike the Qadianis, the Lahoris, led by the well-known Islamic scholar Muhammad 'Ali, insisted that the Mirza was not a prophet but simply a mujaddid or 'renewer of the faith'.

The early hagiographic accounts of Siddiq Hussain say little of his activities until 1924, when he publicly declared what he claimed was his divine mission and established the Deendar Anjuman. The 1920s was a crucial period for Hindu-Muslim relations in India, and witnessed a marked rise of Hindu-Muslim conflict after a brief spell of inter-communal harmony during the short-lived Khilafat and Non-Cooperation movements. In early 1923, the Arya Samaj, a militant and fiercely anti-Muslim Hindu chauvinist group, launched a massive drive to bring into the Hindu fold hundreds of thousands of Rajput Muslims in the north-western districts of the United Provinces. Soon, the campaign spread to other areas of India, and Arya leaders began issuing calls for converting all Indian Muslims. Muslim leaders responded with alarm, and launched efforts to counter the Aryas through various Islamic missionary or tabligh groups. Siddiq Hussain is said to have actively worked with one of the leading tablighi activists of this time, the Amristar-based lawyer, Ghulam Bhik Nairang, to prevent the Aryas from making further inroads among Muslim groups, and also to spread Islam among non-Muslim communities. This is the first evidence we have of what was to become his lifelong involvement in missionary work.

After spending some time in the north with the Lahori Ahmadis and with Nairang and his tablighi group, Siddiq Hussain returned to Hyderabad and established a medical practice. By this time, aggressive communal politics, which had become such a characteristic feature of North Indian life, had made its way into the state. Ruled by a Muslim Nizam and a small feudal class, largely Muslim, Hyderabad was a Hindu-majority state, with a Muslim population of hardly ten per cent. By the 1920s, a growing resentment against the predominance of Muslims in the upper echelons of government service spurred a rising generation of newly educated Hindus on to the path of confrontation, which soon assumed, as elsewhere in India, the form of Hindu-Muslim antagonism. From the late 1920s, relations between Hindus and Muslims became so strained that they threatened to degenerate into civil war. Siddiq Hussain seemed to have been greatly affected by what he perceived as grave threats from aggressive Hindu groups to Islam and Muslim interests at this time. Launching a large-scale missionary campaign, aimed at nothing less than the conversion of all the Hindus of India to Islam, seemed to him the only solution to endemic violence and conflict. This was to become his vocation in life, bestowed upon him, he asserted, by a divine command which he claimed to have received.

Siddiq Hussain began his missionary work among the Lingayats, a community living mainly in the Kannada-speaking districts of the Nizam's Dominions, and in neighbouring Mysore. According to Anjuman sources, once, while on a trip to Gulbarga to the shrine of Kodekkal Basappa, also known as Muhammad Sarwar—the 'Muhammada avatar' of the founder of the Lingayat community, and a Sufi highly venerated by the local Lingayats—he reportedly heard that the saint had predicted the arrival of a saviour of the Lingayats in the form of the 'Deendar Channabasaveswara'. The saviour would be born in a Muslim family and would 'make the Hindus and Muslims one'. This, he went on to claim, was a prophecy heralding his own arrival. Accordingly, he travelled to Gadag, a small town near Hubli, and on 7 February 1924, publicly announced that he was the much-awaited saviour of the Lingayats, the Deendar Channabasaveswara.

Around the same time, besides claiming to be the Deendar Channabasaveswara, he also declared himself to be the kalki avatar, the tenth and last incarnation of the Hindu deity Vishnu, who, the Hindus believe, would arrive to put an end to the kali yug or age of evil. This, he said, had been revealed to him by God Himself, who had told him that he would establish the sat yug, the age of truth, in 1943. As he put it, 'Shri Bhagwan has informed me that I will appear as the kalki avatar. The kali yug is soon to be abolished and the sat yug inaugurated.' Shortly after that, he said, in the second half of the fourteenth (Islamic) century, the Day of Judgement (qayamat) would arrive.

In his *A'ada-i-Islam* ('Enemies of Islam'), a tract penned to convince Muslims of his claims, Siddiq Hussain wrote that in response to the Arya Samaj's success in bringing to the Hindu fold several thousand Muslims, he had received a divine message informing him that 'God had willed that the greatest incarnation (avatar) of the Hindus should emerge to declare to the Hindus that their only hope for salvation lay in converting to Islam.' Elsewhere, he wrote that in the wake of the shuddhi movement of the Aryas, India had witnessed 'heinous assaults' on Islam and on the person of Muhammad. 'God,' he said, 'was watching this, and had decided to take revenge by making all of India Muslim.' By taking on the name of Siddiq Deendar Channabasaveswara he claimed that he was simply fulfilling the prophecies contained in the holy books of the Lingayats

and the Hindus, which, he claimed, had predicted his arrival
and had also indicated the truth of Islam. In his words:

Allah has appointed their biggest avatar in order to make them
Muslim by pointing out the directions contained in the books of
the enemies of the Muslims and he [this avatar] has announced:
'Oh Hindus! If you seek salvation then become Muslim because
you can see that till your avatars recited the creed of confession
(kalima) of our Master, Muhammad, peace and Allah's blessings
be upon him, they did not gain salvation, so how can you be saved
if you do not do so?'

But, the missionary task of 'turning the entire Hindustan
Muslim', as he put it, was, he argued, not to be restricted simply
to pious platitudes and gentle persuasion. Rather, it would be
accompanied by much tumult and conflict. The Deendar
Channabasaveswara, along with his army of Pathan followers, so
he claimed that the Lingayat scriptures foretold, would 'empty the
treasuries of the (temples of) Tirupati and Hampi'. They would
then ensure that 'there is not one idol left standing in any temple'
in the country. Once all the idols were destroyed, the Deendar
Channabasaveswara would set about 'uniting all the 101 castes
(zat)', by making all Hindus Muslim. In the process, the power
of the Brahmins would be completely destroyed. Finally, the
Deendar Channabasaveswara, that is Siddiq Hussain himself,
would be recognized as the 'king of kings' (badshahon ka badshah).

By this time, Siddiq Hussain's messianic appeal and charisma
had won him a small band of disciples. He now set about
training them in the Qur'an as well as in the Lingayat and
Hindu scriptures, taking them along with him on his missionary
tours of Lingayat villages, temples and monasteries. Among his
prominent disciples at this point was a certain Abu Nazir Vitthal,
who was earlier a priest at the Manvi Lingayat monastery at
Belgaum. He gave several of his disciples Hindu names in
order to make them more acceptable to the Lingayats and the
Hindus among whom he was preaching. Thus, four of his
chief followers were given names of Hindu deities—Vyas, Shri

Krishna, Narasimha and Virabhadra. He styled himself as Dharamraja or the 'Righteous King'. Despite all attempts to deliver his message in a form he thought would be acceptable to his audience, Siddiq Hussain's appeal to the Lingayats to accept him as Deendar Channabasaveswara and to convert to Islam raised a storm. 'The Hindu world was shaken to its roots,' says an Anjuman tract, when Siddiq Hussain declared his 'divine mission' to the Hindus. Apparently, several attempts were made on his life by enraged Lingayats. Siddiq Hussain alleged that these were master-minded by enraged Arya Samajis. According to one account, in 1924 alone, twenty-five attempts were made on his life. He was to claim that these attempts failed miserably because he was under divine protection.

Not finding a warm response to his appeal among the Lingayats, Siddiq Hussain now turned his attention to other Hindu groups as well. An interesting shift may be observed here in his missionary strategy. While addressing the Lingayats his focus was largely on himself. He claimed to be the avatar of the revered Lingayat figure Channabasaveswara. When he turned to other Hindu groups, for whom the figure of Channabasaveswara held little or no appeal, the Prophet Muhammad dominated his discourse. Muhammad, insisted Siddiq Hussain, was the much-awaited kalki avatar of the Hindus, the promised saviour who would deliver the world from sin and misery. It is interesting to note that earlier Siddiq Hussain had claimed himself to be the kalki avatar. This status was attributed to the Prophet only later. As during his missionary work among the Lingayats, now once again, Islam was presented not as the negation but, rather, as the fulfilment of Hinduism. Yet, as we shall shortly see, despite accepting the legitimacy of the Hindu scriptures, Siddiq Hussain's attitude towards the Hindus remained hostile. This would soon push him and his followers into a violent conflict with the Hindus of Hyderabad.

In 1926 Siddiq Hussain published his two-volume Kannada book, *Jagat Guru Sarwar-i-Alam*, in which he argued that the Prophet Muhammad was actually the kalki avatar whose arrival had been predicted in the Hindu scriptures, and that, therefore, the salvation of the Hindus lay in converting to Islam. The publication of the book set off a spate of protests. On 9 September 1927, a large rally of Hindu nobles was held at Hyderabad, demanding that the book be banned. A case was instituted in the Nizam's court to this effect. Although the court dismissed their plea, Hindu opposition to Siddiq Hussain continued, and some years later, in January 1932, another large rally of Hindus held at Hyderabad demanded that the Nizam curb Siddiq Hussain's activities, which, they alleged, were calculated to defame their religion and incite communal strife. Accordingly, the Nizam issued a decree banning Siddiq Hussain from addressing public gatherings. The controversial book was confiscated by the state authorities, but later allowed to be circulated without any pictures. According to Siddiq Hussain, because of his untiring efforts to spread Islam among the Hindus, he was sent to jail eighty-four times, and had spent a total of almost ten years in prison.

In his *Jagat Guru*, Siddiq Hussain sought to present Islam, and his own personal mission, as a fulfilment of the Hindu scriptures. He wrote that God had sent prophets to all peoples, including to the inhabitants of India. All the prophets had taught the same religion (din), al-Islam, and the last of these divine messengers was the Prophet Muhammad. Over time the message in the holy books of other peoples had been distorted and the only scripture that had maintained its purity was the Qur'an. Yet, he argued, the previous scriptures had predicted the arrival of Muhammad as God's last prophet for all of humankind, whereas earlier God had sent prophets only for their own particular communities. In other words, Muhammad was the Jagat Guru, the 'Teacher of the Entire World'. His scripture, Siddiq Hussain wrote, 'envisages or comprises the teachings of all the scriptures of the foregone [sic] prophets' and did not in any way 'confront' them. Rather, as the 'Teacher of the Entire World', Muhammad would 'provide protection' to all the previous prophets 'under his banner' on the Day of Resurrection. Therefore, in accordance with what their own prophets and scriptures had allegedly predicted about him, it was the duty of all non-Muslims to accept Muhammad and his teachings.

In effect, therefore, what Siddiq Hussain sought to advance was a plea for non-Muslims to convert to Islam in accordance with what he saw as the teachings of their own holy books. These holy books were accepted as legitimate and of divine inspiration, only to be employed merely as a means to direct their followers to the Qur'an. As Siddiq Hussain put it, 'Islam is like an ocean and all other religions, in comparison, are rivers which ultimately drain into the ocean. In other words, other religions are comparable to the branches of a tree, while Islam is like the seed.'

Siddiq Hussain maintained that all other prophets had predicted the arrival of Muhammad and that 'Allah Almighty has taken from them a covenant regarding the Prophet Muhammad,' 'compelling them' to believe in him as the 'Teacher of the Entire World' and to 'help him in every possible way'. Since all the prophets before Muhammad had attested to their faith in him before God, it was the duty of their followers to follow in their footsteps and do the same. He cited not only the scriptures of the Jews and Christians, but even the books of ancient Pharaonic Egyptian, Confucian Chinese, Zoroastrian, Greek and Roman scholars to prove the coming of Muhammad as the 'Teacher of the Entire World'.

Since his particular concern was to present Islam to the Hindus, a large section in his book sought to show that the coming of Muhammad as the universal saviour had been predicted in many Hindu scriptures. Quoting liberally from the Vedas, the Upanishads, the Bhagwat, Kalki and Bhavishyokt

Puranas, the Ramayana and the Mahabharata, Siddiq Hussain remarked that the arrival of Muhammad as the 'Teacher of the Entire World' had been 'prophesied so vividly and in such detail' in the books of the Hindus as 'cannot be found in any other religious texts'. He wrote that 'they have not spared any incident of his life from his birth till his demise, whether of great significance or of no significance at all', and even went as far as to claim that the 'ancient Hindu seers' had prepared an exact horoscope of Muhammad's life some 3000 years before his birth.

While the Hindus were thus expected to convert to Islam, for Muhammad was said to be the last Prophet of God and Islam the only true religion, Muslims were asked to revise their own views about Hinduism. Siddiq Hussain claimed that before his advent, Muslims were completely ignorant of the Hindu scriptures. They looked upon the Hindus and their avatars as 'kafirs', as people 'without religion', having had no prophet sent to them by God, and lacking in 'truthfulness' and spirituality. But now, because of his work, he claimed, Muslims were convinced that 'there is light (nur) even in the religion of the Hindus,' and that prior to Muhammad, God had indeed sent many holy men, including prophets and saints, to India. He boasted that true Hindu-Muslim unity was being established through his efforts, and prophesied that soon 'Hindustan would be converted into a veritable heaven', an all-Muslim paradise.

Besides ordinary Hindus, Siddiq Hussain also attempted to win over Hindu rulers of various native states to his cause. He is said to have 'challenged all the [Hindu] kings of India to put their heads at the feet of Muhammad'. For this purpose, he penned a special Urdu tract entitled *Hidayat Namah Banam Ghayr Muslim Salatin* ('Letter of Instruction Addressed to Non-Muslim Rulers'). In this tract he presented Islam as signifying 'union' (milap), and argued that Islam aimed at nothing less than uniting all the peoples of the world. He claimed that Islam was 'the constitution of unity', and guaranteed that 'under its shadow' all creatures can live in peace, for the word 'Islam' itself means 'universal peace'. Of all the religions in the world, it was only Islam that could guarantee peace. If all the rulers were to become Muslim, peace would at once be established. On the other hand, he argued, the Hindu religion 'is incapable of guaranteeing peace', and that, in fact, it had caused Hindus to fight among themselves, and divided them into numerous mutually opposed castes.

In 1945, Siddiq Hussain is said to have dispatched groups of his followers to the courts of several Hindu princes and chieftains, with the booklet he had specially penned for them. They were instructed to tell these rulers that if they accepted Islam 'they would gain the wealth of religion (*din*) and the world (*duniya*)', but if they refused, their power would be snatched away from them. According to Deendar accounts, none of the Hindu princes whom the delegations met heeded their advice, and a few years later, all of them lost their thrones.

The Muslims to whom Siddiq Hussain had turned for support in his mission, seem, curiously enough, like the Hindus, either to have ignored him or openly opposed him. Thus we hear of numerous 'ulama issuing fatwas of infidelity against him on account of his claims of being an avatar of Channabasaveswara, and declaring him to be a crypto-Qadiani, an allegation that he strove hard to refute. In the course of his initial work among the Lingayats, several Muslims are said to have joined the Arya Samajis to protest against the activities of the Anjuman. Apparently, an enraged Muslim even went as far as to attempt to kill him. Later Siddiq Hussain claimed that the mission had proved abortive. because God had rushed to his rescue. In an effort to mobilize Muslim support for his cause, Siddiq Hussain made vain attempts to win the favour of the ruling Muslim elite of Hyderabad. In his *A'ada-i-Islam* he wrote that in response to his earnest pleas to God to 'appoint a king to assist him', he had received divine signals that the Nizam, Mir Usman 'Ali Khan Bahadur, had been appointed for this task. It seems, however, that the Nizam was still not flattered. Instead, egged on by the Arya Samaj, he ordered that the maverick Siddiq Hussain be thrown into prison.

In 1934, despairing of making no headway among the recalcitrant Hindus and Muslims, who seemed to consider him little more than a mischief-monger, Siddiq Hussain and a small band of his disciples decided to head northwards, to Yaghestan, near the border with Afghanistan. There, he intended to mobilize the war-like Pathans so that as the head of a grand Afghan army, he could descend to the Indian plains, presumably to fight the British and other non-Muslim powers and establish 'Islamic' rule in the country, with himself as the Imam. On 11 July 1934, in front of a large gathering of his followers he announced that through divine revelation he had learnt that all of India would shortly convert to Islam. 'Rejoice! Oh Musalmans!' he declared, to the obvious delight of his followers. 'The whole of India will soon turn Muslim.' Presumably, the time was now ripe for jihad. However, the British authorities now took serious note of his activities among the Pathans. It is claimed in Anjuman sources with much pride that Siddiq Hussain was promptly branded as 'the most dangerous enemy of the British Empire'. In 1936, following instructions from the British authorities, Farid Khan, the nawab of Darband, captured Siddiq Hussain while he was asleep in a remote village near Peshawar, and handed him over to the British. They immediately arranged for him to be sent to Hyderabad, where they instructed the Nizam to keep him in solitary confinement at the Thugee jail. He was later released, in 1938, but forbidden to leave the confines of the Nizam's Dominions.

After his release, Siddiq continued to maintain contact with his followers in Yaghestan. In 1939, he set up a military training centre at Hyderabad, which he christened the Tehrik Jami'at-i-Hizbullah ('The Movement of the Party of God'), and where his followers were trained in the use of arms. At this time he also penned two tracts, entitled *The Practical Science of War* and *The Principal Armies of Asia and Europe* for his disciples. These, however, were soon banned by the Government of India. Alongside the preparations for war, the Anjuman kept up its missionary work, dispatching letters to or personally meeting several Indian and British leaders, including Gandhi, the Viceroy, members of the Cripps Mission, and King George V himself, asking them to convert to Islam. To the British sovereign Siddiq Hussain declared that if he accepted Islam, his empire would prosper forever. If he refused, however, his imperial glory would soon come to an end. Anjuman sources claim that the disintegration of the British Empire was a consequence of the hard-hearted British monarch not heeding Siddiq Hussain's warnings.

The departure of the British from India in 1947 marked a major watershed for the Muslims of India, including for members of the Deendar Anjuman. During the post-1947 period one discerns a distinct shift in the missionary strategies of the Anjuman—from aggressive proselytization and strident anti-Hindu rhetoric to attempts at presenting the Anjuman as committed to inter-religious dialogue and communal harmony. However, underlying this new approach was the Anjuman's original agenda—propagating the message of Siddiq Hussain and his own version of Islam that other Muslims had almost unanimously branded as heretical.

By the end of 1946, fierce rioting broke out between Hindus and Muslims all over India. Despite still being under the rule of a Muslim king, Hyderabad was not left untouched. Large-scale massacres of Muslims in the western Marathi-speaking districts of the Nizam's Dominions—an area where Muslims were a minority and where Hindu chauvinist groups had managed to secure a firm base for themselves—were reported. Sections of the Muslim elite in Hyderabad began sponsoring a militant Muslim organization, the Razakars ('The Volunteers'), who were later responsible for several attacks on Hindus. Reacting to the massacres of the Muslims, Siddiq Hussain recommended 'defensive fighting' against 'the enemies of Islam' to his followers.

After the British left, almost all Indian native states were incorporated into the Indian Dominion. The Nizam of Hyderabad, however, refused to join India in the hope of either staying independent or else joining Pakistan. In late 1948, egged on by Hindu organizations and intimidated by the growing influence of radical leftists in the Telengana area, the Indian government ordered what it called the 'Police Action'. In a short and swift move the Indian army laid siege to Hyderabad. The Nizam's forces, joined by the Razakars, put up a weak resistance, and were soon overpowered by the Indian army. Interestingly, according to Anjuman sources, Siddiq Hussain and his followers, who had been arrested by the Nizam earlier that year and whose organization the Nizam had banned, fought the Indian army on twenty-seven different fronts, but were soon captured at their headquarters in Asif Nagar.

When the Anjuman headquarters fell to the Indian army, Siddiq Hussain ordered all his male followers to accompany him to prison. A special tribunal was instituted for his trial. Anjuman sources say that he unhesitatingly declared that he had indeed fought the Indian army, 'in accordance with the tradition of the Prophet Muhammad'. The tribunal, it is said, was later declared illegal on technical grounds. Consequently, Siddiq Hussain was absolved of all charges and set free in early 1952. On his release, he is said to have addressed a large gathering at a mosque where he asserted, 'No government can arrest me. I shall uproot infidelity and disbelief. Now the only way for India's salvation is to turn Muslim. The day is not far when the whole of India shall accept Islam.'

Siddiq Hussain remained alive for hardly two months after his release. During this period he is said to have prepared an ambitious programme for missionary work in India, besides giving lectures on the Qur'an to his followers and dispatching his missionaries to various places. In response to the changed political context in which the provocative strategies of the past were no longer feasible, and with Muslims in post-1947 India being a threatened, insecure minority, Siddiq Hussain prepared a new method of missionary work for his followers. This he named the Panch Shanti Marg ('The Five Pillars of the Way of Peace'). The Sanskrit name, it seems, was deliberately chosen to recommend the Anjuman to the Hindus, although it could well have been modelled on the 'five pillars' of Sunni Islam: (i) eko jagadishwar tauhid (belief in the one God); (ii) eko jagat guru (belief in the one guru Muhammad as the 'Teacher of the Entire World'); (iii) sarva avatar satya (belief in all the prophets as true); (iv) sarva dharma granth satya (belief in all religious scriptures as true), and (v) sammelan prarthana ('collective prayer', in other words, namaz, the Islamic form of prayer). Taken together, these beliefs and practices were also given the Sanskrit term of tattva vichar, a rough equivalent of the Arabic word tasawwuf or Sufism.

Although these Sanskrit terms masked core Islamic beliefs and practices, they seem to have been deliberately used, without going into their actual import, by Anjuman missionaries communicating with Hindus, in order to convince them that the Anjuman was committed to a universal faith that incorporated the teachings of Hindu scriptures as well, and had no hidden agenda.

Siddiq Hussain died in April 1952, and was buried in a mausoleum at Asif Nagar. He was survived by four wives, five sons and three daughters. Four of his sons migrated to Pakistan, and one son, Amanat Hussain, stayed behind in Hyderabad, where he is presently the supervisor of the Anjuman. As the head of the Indian branch of the Anjuman Siddiq Hussain was succeeded by his chief disciple, Sayyed Amir Hussain. Under Amir, the Anjuman carried on the missionary work commenced by its founder, but rather than adopting Siddiq Hussain's aggressive mode of preaching, the sect now sought to project itself as a peaceful group, committed to communal harmony and universal brotherhood, in accordance with the *panch shanti marga* that Siddiq Hussain had laid down months before his death. This shift must, of course, be seen as a pragmatic response to the vastly changed political context. Muslims had been displaced from political power in Hyderabad; the ranks of the traditional Muslim elites were rapidly depleting with many of them migrating to Pakistan. A general sense of insecurity haunted the Muslim community in India while the country witnessed an alarming rise of Hindu chauvinism.

In keeping with the new strategy for missionary work laid by Siddiq Hussain, the Anjuman authorities, based at their headquarters at Asif Nagar, focused their energies on training a band of committed missionaries to spread the teachings of the founder through various innovative means. It is estimated that by the late 1990s, the Anjuman had some 15,000 members, mainly in Andhra Pradesh, Karnataka, Maharashtra, and Tamil Nadu. In Pakistan, the Anjuman was led by one of Siddiq Hussain's sons, Zia-ul Hasan, who was based at Mardan in the Pathan borderlands, where he is said to have revived his father's militant outfit, the Jami'at-i-Hizbullah. Little is known about the community in Pakistan, except that it has faced some opposition from traditional Sunnis for some of its apparently 'Hindu' beliefs and practices, and that there have, reportedly, been threats to excommunicate it from the fold of Islam.

After Siddiq Hussain's death, the Indian branch of the Anjuman sought to use peaceful methods of persuasion to appeal to its audience, presenting Islam as but a fulfilment of the prophecies of the Hindu scriptures. Anjuman missionaries visited Hindu temples and attended large Hindu religious congregations, where they set up bookstalls and lectured, wherever allowed, on their beliefs, stressing universal brotherhood and the principles of the panch shanti marga. 'We have not left a single matha, temple, church or gurdwara in India untouched,' wrote an Anjuman activist, 'without explaining there the glory of Muhammad, peace be upon him.' Anjuman missionaries attended Lingayat congregations, where they declared their belief in Basava, but claimed that he was actually a Muslim. In 1977 the Anjuman set up a special booth at the Kumbh Mela in Allahabad where they sold their literature and delivered speeches on their version of Islam. Following in the footsteps of their founder, Anjuman leaders sent off letters to various Indian political leaders, asking them to convert to Islam. In addition, the Anjuman authorities continued to organize the 'international religious conference' every year on Siddiq Hussain's death anniversary, a practice that Siddiq Hussain had himself started in 1929. Speakers from different religious traditions were invited to speak about issues of common concern and interest from their own religious perspectives. This, however, was clearly seen as an opportunity to put the Anjuman's version of Islam across to a non-Muslim audience. The actual aims of the Anjuman remained largely the same. At times its missionary agenda and hostility towards other faiths became clear, as in 1965, when at the end of a tour of Andhra Pradesh, Karnataka and Maharashtra, Anjuman missionaries organized a large rally in Bombay, where they forcefully declared, 'The Hindu religion (dharma) is no religion at all. In the end, all Hindus will have to accept Islam.'

Proselytization was thus still the real goal of the Anjuman, for as a recent Deendar source put it, ' God willing, our work shall carry on till all of India becomes Muslim.'

Given that after 1947, the Anjuman seemed initially to have moved away from the militant approach of its founder, seeking instead to build bridges with people of other faiths by identifying common denominators in various religions, how does one explain the alleged role of the sect in fomenting inter-communal strife in recent years that finally led to it being banned by the Government of India? According to Indian intelligence reports, Anjuman activists are said to have begun travelling to Pakistan after 1992 for military training. If one assumes a degree of truth in this allegation, the timing is significant as it coincides with the destruction of the Babri mosque and the subsequent massacre of Muslims all over India, including Hyderabad. If Deendar activists had been 'lured' into an ISI 'plot' to 'destabilize' India at this time, as Indian newspapers have alleged, it can be seen as a response to the heightened insecurities and fears that plagued the Muslims of India in the wake of the alarming spread of the militant anti-Muslim Hindu right-wing.

As I waded through the carton of books that the maulanas of Asif Nagar had gifted me, I reflected on how similar the Deendaris seemed to be to their Hindutva foes despite their conflicting claims. Both repeated clichés of universality and respect for all faiths. Yet both were impelled by a fiercely intolerant vision, pedalling fury in the name of faith. A shared language of violence and a common commitment to theological terror seemed to unite Hindu and Muslim 'holy' warriors, actually supposed to be fighting each other, against genuine faith and respect for humanity.

7

THE SAI BABA OF SHIRDI

The train pulled into Kopergaon station at mid-day and disgorged an unending stream of passengers—sadhus with matted hair in orange robes and elderly bespectacled couples weighed down by their bed-rolls and food baskets, teenaged boys sporting flaming red and white tilaks on their heads, and scores of families in a festive mood.

'Victory to the Baba,' shouted an excited band of passengers on the platform.

Porters wearing red coats hurried about with piles of luggage on their heads, under a giant poster of a scantily dressed saint in a trance.

A dark corpulent man in a stained olive-green uniform drew up to me and nudged me with his belly.

'Victory to the Baba,' he said in an oily voice. 'You wanting going to Shirdi? I giving you hotel, three star, good price, cheap and best. A/C, colour TV, video movie, hot water, cold beer, ping-pong, morning darshan, conducted Shirdi tour. One day only Rs 5000.'

He handed me his visiting card. It read:

Om Shri Sai Namaha
Messrs. Ram Kumar and Sons
Expert Pilgrim Guider for Shirdi Darshan

He rattled off a well-rehearsed list of other luxuries that were on offer, all for a price of course.

I scrambled into an auto-rickshaw outside the station, working out a deal with the driver for a tenth of the price that Ram Kumar had offered.

The short journey from Kopergaon to Shirdi threw up a picture of abjection and poverty. Mud hovels crumbled under half-eaten thatched roofs. Naked children squatted on the main road relieving themselves into garbage heaps, and a herd of hairy pigs greedily wolfed down rings of falling excrement. Pale blue Buddhist flags hung languidly from bamboo poles, announcing a sprawling Dalit slum. Deep fissures dissected the earth like as autopsied corpse. In the harsh glare of the mid-day sun, old bent women scoured an empty field for leftover roots and nuts.

Ugly, massive, newly constructed ashrams and temples provided an uncomfortable foil to this general hopelessness. Well-fed sadhus, wearing strings of holy beads and layers of caste marks, beamed from posters advertising instant nirvana. Corpulent men in dhotis and safari suits lounged around aimlessly under saffron flags that fluttered on carved pillars. Giant signboards announced five-star comforts: swimming pools, air-cooled rooms, pizza parlours, channelled music, and guided darshans at Shirdi. '*Om Shri Sai*,' they all proclaimed, in unctuous devotion.

Shirdi's main road was abuzz with activity that afternoon. A minor road accident had held up the traffic. Horns blew and curses flew. A pack of young urban pilgrims in blue jeans and Sai Baba T-shirts, ensconced in their Marutis, were close to coming to blows with a hefty Sikh truck-driver. Cows munched meditatively on discarded marigold garlands, oblivious to the display of raw pilgrim passion. Little stalls in canvas shelters sold mandir memorabilia, while, nearby, scores of beggars vied with a pack of street dogs for scraps of food from an overflowing rubbish dump. All around, crooked boards hung on building fronts advertising hotels and inns, extolling their virtues. The 200 hotels or more that Shirdi now so proudly boasted of, had supplanted the original mud-huts, which were no longer to be seen. The town, once a remote village in the poverty-stricken Marathwada region of western Maharashtra, was now an important destination on the crowded Indian pilgrimage map as one of the most popular and wealthy shrines in the country.

The Sai Baba of Shirdi, the town's sole claim to fame, is one of the most widely revered Indian saints of recent times, with a following that transcends all barriers of caste and community. Dressed like a Muslim dervish, with haunting, deeply set eyes, full lips curled into a saintly pout, palm raised in benediction, he reaches out from shop fronts and office walls, roadside shrines under banyan trees and windscreens of beetle-like auto-rickshaws right through from Mumbai to Bhagalpur, and Bhatinda to Bagalkot. A simple, yet compelling slogan, *Sab Ka Malik Ek*, 'Everyone's Lord is One', generally etched below his picture, and one that goes straight to the heart, neatly captures the essence of his life and his teachings—the worship of the one God, and love and harmony among all His creatures.

No one seems to really know when and where the Shirdi Sai Baba was born or who his parents actually were, for the Baba himself was curiously reticent about his past. According to one version of the story, today the most commonly heard one, the Baba was born at the village of Pathri in 1838, in the Aurangabad district, then a part of the Nizam's Dominions, and now in the state of Maharashtra. According to this story his parents, were a Bharadwaj Brahmin couple—Ganga Bavadia, a poor boatman, and his wife, Devagiri Amma. They are said to have been blessed by Shiva and his wife Shakti with a child, who, the divine couple promised, would become a great saint, an incarnation of Shiva himself.

When Devagiri Amma was expecting the child, her husband decided to renounce the world and retire to a forest to meditate, and she followed him. When they got to the forest, Devagiri

Amma sat under a tree to give birth to the child. She pleaded with her husband to wait for her, but he refused. Left with no choice, she wrapped the child up in a bundle of leaves, abandoned him in the forest, and joined her husband.

A short while later, a Muslim fakir from the nearby village of Pathri passed through the forest and found the abandoned child. Being childless himself, he decided to bring it up as his own, giving him the name of Babu. When the child grew up, it is said, the fakir entrusted him to the care of a Brahmin called Venkusha, who accepted the child as his disciple.

Although this is the standard story of the early life of the enigmatic Sai Baba, it is probably a later fabrication and hardly convincing. If Shiva and Shakti had indeed appeared before the Baba's parents, prophesying that Shiva himself would take the form of their son, then it seems impossible that they would have knowingly abandoned him in the forest. Further, if indeed the Muslim fakir found the child abandoned alone in the forest, how was the identity of the child's parents established? Even if their identity had been proved, why was he not returned to them? And further still, one may ask, why would a Muslim fakir entrust his adopted son to the care of a Brahmin?

The entire story seems designed to give the Sai Baba an orthodox Brahmin lineage, and is probably a recent invention, an outcome of the marked Brahminization of the Sai Baba tradition after his death. The similarities that this story shares with the attempts made to give the Muslim Kabir a Brahmin lineage are remarkable. As in the later Kabir tradition, the Brahmins and other 'upper' caste Hindus who came to control the shrine of Sai Baba seem to have made every effort to mould him in their own image, thereby legitimizing their own control and privileges. To recognize a born-Muslim as their guru would have been anathema, and so he was accorded a suitable Brahmin ancestry.

Other sources provide alternate accounts of the Baba's birth. Kamath and Kher, in their biography of the Baba, assert that no firm historical evidence exists that could provide us clues to the Baba's birth and the identity of his parents (M.V. Kamath and V.B. Kher, 1998). They discount the veracity of the story of the Baba's supposed Brahmin origins and claim that it is 'too fanciful to be believed' (Kamat and Kher, 1998). It is, thus, possible that the Baba was actually born in a Muslim family, a fact which some biased writers do not wish to acknowledge. Indeed, one source goes far in refusing to recognize the Baba's obvious Islamic Sufi links by claiming, contrary to what we know of the Baba, that he once asserted about himself:

This is a Brahmin, pure Brahmin. He has nothing to do with black things. No Musalman can dare step in here in the mosque in Shirdi where the Baba lived. He dare not. This Brahmin alone can bring lakhs on the white path and take them to their destination. This is a Brahmin Masjid, and I won't allow any black Mohammedan to cast his shadow here (S.P. Ruhela, 1998).

Sufis as well as the Bhakti saints believe that in order to tread the mystical path, the guidance of a spiritual master is essential. Kamath and Kher write that the Baba left his village of Pathri at the age of eight, in the company of a Muslim fakir, who was probably his Pir or spiritual preceptor, and travelled for many years all over Marathwada. In the course of these travels he met several Hindu and Muslim mystics. It is interesting to note that Pathri was at the time a major Sufi centre dotted with scores of Sufi shrines. Even today the majority of its inhabitants are Muslims. It is likely that the fakir with whom the Baba travelled was a Sufi called Hazrat Roshan Shah Miyan, whom the Baba later identified as his Pir (M.V. Kamath and V.B. Kher, 1998). Some believe that his grave is located at Vavalkar Vada in Shirdi. In her path-breaking study of Sai Baba as a Sufi, Marianne Warren (1999) writes that 'in all probability' it is likely that 'Venkusha' who, some legends claim was the Baba's Brahmin guru, is actually a Hinduized version of the name of this Sufi master. Narayan, on the other hand, writes that the Baba's Pir was the famous Sufi of Dewa, Hazrat Waris 'Ali Shah (B.K. Narayan, 1995).

After receiving instruction on the Sufi path from his Pir, whomsoever he was, the Baba spent many years travelling in the villages and towns of Marathwada. He is said to have stayed for twelve years at Aurangabad, which had for centuries been a major Sufi centre, and received spiritual training from a learned Sufi, a certain Fakir Pir Muhammad. The Baba first came to Shirdi, an impoverished village in the Kopergaon *taluka* of the Ahmadnagar district in present-day Maharashtra, some time between 1868 and 1872. He came here with a Muslim, Chand Patil, from the nearby village of Dhupkhed, to attend the marriage of Chand Patil's sister with a certain Amin Bhai of Shirdi. The Baba stayed at Shirdi for two months, then returned to Aurangabad. At this time he was between twenty-five and thirty years old.

Following his first visit to Shirdi, the Baba is said to have spent some years travelling in the region, after which he again returned to the village, this time in the company of his Pir. When the Baba, dressed like a Muslim fakir, arrived in the village, he was met by Mlahspati, the priest of the local Hindu temple, with the salutation, *Ya Sai* ('Come Sai'). It was after this that he became popular among the villagers as Sai Baba.

Mlahspati was reluctant to allow the Baba to enter the village temple because he was a Muslim. The Baba turned to him and said:

O priest of Khandoba! You have addressed me, saying, 'Come Sai,' but you are resisting my entry into the shrine, thinking that I am a Muslim. O ignorant *pujari* [priest]! Do you think that the touch of this Muslim fakir would defile the God who touches the entire universe with His very touch? The Master of the universe is neither a Hindu nor a Muslim . . . O priest! Do you think that *chaitanya* [consciouness] bears any stamp of caste? Sheer ignorance! Chaitanya is made up of no other caste than chaitanya alone (Chakor Ajgaonkar, 1998).

Initially, the Baba was considered a mad Muslim fakir, but with the stories of the miracles attributed to him, the Baba's following in the village and beyond gradually began to grow. He took up residence in an abandoned mosque in the village, and named it Dwarka Mai Masjid, a term deliberately chosen, it seems, to suggest the unity of Hindus and Muslims. His simple message and constant refrain of *Allah Malik Hai* ('Allah is the Lord') seemed, despite its Islamic terminology, to have appealed to the Hindus as well as the Muslims of the village, who came to behold him as a true man of God. As the message clearly suggests, the Baba preached devotion to and worship of God alone. He never claimed to be God Himself.

The Baba's simple message, 'Allah Malik Hai', sums up his own understanding of religion. God alone was to be worshipped, and no human being could stake claims to that exalted status, although the light of God was present in all things. God being One and the Master of all also meant that all His creatures were part of one big family. This belief was entirely in keeping with both the Bhakti philosophy as well as the teachings of the Sufis, who believed that the light of God exists in every creature, indeed in every particle of His creation. The realization of the unity of God and all His creation (wahdat al-wujud) is thought by the Muslim mystics to be the final stage of the mystical path when they 'die' to themselves (fana) and 'subsist' entirely in God (baqa). In this state of 'union' (jama'a), a state of 'intoxication' (sukr), some Sufis are given to ecstatic utterances (shathat). The classic case in the history of Sufism is that of the tenth-century Mansur al-Hallaj, who cried out in ecstasy, 'I am the truth' (ana al-haqq), for which he was dispatched to the gallows.

In this condition of jama'a, some Sufis, as indeed seems to have been the case with the Sai Baba himself, see all religious paths leading to God alone. Reports of the Sai Baba claiming some sort of divinity for himself or of him being the incarnation of various saints or historical personages, can, from a Sufi perspective, be understood in this light. Yet, we know for a fact that generally the Baba claimed that he was but a humble servant of God, and it seems that he made no claims of being God Himself. In response to a question by a Muslim disciple, 'Abdul Rahim Shamsuddin Rangari, as to why he allowed his Hindu followers to worship him as a god, the Baba said, 'Do in Rome as Romans do. Instead of worshipping their own gods, they worship me as their god. Why should I object and displease them? I myself am a devotee of God' (H.H. Narasimhaswamiji, 1989).

As an antinomian fakir, the Baba's understanding of religion was expansive enough to recognize the presence of the light of God in all beings irrespective of religion. Yet, as Warren notes, 'throughout his life he was simply known as a Muslim fakir' (Warren, 1999). Warren has sought to uncover the essentially Sufi teachings and philosophy of the Baba, which she sees as having been camouflaged, deliberately or otherwise, by later Hindu, mainly Brahmin, hagiographers. Thus, she writes:

While Sai Baba was claimed by both Muslims and Hindus, his core approach to God-realization had a distinct Islamic stance, and he never taught specifically Hindu doctrines and rituals [. . .] Sai Baba has, however, been almost completely assimilated and reinterpreted by the Hindu community.

Likewise, Arthur Osborne (2000) tells us that the Baba 'would repeat Islamic sacred phrases, Arabic or Persian, seldom or never Hindu, but in an undertone, as though not wishing to be heard'. As one of the Baba's close Hindu disciples, Bapu Rao Chandorkar, noted, 'All mantras that Baba spoke were in Persian or Arabic, not Sanskrit, so far as I know' (Ruhela, 1998). And, as Narasimhaswamiji, a close Brahmin disciple of the Baba, remarked 'The ideas which Baba [was] thoroughly soaked up in up to the last were in no way distinguishable from Sufism' (Warren, 1999).

The rituals associated with the early Sai Baba tradition represented a blend of Islamic and local customs, as was indeed the case with several other popular Sufi cults in the Deccan. Warren notes that while Hindus freely entered the mosque where the Baba lived, no Hindu deities were worshipped there, although the Hindus did perform *arti* to the Baba and apply sandalwood paste on his forehead. In the courtyard of the mosque where he lived and preached, the Baba planted a tulsi, sacred to Hindus, for his Hindu followers to circumambulate. A fire (dhuni) was kept burning in the mosque, a practice common to the Nath Yogis as well as certain groups of Muslim Qalandars, such as the Malangs. The Baba would distribute ash from the dhuni as tabarruk or prasad to his followers. In addition, Muslims would regularly offer namaz in the mosque, and the Baba would sometimes join them in prayer (Narasimhaswamiji, 1989). On Thursdays, a special day for the Sufis, the Baba would cook sweet rice and pilaf. After having it consecrated by the maulvi of the mosque, the Baba would send some of it to the priest of the local Hindu temple, and distribute the rest to the poor (S.P. Ruhela, 1998). He would also eat fish and meat along with the fakirs and the poor. This is clearly a Sufi custom. Had he actually been a Brahmin, as is now claimed, he would hardly have adopted such a practice (S.P. Ruhela, 1998). Vegetarian food would be especially cooked and served to the Baba's Hindu followers who did not eat meat.

As for the Baba's own method of prayer, it is said that he did not offer namaz, the Islamic form of worship, regularly, but only on Saturdays, and would recite some verses of the Holy Qur'an and offer fatiha, the recitation of the opening chapter of the Qur'an. He would also often repeat the Islamic creed of confession, the kalima shahdah: *la ilah il alla muhammadur rasul allah* ('There is no God but Allah and Muhammad is the Prophet of Allah'), after which he would distribute sweets to his followers, both Hindu as well as Muslim (S.P. Ruhela, 1998). Bhajans and qawwalis, devotional songs praising God, the Prophet Muhammad and various Sufi saints, would sometimes be sung at the mosque. On Muharrum, *tazias* and *tabuts* marking the martyrdom of Hazrat Imam Hussain, the grandson of the Prophet, would be installed in the mosque.

In 1896, the Baba instituted the annual Sufi 'urs festival, with the explicit purpose of bringing Hindus and Muslims together. In 1912, he agreed to have the 'urs combined with the Hindu Ram Navmi festival, thus reinforcing 'the earlier Sufi initiative for co-operation, symbiosis and tolerance' (Marianne Warren, 1999). Ruhela writes that during the festival Hindus would worship in the mosque along with the Muslims, each following their own rituals. The Baba would put sandalwood paste on the forehead of Mlahspati, the priest of the local Khandoba temple, who would reciprocate the gesture. Then, namaz would be held in the mosque, and the Qur'an would be read out.

Although the Baba seems to have himself worshipped in the traditional Sufi way (S.P. Ruhela, 1998), he would instruct his Hindu disciples to discover God through their own scriptures, recommending them the study of texts such as the *Eknathi Bhagvata*, the *Jnaneswari* and the Bhagwad Gita. God, he believed, was present in different forms in all religions. He insisted that the ultimate aim of all spiritual paths was to reach God, known variously as Allah or Ishwar (Marianne Warren, 1999). Thus, he declared:

Ishwar Aahe Hai, Satya Maan
Ishwar Nahi Hai Khotey Samajh
Sab Allah Hi Allah Hai
Ha Sarwa Allah Miyan Cha Ahe

'Ishwar does exist'—consider this as truth.
'There is no Ishwar'—understand this as false.
Allah is in everything.
Everything belongs to Allah the Master.

The quintessentially Sufi teachings of the Baba are clearly evident in the Deccani Urdu manuscript prepared by 'Abdul, his longest-serving disciple, who came to live with the Baba almost thirty years before the Baba's death. 'Abdul looked after the Baba's dargah till the former died in 1954. It is interesting to note that after this the tradition centred around the Baba underwent a marked process of Brahminization.

'Abdul was born in 1871 at Nanded, and at an early age was placed by his father, Sultan, in the care of a Sufi, Hazrat Amiruddin. At the age of eighteen, he was instructed by Hazrat Amiruddin to continue his spiritual training with Sai Baba. Accordingly, he travelled to Shirdi, where he spent the rest of his life in the Baba's service, receiving instruction in the Sufi tariqat from him. He lived a life of great simplicity, spending much of his time cleaning the mosque where the Baba lived, and reading the Qur'an. Often the Baba would ask him to recite certain verses from the Qur'an for him. The Baba would then explain the deeper meaning of these verses to his disciples. It is said that every day the Baba would teach 'Abdul a part of the Qur'an (Shaila Hattiangadi, 1998).

'Abdul would note down the utterances of the Baba, which finally took the form of a manuscript extending to over 200 pages. The manuscript is presently in the possession of his grandsons who live in Shirdi, and is now in a pathetic state, much of it having already been destroyed by neglect and the ravages of time. Warren has examined 'Abdul's manuscript at length and inferred that the authorities in charge of the Sai Baba shrine at Shirdi have not published the manuscript till date, presumably because of its distinctly Islamic provenance, which would obviously challenge the standard representation of the Baba as a Brahmin. The text very clearly points to the Baba's Sufi background, although it also indicates how willing he was, as a Muslim fakir, to accommodate Hindu concepts and terms insofar as they did not conflict with the basic teachings of Islamic Sufism on the oneness of God.

'Abdul's manuscript begins with the mandatory Islamic praise to God, with which all verses of the Holy Qur'an but one begin: Bismillah hir Rahman hir Rahim ('In the Name of Allah, the Most Merciful, the Most Compassionate'). Then follows a line in praise of the Prophet and the names of his family members (ahl al-bayt) and some Sufis, beseeching them for their blessings. Some of these Sufis cannot be easily identified, while others, such as Hazrat Khwaja Moinuddin Chishti and Hazrat Khwaja Bakhtiyar Kaki, are well known. After this, the names of some Hindu holy figures, such as Brahma and Vishnu, are mentioned. This is followed by an elaborate exposition of key Sufi terms, which are repeatedly interspersed with the Islamic confession of the faith, the kalima shahadah. Curiously enough, parallels are drawn between various Hindu deities and Islamic figures. Thus, 'Abdul writes: 'Vishnu is equal to the Bismillah hir Rahman hir Rahim [...] 'Ali [the son-in-law and cousin of the Prophet Muhammad] is equal to Brahma; Mahadev [Shiva] is equal to the Prophet Muhammad' (Warren, 1999).

The Baba's disciples included both Hindus as well as Muslims. While the Muslims considered him a 'friend of God' (wali), as indeed he himself insisted he was, to many of his Hindu disciples he was an incarnation of their own deity Dattatreya, a common enough name in the Deccan. Several Deccani Sufis, such as Dada Hayat in central Karnataka, Shah Fakir in southern Maharashtra, Sayyed Chanda Sahib Qadri of Daulatabad and Shah Muni were also regarded by their Hindu followers as incarnations of Dattatreya. The association of the Baba with Dattatreya must be seen in this light.

Visitors to Shirdi were taken aback to see Hindus, Muslims, as well as others, living in complete harmony and worshipping together. In many cases this led to a complete transformation in their own attitudes. Thus, for instance, a certain 'Abdullah Jan, a Muslim Pathan from Peshawar, who visited Shirdi in 1913, wrote in his memoirs:

My stay with Baba brought about some changes in my mentality. When I came to Shirdi, I regarded Hindus as enemies of mine. After remaining about three years with Baba, this feeling of animosity passed away and I was viewing [sic] Hindus as my brethren. Now, for instance, I see with regret that in Bombay, Hindus wish to destroy Moslems and their mosques and Moslems wish to destroy Hindus and their temples. If both succeed in wiping out each other, they will only make room for persons of other faiths to establish themselves in place of these two (S.P. Ruhela, 1998).

The Baba of Shirdi breathed his last on 15 October 1918, at the age of eighty. For almost two days after his death, his Hindu and Muslim followers fought over his body. It was finally decided to bury him in a mansion built by a rich Hindu businessman from Nagpur especially for the Baba, in the Buty Wada in Shirdi. The shrine was originally designed as an ordinary grave. Over time, however, as the administration of the shrine came under the control of a small group of 'high' caste Hindus, mainly Brahmin followers, it was transformed into a Hindu-style temple, and is now generally called the Samadhi Mandir.

Rigopoulos, in his comprehensive study of the Sai Baba cult, comments that the consequence of this struggle between Hindus and Muslims over the Baba's legacy after his death, 'marked the end of any Sufi claim, and was the beginning of the Hinduization of Sai Baba' (Warren, 1999). Consequently, this period began to witness a gradual, yet inexorable, process of the Brahminization of the legend of the Baba, and a gradual excising from public memory of his Sufi heritage. The eclipse of the distinctly Muslim Sufi core of the original Sai Baba tradition must be understood in the broader context of the growing assertion of Brahminical Hinduism in Maharashtra from the late nineteenth century onwards. Threatened by the restiveness triggered by Brahminical hegemony of the 'lower' castes, who were represented by people such as Jyotiba Phule among the Shudras, and Ambedkar among the Dalits, a growing number of Maharashtrian Brahmins looked to new, aggressive Hindu supremacist organizations for support. With their violently anti-Muslim agenda, they promised to unite all 'Hindus' in one solid bloc, thus effectively countering the radical appeal of 'low' caste revolutionaries. Vestiges of Muslim traditions among the 'low' castes were now to be stamped out, for they were seen as threatening the 'purity' of the Hindu 'nation'. Bal Gangadhar

Tilak, an orthodox Brahmin himself, and the leader of the Maharashtrian Hindu 'nationalists' of his times, showed the way by leading a strident campaign against the widespread participation of Hindus in the Moharrum observances. His alternative was to invent mass processions to commemorate the Ganesh festival. The Rashtriya Swayamsevak Sangh (RSS), the mother of all anti-Muslim Hindu fascist groups in the country today, was established in Maharashtra in the mid-1920s, and almost all its top functionaries were Maharashtrian Brahmins. The Hindu Mahasabha, too, found strong support among the Brahmins of the region.

With a following that had now grown into several millions, the Sai Baba tradition was now too popular to be left unattended by Brahminical revivalists. New legends were now invented to present the Baba as a Brahmin miracle-worker. He was said to have been born in a Brahmin family and to have studied under a Brahmin guru. The Sai Baba Sansthan, the almost entirely 'upper' caste controlled governing body that had taken charge of the Baba's shrine after his death, claimed that not only was he a Brahmin by birth but that he had explicitly expressed his 'dislike for those who considered him to be a Mahomedan'. This at complete odds with what we know of the Baba's actual life (Swami Sai Sharan Anand, 1998).

In the process of this radical rewriting of the Baba's story, his own bitter critique of orthodoxy and ritualism was conveniently forgotten. If the Baba had always insisted that God alone should be worshipped, or 'Allah Malik Hai' as he would often say, and that he was simply 'Allah's servant' (S.P. Ruhela, 1998), he was now transformed into a powerful god himself, comfortably accommodated in the ever-expanding family of Hindu deities. The observance of Islamic rituals at the shrine, such as singing qawwalis, reading from the Qur'an or performing passion plays during the month of Muharrum, were hurriedly abandoned. These were replaced by Hindu rituals as part of a broader programme presumably of deliberate Brahminization. More tragically, the Baba's own project of promoting inter-communal harmony was subtly attacked by those who now claimed his legacy. In 1954, an idol supposedly of the Baba was installed on his Muslim-style mazar (grave). This was a clear indication of the direction in which those in charge of his shrine were pushing the tradition. By the mid-1990s, this Brahminization of the Sai Baba tradition had gone so far that in 1995 the question of whether a Shirdi Sai Baba temple could be considered as an exclusively Hindu shrine was hotly debated in the courts. The matter went right up to the Supreme Court of India. The state government of Andhra Pradesh sought to have a Shirdi Sai Baba temple in Hyderabad declared a Hindu place of worship. Fortunately, the Supreme Court turned down the appeal, declaring that:

If a temple dedicated to Shirdi Sai Baba was [sic] to be treated as an exclusively Hindu temple, it would be a grave contradiction and negation of the composite religion of universal character, which the saint had preached all his life [. . .] Baba's philosophy was neither exclusively Hindu or [sic] Muslim [sic] or Christian. He believed that God was not bound by the fetters of caste, creed or religion. The Baba used to preach that God did not live in either a temple or a mosque (Warren, 1999).

The appropriation of dissenting voices into the orthodox Brahminical fold by spiritualizing and ritualizing them, and thus effectively robbing them of their radical potential for social transformation and critique, has been the fate of numerous socio-religious movements in India since time immemorial. Unable to combat the pressure of rapidly expanding Hindu assertiveness, the Sai Baba tradition was slowly, yet surely, absorbed into the fold of Brahminical Hinduism, until it was transformed almost beyond recognition.

A flood of pilgrims herded along the narrow lane bursting with traffic and riddled with potholes filled with stagnant pools of grey water. An ornate stone doorway arched over the entrance, leading to a vast open quadrangle. A series of steps led to a row of marble-walled rooms. At the end of the rooms stood a grandiose hall crowned with a shikara draped in saffron flags. The Baba rested in eternal peace under the shikara. People who had queued up outside the hall for over an hour, finally began to file inside.

At the far end of the dimly lit hall rose petals were heaped on a simple grave. Two Brahmin priests, dressed in flaming red dhotis, their holy threads prominently displayed across their breasts, squatted on either side, receiving donations from awe-struck devotees. Ensconced on a velvet-covered platform was a throne with a massive silver idol of the Baba bearing a heavy crown. Below, a long glass case built into the wall displayed some of the Baba's personal belongings—a slender-stemmed copper hukkah, a pair of worn-out sandals, and a large grey grinding stone. Four kitsch alabaster statuettes of Ram, Sita, Lakshman and Krishna, almost certainly recent additions, seemed calculated to give the exhibit a deliberately orthodox Hindu look.

Outside, too, there was ample evidence of efforts undertaken to provide the Baba with the respectable orthodox Hindu credentials that he clearly seems to have lacked in his own lifetime. The short neem tree under which the Baba's Pir, who some said was the Sufi Hazrat Roshan Shah, is believed to have been buried, had now been converted into a little Hindu shrine, containing a small, sleepy-eyed Nandi bull and a linga. Close by, three new small temples dedicated to Shiva, Ganesh and Shani or Saturn had come up.

At the far end of the compound, a long thread of noisy pilgrims wound its way to the vast new puja hall. A steady drone drifted from the hall. Inside, a middle-aged Brahmin sat on a raised pedestal. On the ground, at his feet, rows of small wooden tables had been laid out, on which had been placed little copper pots of water, an assortment of leaves, puddles of red powder and doll-sized statuettes of Krishna, Ganesh and Sai Baba. Men squatted before the tables, their legs curled up in the lotus position.

'We are about to start the Satyanarayan Puja,' the Brahmin announced.

A murmur of delight escaped from the men below.

'Now, take a spoonful of the water and splash it three times on the statue of Sri Ganesh,' instructed the Brahmin.

'Now take, in your right hand, a pinch of the red powder, and place it on the plate.'

The men did as they were told, like school children obeying a stern master.

'Now fold your right hand over your left and . . .'

And so he went on, while the men dutifully followed his every instruction.

I sat through the entire performance on a stool in the corner, marvelling at the genius of the Brahmins who had now succeeded in effacing every trace of Sufi worship at the shrine. If the Baba's own method of worship had been, as reliable sources claim, Islamic and almost indistinguishable from that of the other Sufis, his Muslim heritage had now been completely wiped out by a new breed of 'followers' who now controlled his cult.

The same tragic fate had befallen the Baba's mosque, at a short distance from the grave. The original structure had been demolished, and a new structure built in its place, bearing not the faintest resemblance to a mosque. This, despite the fact that the Baba 'insisted on proper Islamic architecture' (Arthur Osborne, 2000). A new hall had been attached to the 'renovated mosque' to mark the spot where the Baba used to sleep. Resting against it were three large notice boards of the VHP, the Hindu Rashtra Tarun Mandal and the Bharatiya Vidyarthi Sena—the students' wing of the Shiv Sena—all three anti-Muslim Hindu supremacist outfits. The only visible sign of the Baba's Muslim links that remained was the Muslim-style grave of Haji

'Abdul—one of the Baba's closest disciples—that lay under a tree within the shrine complex. I had read that 'Abdul's descendants still lived in Shirdi, and I sought them out. I was led down a narrow street opposite the Baba's mosque to a run-down two-room tenement.

A turbaned middle-aged man smiled and welcomed me. We sat on the floor and talked about 'Abdul, who peered at us curiously from a picture frame that he shared with the Baba on a cloth-covered platform.

The man brought out a bundle of papers carefully wrapped in a silk sheet cloth lying on an alcove built into the wall. He removed the cloth and handed me the bundle.

'Abdul Baba's manuscript,' he explained, 'which he prepared under Sai Baba's instructions.'

He pointed out the running Urdu script, like the trail of a bird's footprints, interspersed with squiggly Marathi letters.

'Abdul Baba was a master of many languages,' he said, beaming at the great scholarly accomplishments of his grandfather.

The pages had yellowed with time. Powdery flakes fell as I turned them. White ants had gnawed through large portions and water stains had washed off the ink in some places.

I leafed through the manuscript hurriedly, for the man had to tend to a family of pilgrims who sat before 'Abdul's photograph with folded hands, their gazes lowered in hypnotic trance-like adoration. A constant reference to Allah and Muhammad filled almost every page of the text, with an occasional mention of one or the other Hindu deity, thus confirming Warren's own analysis of the manuscript.

'This is really a very important document,' I told the man as I readied to leave. 'You must get it published, or at least have it preserved.'

It was clear to me that the 'high' caste authorities of the Baba's shrine were not interested in taking up the task. And so, the Sufi of Shirdi has now been left to gradually turn into yet another of the teeming deities of the elastic Hindu pantheon.

8

THE IMAM MAHDI AND THE BUDDH AVATAR OF PANNA

A bumpy one-hour bus-ride took me from the famed temple town of Khajuraho, to Panna, a dusty, laid-back town on the fringes of a vast forest in north-western Madhya Pradesh, almost at the heart of India. Poverty was etched on the grim faces of the men and women squatting at the bus-stand, many of them dressed in rags. A man, clad in a torn vest, and a striped lungi pulled up till his thighs, revealing a pair of needle-like legs, furiously pedalled his rickshaw towards me. I asked him if he would take me to Prannath-ji ka Mandir. 'Ten rupees,' he answered, and I willingly agreed.

The rickshaw made its way out of the bus-stand, deftly dodging a pack of hairy hogs nosing through a pile of rotting mango skins and cabbage leaves. We rode past Sweetie Chaat Bhandar, with its piles of pakoras and gulab jamuns buried under an army of flies, and the Lovely Chicken Centre. The rickshaw deftly went down the lane by the portals of Hind Mother Teresa School, one of the numerous 'convents' in town. Across the road loomed the abandoned ruins of ancient *chhatris* built over the graves of long-forgotten warriors. Ramesh, the rickshaw-puller, gave a running commentary on the history of the town, pointing out sites of major significance.

'Business is down these days,' he said grimly, beads of sweat gleaming on his face. With his monthly earnings of Rs 1000 he had five mouths to feed, and his wife was expecting yet another child.

The rickshaw abruptly halted at a square in front of the Katchery, the sprawling district court that was once the palace of the raja of Panna. Two roaring stone lions draped in a thick blanket of moss stood at vigil at the entrance. A short brown slate pyramid squatted in front of the building. Its four sides were inscribed with verses stressing the oneness of Hindus and Muslims while a pair of terracotta hands held up in prayer crowned it. On the other side of the road, a narrow lane, bordered on either side with open drains clogged with garbage, snaked its way towards the shrine of Prannath, the saint of Panna whom I had come to visit.

Painted in loud green, pink, orange and yellow stripes, a high wall encircled the shrine complex, shielding it from the din and clutter of the world outside. Holy graffiti—neatly calligraphed verses from the Vedas and the Gita and snatches of Prannath's poetry, declaring the unity of all humankind—covered the wall. A verse from Prannath's holy book, the *Kuljam Swarup*, caught my eye, and I scribbled it down in my notebook, much to the curiosity of passers-by. It read:

ek kahya bed kateb ney, so juda rahya saban
tinko saro dhundya par ek na paya kin
judey judey namey gavahi, judey judey bhesh anek
jin koi jhagdo aap mai, dhani sabo ka ek

What the Vedas say, the Qur'an says, too,
But still those who claim to follow them oppose each other.
They all search for Him, but no one finds Him.
He is known by various names, and appears in various forms.
They all quarrel about him [but forget that],
The Lord of all is One.

I had arrived at the shrine of one of the most intriguing, yet least known, holy men of India. Hindus and Muslims both claimed him as their own, along with a third group, the Pranamis, named after him. All agreed, however, that this mysterious man of God had preached an ethical monotheism through which he had tried to bring people of different, warring faiths together in worship of the one formless God.

An enormous wooden door opened out into a vast complex, dominated by the Gummatji, the imposing tomb-complex of Prannath, and the Banglaji, a house with a slanted roof where the saint used to deliver his religious discourses. The Gummatji is a fine specimen of Muslim-Rajput architecture. Its vast domes, turrets and graceful arches seemed to have effortlessly combined Hindu and Islamic motifs. Perched on a series of golden bulbs on the main dome, a golden outstretched palm or panja pointed towards the heavens—probably symbolizing both the panjatan pak, the 'five pure ones' of the Prophet and his immediate family, and the panch tattva or 'five elements' of the Hindus.

Seated on a mat at the entrance, a handsome young man poured over a holy text, rocking himself to and fro as he recited sacred verses in a soft, mellifluous drone. With his pale ivory complexion, his carefully carved nose and his sky-blue salwar kameez, he could have easily been mistaken for a strapping mountain Pathan. He looked at me with his large, round eyes and smiled.

'Welcome, brother,' he said, putting down his book on a wooden lectern and rising to shake my hand.

He introduced himself as Anirudh Dhami, one of the several priests attached to the shrine.

'People call me Dada Bhai. You could call me that too,' he said with disarming cheerfulness.

I followed Dada Bhai into the shrine, through the cool inner circular corridor. Stucco statuettes of Krishna and his *gopis* frolicking in Brindavan—holding hands and skipping along in child-like glee—peered down from the roof and the walls. The spaces between the statues were filled up with lotus flowers in full bloom and curved tendrils bearing tender buds. A tin board nailed to the wall sternly warned, 'No permission to do arti wearing pants.' A handcrafted silver door opened into the sanctum in front, where, covered with layers of velvet and roses, the tomb of Prannath rested in an underground chamber, accessible only to the officiating priests. An impressive silver throne sat over the grave, and on it, reclining in the soft comfort of a row of bolsters, was a gilt-edged copy of the *Kuljam Swarup*, draped in a delicately embossed silk sheet. A golden crown studded with semi-precious stones and shaded by a little protective silver umbrella dangled above it.

A line of pilgrims filed inside, circumambulated the grave with folded hands and half-closed eyes and prostrated themselves before the grave. A priest dressed in a neatly pressed dhoti and kurta and a cone-shaped brocade cap, a deep red tilak smeared on his forehead, sat outside the sanctum, dispensing holy water, bits of sugar, and wheat flakes cooked in ghee. An old man bent over his stick dipped his bony finger into a pool of sandalwood paste in a gleaming oyster shell, and, peering into a plastic-bordered mirror, applied a dot on his forehead.

Outside, a group of women had gathered in preparation for the night prayer, the last of the five collective prayers held at the shrine every day. Dressed in soft-coloured chiffon saris, their heads neatly covered with their pallus, the women squatted on the marble floor at the entrance, singing an ode to Prannath to the accompaniment of a dholak:

'Yes, Momins! He it was whom you saw in Braj with the gopis, and it was he you saw in Medina wrapped up in a black blanket.'

A reference to Krishna and Muhammad respectively.

Tears ran down the cheeks of an old, toothless woman dressed in a faded white sari, a widow from Nepal, who seemed to be in a state of divine ecstasy.

The singing suddenly stopped with the deafening ring of a metal gong, a sign for the women to give way to a group of men, who now began to sing the verses of the *Kuljam Swarup* in a loud chorus. The priest stood up, a copper butter-lamp with seven long wicks in his hand, and began the arti. He waved the lamp before the holy book, sending clouds of sweet-smelling smoke up into the air. Two bearded men standing on either side of the priest gently waved what seemed to be yak-tail whisks.

The elaborate ceremony lasted a quarter of an hour ending with the distribution of lumps of sugar and holy water ladled out of a copper pot with a small metal spoon. A velvet curtain was drawn across the door that led to the grave, leaving Prannath to sleep in peace. The worshippers then followed the priest to the Banglaji, where, after the ritual worship of the *Kuljam Swarup*, a community elder read out verses from the holy book, explaining their import and exhorting his listeners to hold on firmly to the 'true religion'.

'It was here that Prannath-ji would expound his doctrines, reading out from the Qur'an and the Vedas to explain the inner truths of the two faiths to his Hindu and Muslim followers,' whispered the awe-struck Dada Bhai.

The centuries of Mughal rule constituted a period of enormous religious creativity, spawning numerous initiatives to bring Hindus and Muslims closer. Numerous Sufis, Bhaktas and yogis freely borrowed from each other, giving birth to several religious sects that attracted followers from across the Hindu-Muslim divide. One such sect was the Nijanandis, more commonly known as the Pranamis, followers of the seventeenth-century Meher Raj Thakur, known to his followers as Mahamati Prannath, 'The Enlightened One', or 'The Lord of the Souls'. Today, there are roughly eight million Pranamis, living in scattered groups throughout western India, particularly in Gujarat, Rajasthan and Madhya Pradesh.

The origins of the Pranami tradition are as obscure and fiercely contested as the identity of the community today. According to one version, the generally accepted one for contemporary Pranamis, Meher Raj Thakur was born in 1618.

He was the youngest son of Keshav Thakur, a Lohana from Jamnagar in present-day Gujarat. As a child, he is said to have displayed strong mystic leanings, and, at the young age of twelve, he became a disciple of one Dev Chandra, a Kayasth from Umarkot in Sind. Dev Chandra is said to have been commanded by God to preach to a world weary of inter-communal strife a simple monotheism, stressing the essential unity of Islam and Vaishnavism, and to crusade against polytheism, empty ritualism and the tyranny of the Brahmins and the Mullahs. Impressed with the young lad's dedication, Dev Chandra is said to have revealed to him the inner secrets of satya dharm, 'the true faith'—the core that is common to all religions. Then, it is believed he instructed Meher Raj to go out into the world to preach the faith saying as one informant put it:

The followers of different religions have spread hatred in the name of God. Go and explain to them from within their own religions the truth about God. Tell them that the light of God shines in every human being, for there is no difference of *varna*, caste, sect or class. Unravel before them the true meaning of the Qur'an and the Vedas and show to them that just as God is one, religion, too, is one. Go forth now and spread the light of the satya dharm.

Having come under Dev Chandra's influence, Meher Raj is said to have lost all desire for worldly possessions and distributed all his wealth among the poor. Distressed at his abandoning the world at such a young age, his family thought of a way out. They arranged to send him to Arabia to bring back a relative who had been living there for many years. Meher Raj is said to have spent five long years in Arabia where, it seems, he met numerous Muslim Sufis and scholars from whom he learnt about the religion of the Prophet. His knowledge of Islam is said to have astounded many Muslims, not least the Khalifa himself.

When Meher Raj finally returned to Gujarat, he was arrested by the local raja, who had been told that he was carrying with him much money and gold. Some months later, however, he was freed, after which he took up the post of diwan at the court of the raja of Dharol. Soon after, he left the job and joined Dev Chandra, who, by now, was nearing his last days. Shortly before he died, Dev Chandra handed him his cloak and appointed him his deputy, commissioning him to preach the message of the 'true faith'. Dev Chandra's own son, Bihariji, a staunch upholder of the caste system, is said to have fiercely opposed him, and the nascent community of the Momins ('The True Believers') or the Sundar Saath ('The Beautiful Companions') split over the caste issue, with the majority choosing to side with the anti-caste Meher Raj, who now assumed the title of 'Mahamati Prannath'.

As Meher Raj now began travelling through Gujarat, making scores of disciples, he met with stiff opposition from rulers and priests, both Hindu as well as Muslim. His teachings on the futility of caste, his bitter critique of the corrupt practices of the Brahmins and the Mullahs and the oppressive ways of the kings, his fierce opposition to idolatry and polytheism and his appeal for a faith in God transcending community barriers, were perceived as a grave threat by the establishment. The Hindu ruler of Jamnagar had him and his disciples arrested and thrown into prison, where they languished for a year while the raja was engaged in a long battle with Qutb Khan, the Muslim governor of Ahmedabad. Some time later, Meher Raj was released only to be taken captive again, this time by Qutb Khan. After spending a short spell in jail, he was set free. He then headed for the coastal settlement of Diu. From here he took a boat to Muscat, where he is said to have made several disciples among the Arabs, including some fierce dacoits who repented for their sins at his hands.

On his return to Gujarat, the governor of Surat is said to have ordered his arrest. Unable to trace him, the guards arrested his wife instead. Fearing that they might molest her, a Brahmin disciple of Meher Raj came to her rescue, telling the guards that she was his sister. The guards, suspecting that he was lying, said they would believe him only if he ate food cooked by her. The Brahmin had been brought up to believe that all other castes were polluting and that food cooked by them could not be touched. Having joined Meher Raj's community, however he could no longer abide by such taboos.

That day, he, along with Meher Raj's wife and the rest of the Momins or Sundar Saaths present—Hindus, Muslims, Brahmins, Kshatriyas, Vaishyas and Shudras—all sat down together for a communal meal.

Till date in every Pranami shrine, the followers of Prannath share an annual ritual meal in commemoration of this event, a powerful symbolic defiance of Brahminical orthodoxy and its notions of pollution and purity.

From Surat, Meher Raj and his band of disciples proceeded to Sidhpur Patan, and from there to Merta, near the city of Nagaur, in present-day Rajasthan.

One evening, while taking a stroll, Meher Raj heard the call to prayer of the Mullah from a nearby mosque. All of a sudden, it is said, he was filled with a strange divine bliss. It struck him that the Allah of the Qur'an and the Ishwar of the Vedas were one and the same. Vimla Mehta, clearly the most prolific contemporary Pranami writer, describes the event in the following words:

It seemed to him that the Prophet Muhammad had himself entered him, and had given to him the true knowledge not only of the Qur'an, but also of all the other holy books, explaining to him the underlying unity between them. Till then, Prannath had restricted himself largely to preaching among the Hindus the true knowledge of the Vedas that he had been given by Shri Dev Chandra, but now he began explaining the unity of religions from the Qur'an as well [Vimla Mehta, 1979].

Like the Bhakti saints and Sufis before him, Meher Raj now set about composing mystical verses to preach his message of the oneness of God and the unity of humankind. Later, these verses—over 18,000 of them spread over fourteen books—were put together in the form of a holy scripture, called the *Kuljam Swarup* ('The Form of the Total Wisdom'). Four books of the scripture deal with Islam, four with Hinduism and the rest consist of verses on personal piety, righteous conduct and the love for God. It is also known as the *Tartam Sagar* ('The Darkness-Dispelling Ocean'), for, as Dada Bhai, the priest explained to me, 'Just as the rivers that flow into an ocean lose their separateness, so, too, it is in this book with Hinduism and Islam.'

Written in various languages, including Arabic, Persian, Sindhi, Gujarati and Khadi Boli, these verses speak of the love for God and the painful path of union with Him. Knowledge of God is to be gained only through the path of love. Neither highbrow scholarship nor noble birth can lead to Him. God sees no difference between a Muslim and a Hindu, or a Brahmin and a Shudra. Rituals and sacrifices, and pilgrimage to shrines and temples are all meaningless—they have been invented simply to fill the bellies of rapacious priests. True salvation can only be gained by abandoning one's love for the world and dedicating oneself totally to God and to the humble service of all His creatures, beyond religion and caste.

Rather than claiming to preach a new religion of his own, Meher Raj insisted that he was simply reviving true religion in its primal form—*haqiqi din-i-islam* ('The True Religion of Islam') and *saccha sanatan dharm* ('The True Eternal Faith'], as he called it.

The *Kuljam Swarup* is replete with equivalences drawn between Vaishnavism and Islam, that seek to prove the hidden oneness of the two creeds. Muhammad is equated with Krishna, while Noah, or Nuh as Muslims call him, is said to have been the same as Vasudev in the story of Krishna, both having survived a terrible flood by the grace of God. The garden to which Noah's son Sam took his people is said to be Brindavan, the play-field of Krishna and his gopis. Jesus, the 'Spirit of God' (ruh allah), and Dev Chandra, Meher Raj's guru, are one and the same. The angel Mikhail is synonymous with Brahma, the Islamic Azazil with Vishnu, Israel with Shiva and Israfil, appointed by God to blow the horn announcing the Day of Resurrection, with the Buddha. The true believers are the Momins, while the sinners, no matter what their religion, are kafirs. While the former shall enjoy eternal bliss in heaven (bihisht or paramdham), the latter shall be thrown into the raging fires of hell.

Meher Raj saw himself as the messiah appointed by God to lead the world out of ceaseless internecine strife. He declared himself to be the Imam Mahdi ('The Rightly Guided One'), whom the Muslims expected when the end of the world was near, and the Buddh Nishkalank Avatar ('The Enlightened Spotless Incarnation') of the Hindus. He went so far as to claim that the Prophet Muhammad had himself predicted that he would usher in the Qiyamat, the Day of Judgement. Referring to an alleged Prophetic tradition that on such a day, the sun would rise from the west but its light would be seen only in the east, he claimed that it actually referred to his own advent. This meant, he said, that the real meaning of the Qur'an would finally be made manifest in the east, in India, where the flag of 'true Islam' or satya dharm would finally be unfurled. This, he claimed, was his divinely appointed mission—to revive the 'common faith' of Muhammad and Krishna. The 'command' (hukm) of God, in the form of the spirit of Muhammad and the 'power' (shakti) of Krishna had entered him, he said and instructed him to explain the esoteric truths to the Hindus and the Muslims, revealing to them the actual import of the Vedas and the Qur'an, which it seemed they had long forgotten.

The motif of the oneness of humankind, transcending the Hindu-Muslim barrier, and based on devotion to God and to a life of piety and noble conduct, is a constant refrain in the *Kuljam Swarup*. Despite being brothers and fellow creatures of God, Hindus and Muslims constantly fight in the name of God while actually failing to recognize Him. Thus, Meher Raj says:

jo kacchu kahya kateb ney soi kahya bed
dou bande ek sahib ke, par ladat bina paye bhed
brahmin kahe ham uttam, musalman kahe ham pak
dou mutthi ek thor ki ek raakh dujey khaak

Whatever the Qur'an says, the Vedas say the same,
But the two servants of the same God fight without attaining the Secret.

Both [Hindus and Muslims] accept the One God and say that there is One Soul in all.

The Vedas and the Qur'an teach the same thing, but no one understands them in fact.

The Brahmin claims he is the most superior, the Muslim says he is pure,

But both are simply a handful of mud, one turns to ashes and the other to the grave.

The same message is put differently in another stirring couplet:

dohe kahen wujud ek hai, arbah sabon mai ek
bed kateb ek bata vahon, par pavai ne koi vivek

Similarly, Prannath says:

lad firkey judey hindu musalman
aur khalaq keti kahun sab mai lagey guman
kahey sab ek wujud hai, sab mai ekai dam
sab kahey sahib ek hai, par sabki ladey rasam
boli sabon judi padi, naam judey dharey saban
chalan juda kar liye, taathey samajh na paari

Hindus and Muslims, constantly at war,
All base their claims on mere guesses.
Yet, they agree that there is only a single Existent One,
And say that there is just one Lord, known to them by different names,
For they speak different tongues and call him with different words,
And so they have made differences, which they themselves fail to understand.

And again he cries out at petty religious distinctions, while putting forward, at the same time, his own spiritual claims:

jaat ek khasam ki aur na koi jaat
ek khasam ek duniya aur ud gayi duji baat
mahamat kahe aye momino dekhey khasam pyar
isa muhammad andar aye ke khol diye sab dvar

There is only one caste, and that is of God,
Realize that God is one and so are all His creatures,
And then, all duality shall vanish.
Mahamat says, 'O Believers! On seeing the love of the Lord,
Jesus and Muhammad have entered me, and have opened all the doors.

Muhammad and his own guru Dev Chandra or Shyam—Krishna in his form as lover of the gopis—have the same message for humankind, for, Meher Raj says, 'There is no age without a Muhammadi,' or 'God's command'. Thus, he tells both Hindus and Muslims:

to sifat sab muhammad ki,
so muhammad kahya jo shyam
Abal akhir dou din mai, ek muhammad bujarg naam
Trigun tirthankar avtar, kai farishtey payghambar
Tin sabki shobha se shyam, aya muhammad par.

The attributes of Muhammad.
What Muhammad said, so did Shyam.
The first and the last, in the two religions, repeat the name of one Muhammad the Master.
The incarnation with the three properties, and many angels and prophets.
Their glory is Shyam, Muhammad who has come.

Claiming to have been appointed by God as the Mahdi and the Nishkalank Buddh Avatar to put an end to Hindu-Muslim strife by explaining the hidden truths of both the Hindu and the Islamic scriptures, Meher Raj declares:

hindu maney buddh ko, musalman imam,
dono utarey paar jo tamas tajey tamam

Hindus revere the Buddh, while Muslims the Imam,
Only they can cross the ocean, who conquer their base selves.

Elsewhere, he writes:

ya qur'an ya puran ye kagad dou parvan
ya ke magaz mayney ham pas, andar aye ko kholye prannath
ved kahey brahma ek hai, kateb kahey ek haq
leney na devey mayney, dil ada dushman fareb

The Qur'an and the Puran, these two scriptures from God—
Their inner truth is with me, and Prannath has explained them.
The Vedas say that Brahma is One, and the Qur'an says God is
One,
But the heart, the devious enemy, has kept this truth concealed.*

Pranami sources credit Meher Raj with having made so
bold as to admonish the Mughal Emperor Aurangzeb against
his wicked ways, and against his oppression of the Hindus,
which for Meher Raj had been based on a distorted
understanding of the Qur'an. Accordingly, it is said, he arranged
for a band of twelve of his Momins, ten Hindus and two
Muslims, to accompany him to Delhi. On the way they halted
at the Hindu holy town of Haridwar, where Meher Raj was
bitterly opposed by the Brahmins. It seems, however, that he
finally convinced some leading pundits of the truth of his
claims. When he arrived in Delhi, large crowds of Hindus and
Muslims gathered at the *haveli* where the group had put up,
astonished at 'the fakir who takes the Puran and the Qur'an
together' and had the courage to defy the wrath of the emperor.
Meher Raj then dispatched a letter to Aurangzeb, declaring
himself to be the Imam Mahdi, and expounded the spiritual
truths of the Qur'an and the virtues of a true Muslim, while
rebuking the emperor for his un-Islamic ways despite his
pretence of being a faithful follower of the Prophet. Then he
sent his twelve Momins to the Jami'a Masjid, the imposing
Friday mosque near the emperor's palace, where they began to

---

*As narrated to the author.

loudly recite verses in praise of Muhammad and the Imam Mahdi. Greatly impressed with their piety, or so the story goes, the chief Mullah of the mosque took them to meet Aurangzeb, who promptly had them imprisoned.

When the news of his jailed companions reached Meher Raj, he appeared in the emperor's court. Aurangzeb agreed to release the Momins if they would abide by the shari'at law. In return for that he offered Meher Raj a vast estate. Meher Raj spurned the offer, saying that it was precisely to release people from the bonds of rituals and religious laws that God had commissioned him. That night Aurangzeb had a strange dream: a band of Muslims were fleeing from the sight of the Qur'an, while a group of Hindus were circumambulating it. It was said to be a divine message that meant that he, and other followers of the shari'at, had forgotten the true, inner, mystical meaning of the divine revelation.

With Aurangzeb now refusing to listen to reason, Meher Raj decided to leave Delhi. Pranamis claim that, having failed to bring Aurangzeb to his senses through the 'path of love', Meher Raj was forced to seek more direct, forceful means. Accordingly, he and his disciples marched southwards, to Anup Shahr, Ajmer, Jaipur, Udaipur, then to Deogarh and Mandsaur on to Aurangabad. On their way they appealed to local rulers to rise against the Mughal monarch, and made a large number of followers, Hindus as well as Muslims. Finally, the band of roving Momins reached Gadha, where they learnt of a certain Chhatrasal—a young Bundela Rajput—who had risen in revolt against the Mughals. Pranami sources present the meeting of Meher Raj with Chhatrasal as the dawn of a new age of religious freedom, and the august beginning of an experiment in righteous rule. When they met at the town of Mhow, Chhatrasal accepted Meher Raj as his guru, who, in turn, handed to him a special sword, the Zulfiqar, named after the sword that Muhammad is said to have given to 'Ali, his son-in-law and the chief of the Sufis. Meher Raj blessed the prince with a long life and victory in his struggle against Aurangzeb. He instructed him to set up his capital at Panna, then in the middle of a thick forest, where, he told him, he would find a diamond mine to finance his court. Today, Panna is one of the few diamond extraction centres in India.

Along with Chhatrasal, Meher Raj and his disciples then shifted to Panna, where, it is said, Chhatrasal ushered in the Kingdom of God, with Hindus and Muslims living in complete harmony. Meher Raj spent the last decade of his life in Panna, preaching his doctrine of the oneness of all religions, breathing his last in 1694.

This, briefly, is how most contemporary Pranamis understand their history, and this is the way it is taught by their priests and presented in their literature. There is, however, an interesting view that presents a very different picture of the origins of the cult. The story, which I heard from several Muslims as well as a Sanatani Hindu in Panna, runs as follows:

When Aurangzeb ascended the throne of Delhi, he set about killing his brothers. Dara Shikoh was beheaded on the specious grounds that he had renounced Islam, and Murad met with a similar fate. Aurangzeb's third brother, Shah Shuja, managed, however, to escape, and sought refuge first in Bengal in the east, then in the jungles of Panna, in the guise of a sadhu, taking on the name of Prannath. As part of his regal retinue, he brought along with him from Bengal a number of servants, whose descendants are known today as the Purbiyas or the 'Easterners', and who, although Pranami by faith, live in a separate locality in Panna and are generally held in contempt.

Shuja was a pious Muslim and a great devotee of Krishna at the same time. So he set about trying to bring the followers of Muhammad and Krishna together. Taking him to be a great saint, Chhatrasal of Panna accepted him as his guru, not realizing his true identity. Shuja wanted to take revenge on his brother, and encouraged Chhatrasal to organize a revolt against him. As elsewhere, religion and politics joined hands, and the valiant Rajput was goaded into launching a religious struggle against the emperor by his disgruntled, brother, now turned sadhu.

Needless to say, this is a version that most Pranamis reject violently.

A third and certainly more plausible theory is that Meher Raj and his guru Dev Chandra were actually missionaries of the Ismai'li Shi'ah Muslim faith, also known as the Sat Panth or the 'True Path', and that, like the Isma'ili missionaries before them, they had deliberately adopted Hindu names and practices in order to communicate their message in a more intelligible manner to their largely Hindu audience. In the early 1920s, Khwaja Hasan Nizami, a reputed Urdu scholar and a leading Sufi practitioner, prepared a book on the history of secret Isma'ili communities in India which, although in some sense Muslim, had adopted several Hindu customs and traditions. He listed the Pranamis as one of these. (Khwaja Hasan Nizami, 1338 A.H.). Shortly after, in 1935, Sadruddin Dargawala, the head of an Isma'ili shrine in Gujarat, wrote that the Pranamis were an offshoot of the Imam Shahis, themselves a breakaway group of the mainstream Isma'ili Sat Panth. Like the Isma'ili Sat Panthis, the Pranamis rejected the shari'at but accepted Muhammad and developed an elaborate esoteric explanation of their creed.

A critical examination of original Pranami sources and of early Pranami history lends considerable credibility to this argument. Dominique Sila-Khan—a French scholar whose work on the forgotten and now Hinduized branches of the Isma'ilis of Gujarat and Rajasthan is a classic and has forced us to revise our own understanding of Hindu-Muslim relations in mediaeval India—is convinced of the Isma'ili roots of the Pranamis, and argues that it is quite likely that Meher Raj was actually an Isma'ili missionary in a Hindu garb (Dominique Sila-Khan, 2001).

Pranamis are ambiguous about their own identity. Some insist that they are 'true' Hindus, and claim that Prannath had been commissioned by God to revive Hindu rule in the face of 'Muslim aggression'.

'If Prannath-ji had not appeared, all the Hindus would have forcibly been made into Muslims by Aurangzeb or else put to the sword,' insisted a young Arya Samaji who had recently joined the community. 'He is indeed a symbol of Hindu pride.'

My young Pranami friend, who must remain unnamed, did not agree. 'That's what some people have now started saying, but the truth is that we are neither Hindu nor Muslim, or perhaps just a little bit of both, and something else, too.'

The Arya Samaji tried to intervene but my friend cut him short. 'You've only just joined our fold,' he said, visibly irritated, 'and you know but little about it. The last thing we want is an Arya Samaji take-over.'

Like other liminal communities, the Pranamis, it seems, simply refuse to be put in a box.

The fuzzy nature of the Pranami community is not a new phenomenon. In 1764, not long after the death of Meher Raj, a certain Murtaza Hussain passed by Panna on his travels, where he noted, with barely concealed curiosity, that the Pranamis worshipped a pile of books on a bed. On one side was a copy of the Qur'an, and, on the other, of the Puranas, with 'learned men of both religions in attendance'. A little more than a century later, the Christian missionary John Thomas wrote of the Pranamis of Panna:

When the Pranamis make a new disciple, in order to test whether he actually accepts their belief in the oneness of Hinduism and Islam, they make him participate in a communal meal along with both Hindus and Muslims. Other than this custom and the belief that the principles of both religions are the same, nothing exists which can distinguish them from the Muslims in matters of practice and religion. They follow the customs of their ancestors, whether Hindu or Muslim, and generally accept that there is one God present in all the various religions (Padri John Thomas, 1898).

Traditionally, most Pranamis kept their faith a secret, fearing persecution and ridicule by both Hindus and Muslims. Things, however, began to rapidly change from the early decades of the twentieth century, pushing the community to rapidly redefine its identity, urging it on to identify itself more directly with Brahminical Hindu Vaishnavism, thus seriously undermining the unique tradition of Hindu-Muslim brotherhood that Meher Raj had himself sought to promote.

The story of the visible Hinduization of the Pranami tradition goes back to the early 1930s, to a small, obscure village in the hills of Nepal. Two tales are told about what actually transpired there at the time. According to the first one, a Pranami peasant refused to accept the prasad or temple offering given to him by his Sanatani Hindu landlord, on the grounds that this was forbidden for the followers of the Nishkalank Buddh Avatar. The enraged landlord, offended at what he took to be an affront to his religion, gathered the local Sanatani pundits and challenged the Pranamis to a debate. Leading Pranami scholars from India were called, and a heated discussion took place with the Sanatanis. In order to prove their claims, the Pranami priests insisted that they were actually Krishna worshippers—followers of Krishna in his form of 'lover of the gopis'. They referred to a verse in the Mahabharata where Krishna is reported to have said that 'the souls of all those who offer pranam to him will be saved,' claiming that it actually referred to them, 'pranam' being their standard mode of greeting. They stressed that they were true, full-blooded Hindus, in order to quieten the Sanatanis. From then on, a major section of the Pranamis began styling themselves as followers of the 'Shri Krishna Pranami' religion.

According to the second tale, in the 1930s, Pranami missionaries began preaching their faith in the villages of Nepal, attracting numerous poor people to their fold. At that time, and till recently, non-Hindus were sternly prohibited under Nepali law from engaging in missionary work among the Hindus of the kingdom, and the Pranamis were suspected by some of being a neo-Muslim group. Hence, in order to conceal their real identity, the Pranamis declared themselves as Krishna-worshippers and presented themselves as just another of the innumerable sects of the Hindus.

Other factors egged the Pranamis on to increasingly identify with Brahminical Hinduism. This was a time when Hindu-Muslim antagonism was on the rise. Many Pranamis, finding themselves sandwiched between Hinduism and Islam, were forced to choose one or the other. A leading Pranami priest in Gujarat changed the colour of the robes of the priesthood from white to ochre in order to pass off as Hindu. Some Pranamis came under the influence of the fiercely anti-Muslim Arya Samaj when some Arya Samajis also joined the community. As a result, the group's Islamic legacy was increasingly concealed or else denied, as if it were a major embarrassment.

Moving in the direction of Hindu orthodoxy also seemed to pay rich dividends for many Pranamis.

'We were considered as polluting by high-caste Hindus because of our Muslim customs and beliefs, and because we do not believe in caste and untouchability,' said a young Pranami who was struggling to keep alive the unique shared religious culture of his community. 'They would refuse to eat food cooked by us or drink the water we had touched.'

Denying their Islamic legacy and stressing claims to 'true' Hinduhood seemed to be a carefully worked out strategy for upward social mobility, as the community attempted to become more acceptable to the dominant orthodox Sanatanis.

On the other hand, and paralleling this development, a growing number of local Muslims, whose forefathers are said to have been among Meher Raj's disciples, gradually began moving away from the sect, increasingly identifying themselves, instead, as unambiguously Muslim. While in earlier times, scores of Muslims would flock to the shrine, particularly on Thursdays, to invoke the blessings of the saint, today their number has dropped dramatically. Scattered groups of Muslim Pranamis still exist, particularly in western Uttar Pradesh, but, so say the Pranamis of Panna, several others, while continuing to revere Meher Raj as the Imam Mahdi, keep their faith concealed for fear of the wrath of the Mullahs. 'Many Muslims may also have moved away from the tradition because perhaps not all of them were treated as equals by the other Pranamis,' I was told. The hold of deeply rooted prejudices could still overshadow Prannath's teachings. Today, there are only a few identifiable Muslim Pranamis.

Local Muslims in Panna are divided on the issue. Some agree that he was a great saint, but not one to be especially revered because, as I was told, he lacked a confirmed spiritual link through various Sufi masters to the Prophet. On the other hand, influenced by Islamic orthodox reformists from outside, others insist that the cults of the saints, whether Hindu or Muslim, are strictly forbidden in Islam.

All the same, old ties, like old habits, die hard.

Down the lane leading from the Gummatji, adjacent to an old mosque, is the house of the mild-mannered, middle-aged Muhammad Kamaluddin. His fine nose and his pale cream complexion suggest a remote Central Asian ancestry. He is the head of a local wrestling club, the Mohsan Akhara, established in Panna some three centuries ago. Boys of the locality—Hindu, Muslim and Pranami—train here every morning. Kamaluddin carries on the tradition of his forefathers—leading his students every year on the tenth day of the Islamic month of Moharrum to the shrine of Meher Raj.

'We gather in front of the shrine and chant elegies to Imam Hussain to mark his martyrdom,' he said, as he beckoned to a seat. 'We read out the fatiha and invoke Allah to bless the saint. The priest then gives us the prasad, after which my boys display their martial skills, wielding sticks and swords, invoking the names of the martyrs of Kerbala.'

'Fewer Muslims go to the Gummatji now,' admitted Kamaluddin, 'but there are still some who carry on the tradition.'

He told me of a certain Maulvi who used to regularly be invited by a Pranami guru to explain to his disciples the meaning of portions of the Qur'an, and various Islamic terms that abound in the *Kuljam Swarup*.

'But all this is slowly dying out now,' he lamented. 'The Hindu-Muslim divide is getting worse by the day.'

The marked Hinduization of the Prannath tradition is most visible in the architectural changes that have recently been introduced in the shrine at Panna. At the entrance of the Gummatji, just above the main door, are three old inscriptions in the Persian script, neatly white-washed to keep them out of sight. The first of these reads: dargah-e-muqaddas imam mahdi-uz zaman ('The Dargah of the Rightly Guided One of the Time'). The inscription on the left contains the kalima, the Islamic creed of confession of the faith: la ilah il allah muhammadur rasul allah salallahu aleihi wasallam ('There is no God but Allah, and Muhammad is the Prophet of Allah, may peace and the blessings of Allah be upon him'). To the right, the third inscription announces: nijnam shri kishanji anand aksharteerth so to ab zahir bhey ('He, whose name is Shri Krishna of the Highest Heavens, has now been made manifest'). Together, they neatly encapsulate Meher Raj's personal claim of being the Imam Mahdi of the Muslims and the Nishkalank Avatar of the Hindus.

I was told that it was under the pressure of some influential Krishna Pranamis, anxious to conceal the more obvious Islamic dimensions of their past, that the inscriptions have now been obscured by layers of paint. The shrine now proudly announces itself as the Anant Shri Prannathji Ka Mandir Muktipeeth Padmavatipuri Dham. There are no references whatsoever to it ever having been a dargah. The inscriptions on the inner wall of the terrace surrounding the main dome have met with the same tragic fate. A friendly priest, concerned with the way his co-religionists were seeking to distort their faith, led me up a flight of narrow steps to the terrace, and pointed out a row of recently white-washed inscriptions. Not knowing Urdu himself, he asked me to read them out to him. Under a gently rounded turret, a long horizontal stone slab announced one of Prannath's many epithets: hazrat imam muhammad mahdi sahib akhir-uz zaman ('The Honourable Imam Muhammad the Mahdi, the Master of Time'). Adjacent to that stood a roughly crafted box-shaped stone with the Islamic kalima inscribed on it. Built into the rear end of the wall was the sole inscription in Hindi— an elaboration of a similar inscription on the entrance wall: nijnam shri kishanji anadi aksharteerth so to ab zahir hue bidh vatan sahit brij ras navratanpuri in bha ma ('He, whose name is Shri Krishna of the Highest Heavens, has now been made manifest in Panna, the City of the Nine Jewels, in his Form of the Lord of Braj').

The priest nodded gravely as he listened to me intently as I read out the inscriptions.

'Yes, yes, all this is true, but some people are trying to hide it,' he said, worry, distress and helplessness writ large over his face.

I asked him why, and he answered, 'Some think that today it is Hindus who have power, so, they say, let's identify with Hindus only. But, to be honest, we are simply followers of the universal religion of humanity, neither Hindu nor Muslim.'

Idol-worship is anathema to the Pranamis, as it is to the Muslims. Meher Raj preached an ethical monotheism, bitterly critiquing idolatry. Due to this he had to contend with fierce opposition of the orthodox Brahmins of his time. But, as the Pranamis had moved towards a greater identification with Hinduism, things had begun to change. The inner walls of the Gummatji, which are once said to have been adorned with verses from the Qur'an or other Arabo-Persian inscriptions, were now covered with slabs of white marble and kitsch terracotta statues of Krishna playing the flute in child-like wonder, traipsing down wooded glades in the company of gopis, who were demurely dressed like Victorian maidens. Likewise,

inside the Banglaji, where once upon a time the devout would
sit and listen to the Qur'an and the Vedas being read out
simultaneously, colourful pictures of youthful goddesses perched
on swings, modestly clad in saris, or dancing the *dandiya* with
the Lord of Brindavan, graced almost every inch of the walls.
The portrait of a sombre-looking Chhatrasal, his chest laden
with strings of pearls and jewels, nudged against a large oil
painting of a fierce-looking Shivaji—the icon of militant anti-
Muslim Hindutva, sword in hand, ready for battle.

Yet, curiously enough, these portraits and statues were not
worshipped as idols and the shrine was thus, strictly speaking,
not comparable to a Hindu temple.

'We don't worship images,' my young Pranami friend
informed me as we sat under a tree in the courtyard of the
Banglaji. 'These have been put up only for decoration. We
worship only the one formless God, and bow our heads only
before his bani, his word, the *Kuljam Swarup*.'

Why then the idols, even for simple decorative purposes, I
asked him. Would that not gradually degenerate into idolatry?

'It's like this,' he answered. 'We worship Krishna only in his
aspect of the lover of the gopis, that is, in the prem bhav. These
pictures are simply a means to help recreate that particular mood,
to worship God in the aurat bhav, as a woman worshipping her
Lord, for God can be attained only through the path of love.'

'Say whatever you want,' said an old man contorting his nose
in visible disgust, 'but I think it's just a ruse to pass off as
orthodox Hindus.' A humble Purbiya, he seemed bitterly opposed
to the Krishna Pranamis, most of whose leaders were, he revealed,
either Brahmins or those who at least claimed to be Brahmins.

The Krishna Pranami-led drive to Hinduize the Pranami
tradition had not gone unchallenged. Sanatani Hindus,
Muslims and even followers of Meher Raj questioned its intent.
A Sanatani I met in Panna dismissed the Pranamis with a
casual wave of the hand.

'They are neither Muslims nor Hindus,' he insisted.

'But, then, what are they?' I asked in exasperation.

'See, there are just two religions in the world, Hinduism and Islam, so where did this third religion come from?' He seemed genuinely perplexed.

'If you ask me,' he said, 'they are now trying to pass of as Hindus, but we know them for what they are, trying to corrupt our religion.'

'Their claims to being Krishna worshippers are just a convenient means for them to carry on with their missionary work among the Hindus,' he fumed.

A Muslim I chanced upon in the old city voiced much the same opinion.

'They keep changing their colours with time,' he insisted. 'When the Muslims were dominant, they claimed to be some sort of Muslims, but now that the Hindus have the power they claim to be Hindus.'

'How could Meher Raj claim to be the Imam Mahdi?' he asked, visibly vexed. 'The Prophet says that the Mahdi would descend at the end of time on top of a minaret in the grand Ummayyad mosque in Damascus. Now, you tell me, why would he choose a godforsaken place like Panna to manifest himself?'

'In any case,' he huffed in anger and declared, 'the cults of the saints are definitely un-Islamic.'

It was not that all, or even most Pranamis willingly acquiesced the way in which their own history was now being rewritten. Nek Chand, as I shall call him, was a young Pranami the son of a daily wage earner. He, along with a group of his co-religionists, met every evening to read from the *Kuljam Swarup*.

'Many of the new converts to our religion are still intoxicated by their newly acquired Hindu superiority,' he admitted ruefully, 'and that is why some of us are definitely anti-Muslim, and just too embarrassed to admit the Muslim side of our heritage.'

'But,' he hastened to add, 'Muhammad and Krishna occupy an equally important place in our tradition, and our holy book is replete with references from both the Qur'an and the Puran, a living proof that no one can deny.'

Nek Chand complained of how the temple committee was now controlled almost entirely by people who claimed to be Brahmins. 'Flaunting caste titles like Dubey and Sharma, although Prannath-ji was virulently opposed to caste distinctions,' he lamented.

'Some influential people in the community seem to want to present our religion as just another Hindu sect,' he said gravely, 'But it was precisely to demolish these barriers between Hindus and Muslims, to transcend religious differences and establish the religion of man, manav dharam, that Prannath-ji came into this world!'

What struck me as I encountered these divergent, often mutually opposed, views of the Pranamis was how contestations over the identity of the community have dealt with Meher Raj's principal mission: bringing together Hindus and Muslims in common worship of God. Followers of Meher Raj, whether mainstream Nijanandis or Krishna Pranamis, insisted that he preached a broad humanism that transcended narrowly inscribed boundaries of caste and creed, and upheld the principles of tolerance and harmony. Yet, in the same breath, it was striking how, for many, Muslims had come to be viewed as the intolerable, menacing 'Other', while, at the same time, Muhammad was being accommodated into a decidedly Hindu framework.

An ex-Arya Samaji, who had now acquired a considerable following among the Pranamis as a saint of sorts, insisted, 'Yes, Prannath-ji had great regard for Allah and Muhammad and for the Qur'an, but how can we tolerate the Muslims of today?'

'Muslims are asuras by nature—violent and blood-thirsty,' he argued. 'They insist on eating meat, but Muhammad ate only dates and fruits, like a true yogi. In fact, Muhammad was a Hindu, no doubt about that,' he said, pleased at his own discovery.

'In any case,' he declared with an air of finality, 'the Vedas are the highest form of spirituality, and everything must be judged using them as a yardstrick.'

All Pranamis may not have radical anti-Muslim ideas today, but these have gained sufficient ground to merit attention. Belief in Muhammad then, need not translate into respect and tolerance for Muslims, for Muslims are alleged to have a completely faulty understanding of the faith which they claim to follow, unlike the followers of Prannath who, it is said, have access to the hidden truths of Islam. Meher Raj and, through him, his followers alone are said to possess the true knowledge of the Qur'an, while the Muslims have strayed far from the truth. The commonly given explanation is:

God's revelation to Muhammad consisted of 90,000 divine words. Of these the first 30,000 related to the shari'at, the external law, which Muhammad relayed to the general mass of Muslims. The second set of 30,000 words concerned the mar'ifat or secret wisdom, which the Prophet transmitted to only some of his chosen followers, the chief of whom was 'Ali, the head of the Sufis. The last 30,000 words, dealing with the Truth or haqiqat, the hidden secrets of the Qur'an, he kept to himself, for God had instructed him to keep them concealed till the arrival of the Imam Mahdi, whose task it would be to make them manifest. This, Meher Raj is said to have done when he appeared as the herald of the Day of Resurrection.[*]

Thus, knowledge of the truth of the Qur'an (as, indeed, of the Vedas) is said to have been granted as a special gift from God to Meher Raj, and to have been inherited by his followers.

The Muslim as a terrorist was an image that repeatedly cropped up in conversations, even to justify the visible Hinduization of the Pranami tradition.

'If we had let all the Arabic inscriptions remain on the walls of our shrine,' claimed a young Krishna Pranami, an ardent

---

[*]*As narrated to the author by several Pranamis at Panna.*

supporter of a certain right-wing Hindu political party, 'who knows, by now the Muslims would have started a ruckus claiming the place as their own! And so our elders thought it best to remove all such traces from the building which might even remotely suggest its Islamic past.'

'The party I support stands up for Hindu rights in this sea of Muslim terrorism,' he proclaimed defiantly.

Election posters of this party littered the walls of several houses in the Pranami *mohalla*. A sticker on the door frame of a Pranami-owned shop boldly declared, 'If Hindus Decline, the Country Is Divided. If Hindus Unite, the Country Is Strengthened.' Next to it was a picture of a benign Meher Raj and his guru, Dev Chandra, both deeply engrossed in prayer with halos around their heads. A simple and compelling logic for some. Yet I could not help feeling, a far cry indeed from Meher Raj's own breadth of vision.

Dada Bhai nodded in agreement. 'Prannath-ji,' he said earnestly, as we walked past the shop, 'believed that we should love all of God's creatures, Hindus and Muslims.'

Given the fluid and confusing identity of the Pranamis, I asked a young man how he had identified himself in the recently held census, which, following in the tradition of colonial times, insisted on knowing people's religious affiliation.

'That's simple,' he answered, 'many of us entered ourselves as Pranamis, in the column reserved for sundry Others.'

For many who claim to follow Meher Raj today, the Pranami tradition was precisely seen as that—a separate religion by itself. Such, indeed, was the fate that Meher Raj seemed to share with other reformers such as Nanak, Kabir and Dadu, men who spent their lives crusading against religious divisions, pleading for a simple faith in the one God. Thus, Meher Raj was now seen as God's final messenger who had been commissioned to reveal to the Hindus and Muslims the truth of their faiths, the *Kuljam Swarup* being God's final revelation.

Further demarcating themselves from others, Hindus as well as Muslims, thus asserting their own sectarian identity, marriage outside the community was discouraged, unless the non-Pranami spouse agreed to convert to the faith. Despite Prannath's own crusade against caste, invidious caste-based distinctions still persisted, and although they followed the same faith, Rajput, Brahmin, Punjabi or Dalit Pranamis were conscious of their separate identities and marriages generally took place within the caste. Untouchability, however, was unknown, and Dalits could officiate at Pranami temples, although the main temple at Panna has never had a Dalit priest so far.

On my way back to Khajuraho, Dhan Prasad, a young Pranami social activist with a local Bundelkhandi performing group, accompanied me to the bus-stand. The bus, as was the norm in these parts, was late by more than an hour.

'It has not left Khajuraho as yet, although it should have been here by now,' said a uniformed man at the ticket-counter. 'It is still waiting to fill up with passengers before it departs.'

We headed for a tea-stall built on wheels to escape a sudden shower, and settled down to a plate of freshly fried onion *kachori*s dipped in mint chutney.

'I was here last night,' Dhan Prasad said, as a stream of hot air from a kachori straight out of the frying pan escaped from his nose. 'Some of my Muslim and Hindu friends were here too, and they were discussing the Ayodhya issue. The Hindus insisted that a temple should be constructed on the spot and the Muslims said no. I offered a compromise solution. Let a Pranami shrine be built there, I told them, and then both Hindus and Muslims would be satisfied.'

He broke into a hesitating smile and ordered another round of kachoris.

If only it could be that simple, I thought to myself, as the bus pulled into the stand.

9

GOGA
THE 'PIR OF POISON'

As the bus rumbled across from Haryana into Rajasthan, the lush fields of buckwheat criss-crossed with gurgling water-channels gave way to vast empty stretches of sand pockmarked with scrawny scrub. Mud huts with thatched roofs lined the road in small clusters, huddling together against the harshness of the Thar. Little colonies of dal and *bajra* straddled the towering dunes, bravely resisting the constantly encroaching desert. Black pots painted into fearsome fang-bearing ghouls stood on bamboo poles to scare away the birds. Women draped in bright earthy colours, their faces wrapped in veils, perched atop lazily moving camel-carts. Peasant men laboured in the fields, moved about on little wooden donkey-carts, or simply whiled away time on charpoys in the niggardly shade of khejdi trees, puffing away at their clay hukkahs. A giant signboard announcing 'Anup Macro-Man Underwear' displayed an old-fashioned pair of boxer shorts exhibiting an enormous bulge. Tin and mud walls of village shops advertized a variety of other new products that were now flooding the countryside—biscuits, locks, pens, tea, soaps, mill-made cloth, the ubiquitous Coca Cola and the services of a certain Dr Hansraj Gupta, 'World Renowned Specialist in the Cure of Secret Embarrassing Diseases'.

It was almost noon, and the sharp September sun dominated the sky when the bus dropped me off two miles north of the village of Gogamedhi, at an intersection in the middle of a vast lake of sand. A narrow clearing between the dunes led to a settlement visible at a distance. I trudged through the sand with difficulty, shading my eyes from the relentless glare of the sun with my leather bag, musing on the carelessly scattered heaps of plastic packets, empty cans and bottles, torn dhotis and scraps of paper that lay around. A rusted board across the entrance of a tin shed painted a loud red announced the 'Shri Goga Maharaj Gaushala', a home for cows in a land where most people struggled to survive in mud hovels, even tents made of used plastic packets sewn together with twine.

The clearing in the sand ended as abruptly as it had begun, at a massive white-washed gateway decorated with tall scalloped arches protruding from a long wall topped with little turnip-shaped domes. In front, in a small square that opened out into a vast field, canvas tents pitched on wooden poles displayed customary pilgrimware—pictures of a warrior-saint armed with an assortment of weapons, astride a pale blue horse, with a menacing cobra coiled around his neck; bunches of frilly marigolds and needle-like incense sticks; plastic white-faced and blond-haired imitation Barbie dolls; strings of stone and plastic beads that dangled from rusted nails; little pyramids of holy powder; stacks of soggy samosas and syrupy jalebis covered by an army of flies.

A series of steps led up from the entrance door to the main structure, an unpretentious building shaped like a mosque. Its outer walls were built of pale cream marble. At each corner slender minarets sloped inwards at an angle, tapering off into copper balls shaded by metal umbrellas with gold-coloured metal tassels. A marble slab, carved in crude Arabic calligraphy, displaying the Islamic creed of confession, 'There is no God but Allah,' stood just above the door leading into the shrine. Below it, another stone slab commemorated the renovation of the shrine, sometime in the early twentieth century, by Ganga Singh, the maharaja of Bikaner. A long list of his unpronounceable regal titles made up for most of the inscription.

It was cool and dark inside, and the heady scent of rose water and incense hung in the air like an invisible presence. The walls were bare, except for a clock in a plastic frame and a kitsch picture, obviously recent, of Goga astride his horse, with a group of militant-looking followers behind, bearing swords, spears and yak-tail whisks. The lord of the Yogis, the legendary Guru Gorakhnath, was perched on a cloud in the corner of the picture, and emitted a ray of light that engulfed the imperial army. A soft white marble grave with the Hindu insignia of the Om and the Swastik painted in kumkum powder, and shaped like a Muslim *qabar*, rose from the ground. A party of peasants lay prostrate before it mumbling their prayers.

Outside, in the glare of the merciless sun, sat Alauddin Khan the Mirasi, tightening the rope stretched across his dholak. Next to him, squatting on his haunches in the cool shade of a stone pillar, Chandu Ram the Sansi fiddled with his one-stringed *rawanhattha*, carved from the dried skin of a pumpkin. A group of what seemed like well-heeled urban pilgrims, flashing their cameras and mobile phones and eating Cadbury's chocolate, strode into the courtyard. The uniformed team was clad in ill-fitting safari suits, tennis shoes and cheap plastic goggles.

The duo set about trying to win their attention. Alauddin tickled his dholak with a pair of sticks carved like an antelope's horns, while Chandu cradled his instrument in his bosom, pouring out a plaintive desert wail. Together they sang of the Pir of Gogamedhi, telling of his spoils, his great miraculous powers and his love for the poor and the sick.

'Take us in your arms, oh great Goga-Ji,' they burst forth, shutting their eyes and rocking their heads. 'Help us to cross to the other shore.'

'Hindus and Muslims, they both recall his great mercy,' they cried out, extolling the awesome Pir.

The urban pilgrims ignored them, and bowed their heads before a fierce weapon-wielding idol, and stuffed notes into a tin donation box. Alauddin and Chandu peered at them expectantly from the corner of their eyes, raising their tempo, further extolling the great powers of Goga Maharaja as the pilgrims emptied their purses before the idol.

'Give us Rs 5 in Goga's name,' cried Chandu pathetically, adopting the direct method after the subtle and more sophisticated technique of song-cum-praise had failed to melt their stony hearts.

'Yes, yes,' Alauddin chimed in, 'and Goga will grant you your heart's desire. Many, many children and a lifetime's supply of money.'

The leader of the pilgrims, an enormous chinless apparition, slid a hundred-rupee note into the donation box and folded his hands in prayer, his thick black lips quivering in piety. Then all at once he hauled himself up, and, flinging his arms about in the air, hurled the choicest imprecations and shooed the singing duo out of sight.

Goga Pir is one of the most popular folk deities of northern India, with a following running into several millions. The legend of Goga, like those of other Rajasthani folk heroes, is shrouded in mystery. Several versions exist. However, all versions present a common structure although they vary in matters of small detail.

Legend has it that Jhevar, the Chauhan Rajput ruler of Dadreva in Churu, had been driven to despair for lack of an heir and a son who could consign his mortal remains to flames after his death, thereby ensuring his safe passage to the heavens. One day, a wandering sanyasi named Kanhaiyya appeared at the royal palace. On learning from Bachal, the king's chief wife, that she was childless, he advised her to seek the favour of Guru Gorakhnath, the king of the Nath Yogis, who had

settled in a forest outside Dadreva. Heeding his advice, Bachal
now began serving the guru, secretly slipping out of the palace
every morning so that her husband would not notice her
absence. Meanwhile, unknown to Bachal, her sister and Jhevar's
second wife, the wily Achal, also heard about the sadhu and his
miraculous powers. She too began secretly serving him, in the
hope of begetting a son who might one day become king.

Finally, after spending months in a trance, Gorakhnath opened
his eyes. Looking around, he discovered to his pleasant surprise
that his hermitage had been swept clean and carefully tended to
while he had been deeply engrossed in his spiritual exercises. It
so happened that just then Achal passed by, and mistaking her
for the devoted disciple Bachal who had kept his hut so tidy,
Gorakhnath blessed her with two sons. Later, when Bachal arrived
at the hermitage, he discovered his mistake, and promised her
that she would give birth to a brave son who would go on to
fight many battles. In due course, Achal gave birth to two sons,
Arjan and Sarjan. Bachal had a boy, who was named Goga.

The different versions of the legend of Goga suggest widely
varying dates of his birth, ranging from the eighth to the
fourteenth century.

Each version has its fair share of intrigues, wars and
succession squabbles, in keeping with the narrative tradition of
Rajasthani ballads.

When Jhevar died, Goga succeeded him, but soon enough
his envious half-brothers set about plotting to usurp his throne.
They demanded the kingdom for themselves, and the large-
hearted Goga is said to have willingly agreed to let them have
half of it. Arjan and Sarjan spurned the generous offer, and
started preparing for war instead.

According to some versions of the legend, they appealed to
the 'Muslim Sultan' of Delhi to assist them (named variously
as Muhammad bin Qasim, Mahmud Ghaznavi, Muhammad
Ghori, Ferozeshah Tughlaq, the fictitious Badshah Abufar of
Iran or the much-maligned Mughal Emperor Aurangzeb. These

figures span a period of almost a millennium and have little in
common except for being Muslim). The 'Muslim sultan'
marched on Dadreva, and a fierce battle ensued in which
'thousands' were killed. Ultimately, the villainous Arjan and
Sarjan were slain and Goga marched off the battlefield victorious.

When Bachal heard of the death of Achal's sons at Goga's
hands, she flew into a rage, for despite their wickedness she loved
her nephews dearly. She forced Goga to abdicate the throne and
go into lifelong exile. A true Rajput that he was, Goga willingly
obeyed his mother's orders. He set off on his blue horse into the
wilderness of the desert. After roaming in the dunes for days, he
chanced upon Gorakhnath's hut. He pleaded with Gorakhnath
to take his life, but the sadhu answered, 'He who has given life
to you cannot take your life. Go to Baba Rattan in Bhatinda. He
knows both the religions [Hinduism and Islam]. He will help
you to enter the earth.'

Goga then headed north, travelling to Bhatinda in Punjab,
where Baba Rattan, said to have been a 700-year-old companion
of the Prophet Muhammad, and himself a convert to Islam,
administered him the kalima—the Islamic creed of confession.
Another version of the legend does not refer to Baba Rattan at
all. According to this version, in desperation, Goga pleaded
with Dharti Mata (Mother Earth) to take him in. The Mata
answered him, saying, 'Only a Muslim can enter the earth
with his body. Recite the kalima and I shall accept you.' So
Goga became a Muslim, and at once the earth split open and
swallowed him along with his blue horse.

This, then, is the popular story cast in songs sung by wandering
Mirasis and Bhats, the musician castes of Rajasthan, and by
'low' caste followers of Goga, who, till recently, formed the vast
majority of his devotees. Today, a very different legend of the
Rajput-turned-Muslim warrior hero can be found in the little
tracts that are sold at pavement stalls on the streets of Jaipur

and Jodhpur, in the voluminous modern literature on traditional Rajasthani folk deities, penned, almost entirely, by Brahmin and other 'upper' caste writers, and in official documents issued by various government authorities. As the cult of Goga now grows out of its hitherto largely 'low' caste constituency, and as Muslim followers of the tradition gradually abandon it under the influence of reformist Islamic groups, the legend of Goga is being hurriedly rewritten. In the process, the remarkably fluid religious identity of Goga and the cult centred around him are being suitably modified and firmly cast in an orthodox Hindu, if not distinctly anti-Muslim, mould.

In this new genre of writing, Goga is presented as a Hindu warrior, bravely fighting Muslim 'interlopers', something that guarantees him an important place in that steadily expanding pantheon of 'nationalist' heroes. The confusion stems from the fact that there are at least three different Gogas who are revered as popular heroes: our own Goga of Dadreva; Goga, the ruler of Ajmer; and Goga Rao, the king of Sambhar, near Jaipur (Satyendra, 1975). The new rendition of Goga Pir introduces elements hitherto absent in the popular oral tradition about him but borrowed from the stories of the other two Gogas.

Thus, for instance, new, Brahminized versions of the legend talk of how the crafty 'Muslim' general of the Delhi sultan sought to trick Goga into submission by shielding his own army behind a row of cows, convinced that the pious 'Hindu' warrior would never dare attack the holy animals. Goga, now hailed as 'Protector of the Mother Cow', is said to have cleverly outmanoeuvred the Muslims and rescued the cattle from them in a surprise attack. Through a cunning play on words, the battleground where this terrible war is said to have been fought has been cleverly shifted from Baghar, the area around Dadreva, to Baghdad, and Goga is also shown taking on the might of none other than the Abbasid Khalifa himself, the most powerful ruler of the world of his times and the head of the House of Islam.

For his part, Goga has now been promoted from the chieftain of the remote village of Dadreva to the powerful ruler of a vast Rajput kingdom. Goga's encounter with the 'Muslim sultan', a petty feud in the oral tradition, is now represented as a decisive war between two religions. The skirmish between two factions of a Rajput family, in which the sultan of Delhi plays only a minor role as an ally of the opposing party, now takes on the shades of a momentous clash of civilizations, between Hinduism, standing for patriotism and undying love for the motherland, and Islam, identified more or less as a barbaric creed bent on the destruction and rape of Mother India. Thus, for instance, the *Census of India Report* of 1961 (Manager of Publications, Government of India) tells us: 'Gogaji fought many battles against the Muslim invaders and emperors to save his principality from their yoke. He was a protector of cows and saviour of the Hindu religion.' It acknowledges the existence of the legend of Goga's conversion to Islam but adds that the legend is 'highly improbable'. Other writings are less charitable, and make no mention at all of the legend of Goga converting to Islam, not even in order to refute it, for to even conceive of the possibility would be sinful. Instead, ironically, in the new versions of his legend, Goga is said to have been killed by 'blood-thirsty' Muslims, thereby dying the death of a 'true' Hindu hero, giving up his life for Bharat Mata and the Sanatan Dharam, the great Hindu religion. In some accounts his death on the battlefield fighting the 'Muslims' is said to have occasioned the first jauhar or collective suicide by women in the history of Rajasthan. Following the death of forty-five sons and sixty nephews on the battlefield, Goga's thirty-five queens are said to have consigned themselves to the flames, thereby saving themselves from humiliation at the hands of the Muslims. Needless to say, no one I met in Gogamedhi, Hindu or Muslim, had ever heard of the story of Goga being slayed by Muslims, or of the gory events that were supposed to have ensued thereafter that this new breed of writers refer to.

What seems to be a fairly recent retelling of the legend of Goga Pir is accompanied by strikingly visible transformations in the shrine complex of Goga. The process goes back to the early years of the twentieth century, when, in 1911, Ganga Singh, the maharaja of Bikaner, ordered that the shrine be repaired. Besides the stone slab commemorating his assistance, he had a bell installed inside the entrance door, and a carving on Goga's grave depicting a warrior atop a horse, surrounded by the sun and the moon—regal emblems of the Rajputs and visible 'Hindu' markers. It is said, so I heard, that earlier some Muslims had questioned the wisdom of tampering with the structure of the dargah. Later, however, they acquiesced in the hope that a minor concession to Hinduism might bring in more Hindu followers and a steady stream of donations. The lure of lucre and plain prudence, it seems, had stolen a run over religious scruples.

Following the take-over, in or around 1950, of the shrine by the Devasthan Board, the body appointed by the Rajasthan government to look after the affairs of Hindu temples in the state, more visible changes were made. The entrance to the shrine now had a board affixed to it by the Devasthan Department, announcing the 'Mandir of Jahar Vir'. What had, for centuries, been a Sufi dargah had thus officially, with the blessings of the government, been transformed into a mandir, and Goga's obviously Muslim title of Pir had been replaced with the Hindu epithet of Vir—a valiant Hindu warrior fighting the Muslim 'Other'.

The Muslim aspects of the Goga cult, which the recent retellings of his legend seek to deny, are still visible, however, in the form of the Muslim family of the Chayal caste that has tended the shrine as caretakers or pujaris ever since it was established. The Chayals, a clan of Rajput Muslim Ranghars, are said to be the direct descendants of Goga, thus lending credence to the story of Goga's conversion to Islam. Although the claims of the Chayals as administrators of the shrine have been challenged of late on the grounds that 'Muslims' cannot control a 'Hindu' 'temple', the courts have ruled in favour of the Chayals, citing their long and continuous and previously undisputed control of the shrine. And so, till this day, the Chayals are officially the hereditary custodians of the grave of Goga, and receive all the money that is donated to the shrine, except the income received during the grand mela in the month of Bhadon, which is taken by the government.

'What is your caste?' asked the Brahmin pilgrim from Jaipur, who sat like a mediaeval monarch on a red plastic chair and fiddled with the holy thread that snaked provocatively over his belly.

A strange first question to ask, I thought. But this was Rajasthan, where caste is generally the first thing that one inquires about when one meets a stranger. One's subsequent dealings are carefully calibrated according to the response received.

'Oh, I don't believe in this caste business. I'm not a Hindu in any case,' I said.

'You may believe what you want, but that still can't stop you from having a caste,' said the Brahmin matter-of-factly. 'Even Muslims have castes here.'

'Well, I'm just me, I guess,' I answered.

'Ah, I've heard that one before,' the Brahmin replied, twisting his mouth into a mocking smile, 'from a wretched untouchable who wanted to conceal his low caste origins. But we found him out finally,' he said triumphantly.

'You must follow some religion,' he insisted, pressing ahead with his inquisition.

'I am an Isai,' I lied without a wink, not wanting to be identified as either Hindu or Muslim, although I had not the remotest Christian links.

'A *kasai*!' he exclaimed in horror, muttering a curse.

'Kasais! Slayers of our holy cows!' one of his admirers who sat at his feet spat out in disgust.

I hurried to dispel his ignorance of the followers of Christ, rescuing them from being unfairly banded together with blood-thirsty butchers of 'holy' herbivores. He calmed down somewhat, but continued to spy on me from the corner of his eye.

'How old are you?' he asked as he stopped fiddling with his holy thread and moved on to pluck his penis from under the folds of his dhoti.

'Thirty-four,' I said, averting my gaze from the unseemly sight.

'How many children do you have?' he demanded to know.

I was now convinced that he was either a secret agent keeping a close tab on me or else had received a commission to write my biography.

'No children at all,' I said, 'I'm not married.'

'Not married? At your age? I don't believe it!' he cried in disbelief.

'You must get married. The *shastras* say you must. After all, you need someone to carry on your name after your death, no?' he said gravely. 'All the gods got married you know, and most of them had many, many children. You must follow their example.'

The party of his fellow pilgrims nodded gravely in agreement.

Determined to put an immediate end to his banter, I said, 'Enough of this, and stop being so nosey.'

His eyes almost toppled out their sockets as he glared at me wide-mouthedly, stunned at the non-Brahmin insouciance that he must have encountered for the first time in his life.

The last of the pilgrims boarded their mini-buses and taxis and sped off into the great breast-shaped dunes, leaving the desolate shrine enveloped in stillness. A million stars danced in the clear night sky of the desert. In the distance a string of camels moved in slow, measured steps towards a clump of mud huts.

I sipped tea at a makeshift stall—a kettle bubbling on a pair of bricks placed around a fire of twigs and leaves. Rana sat next to me, pulling at his cigarette. A lock of hair fell on his forehead, and his long, camel-like nose ended in a great bulb. His teeth were stained a rich yellow-brown and when he spoke, his almond-shaped eyes danced with child-like innocence.

'Only thirty-odd Chayal families remain,' Rana was explaining. 'In 1947, many of our people fled to Pakistan and several others were slaughtered.'

'Not many Muslims, not even Chayals, come to the shrine any more,' he said. 'The Tablighi Jama'at tells them that it is un-Islamic to beseech Pirs for assistance.' Yet, some Chayals, he said, were still carrying on with their ancestral tradition, struggling against both the wrath and ridicule of their co-religionists, and the overwhelming pressure of Brahminization to which the Goga cult was now fast succumbing.

Rana invited me to his room, located in a corridor that ran along the length of the inner wall of the shrine of Goga Pir. I seated myself on a string cot, which gently groaned under my weight. A three-year-old calendar, depicting the Ka'aba in Mecca and the Prophet's mosque in Medina, hung from a nail driven into the recently white-washed wall. Shirts and trousers were neatly stacked on a tin trunk in a corner. A prayer mat decorated with Islamic motifs was spread out on the floor.

Rana busied himself in the kitchen while I leafed through a book of Islamic prayers lying on the alcove. After dinner, I slipped into my lungi, while Rana went about making preparations for the late evening prayer. He bent over a tap to perform his ablutions. He washed his hands first, then his face, finally moving on to his feet, carefully following the method employed by the Prophet himself 1400 years before. He wiped his face with a towel, then stood on the prayer carpet, his hands by his sides. He murmured an incantation, and lifted his fingers to his ears. 'Allah-o-Akbar,' he said softly with his hands across his waist, his eyes transfixed before him. Then he fell to the ground in humble adoration of the one invisible God.

I watched Rana as he stood up and knelt down in silent prayer, as he held up his hands before his face after the series of well-rehearsed genuflections gave over, communing with God in low whispers. What a stark, dignified contrast the Muslim namaz seemed to be, I thought to myself, to the clanging of bells, the billowing clouds of overpoweringly sweet-smelling incense, the splashing of holy water, the loud shouts and display of emotion that had marked the evening puja at Goga's shrine next door. Rana had been present there too, but he and a fellow Chayal had simply sat on either side of a metal pan into which throngs of pilgrims, all Hindus, dropped their coins. The Hindu-style arti had been conducted by a government-appointed Brahmin, dressed in a starched white dhoti, a long shirt that reached down almost to his knees, and a saffron scarf thrown loosely around his neck. He rang a little copper bell in one hand, and, with the other, took a little brass lamp around Goga's grave. The mellow light from its seven cotton wicks cast long, eerie shadows on the bare walls. Then he knelt down to apply tiny red dots of kumkum powder on the grave, and to paint on it the sign of the Om and the Swastik. All along, the pilgrims murmured their prayers while outside a *nagara* boomed like a cannon. The arti gave over with the pundit raising slogans in praise of Shiva, Vishnu and 'Jahar Vir', that finally culminated in a full-throated ode to the Hindu religion, Sanatan Dharam Ki Jai Ho, 'Victory to the Eternal Faith'. The mesmerized pilgrims shouted out after him.

This Brahminized puja, I was told, was a recent invention, probably dating back to the 1950s, when the shrine was taken over by the Devasthan Board. It was stunning to see the caste system being subtly introduced in a government-administered 'temple'. The priest was a Brahmin, and the handsome but rather garrulous and officious manager, charged with the responsibility of sending an endless stream of files to various government departments and making arrangements for the annual mela, was a Brahmin too. The cleaner, another government employee, was, predictably enough, a Dalit of the hereditary sweeper caste, the 'lowest' of the 'low'. With almost no Muslims visiting the shrine, the Chayals no longer had any priestly duties to perform. Their role was now limited to simply receiving the money that pious pilgrims offered at the shrine. For the occasional Muslim visitor they might recite the fatiha, the opening verse of the Qur'an, but that was now rare, and becoming rarer still.

Rana and I sat on the roof of the shrine, talking deep into the night about Hindus, Muslims and the mysterious Goga Pir. I asked Rana what the Muslims thought about the Hinduization of the shrine.

'Most Muslims,' he said indifferently, 'are simply not bothered. They've abandoned their faith in the power of saints and Pirs to intercede with God on their behalf. Allah suffices for them now.'

For the other Muslims who still preserved their faith in Goga, he added, there was little they could do, being heavily outnumbered by the Hindus. 'Don the dress of the country where you live,' he advised, shrugging his shoulders. As long as their status as custodians of the shrine and recipients of its income were guaranteed, the Chayals felt they had little to lose from the way in which the cult was being reshaped. Indeed, Rana said, they might even stand to gain, for a more distinct Hindu identity for Goga might actually attract more Hindu pilgrims to his shrine, particularly from the richer, 'higher' castes who would shudder at the thought of entering a Muslim shrine and worshipping a Muslim saint. That was why, he admitted, the Chayals had tolerated pictures of Goga and Gorakhnath being put up on the inner walls of the shrine, thus helping to convert the dargah into what, for all practical purposes, it had now become—a temple.

While the Hinduization of the Goga cult is directed primarily against what appear to be the 'embarrassing' Muslim associations of the tradition, it also represents a major challenge to lower caste popular forms of religion. Excluded, on pain of death, from Hindu temples, the lower castes found in the traditions of local heroes, including Muslim or Sufi saints, a means to express their sorrows and their hopes for a better world. Hence, they formed the vast majority of Goga's followers. As a system of parallel priesthood, low-caste Goga worshippers, particularly among the sweeper castes, would function as medicine men, offering cures for various illnesses. To them, Goga, in his form of Jahar Pir, the 'Pir of Poison', was a dispenser of great miracles. Invoking his name, low-caste shamans would travel from village to village armed with tall bamboo poles decorated with tassels, begging for alms and curing snakebites.

The Goga cult also managed to find many followers among marginalized tribal groups. Thus, for instance, just outside Goga's grave is a small temple dedicated to two tribal Bawariya followers of the Pir, that is presided over by a Dalit priest. As the Goga tradition is now being gradually Brahminized, it seems entirely possible that the story of the two Bawariyas would also be 'suitably' modified to fit in with more orthodox Brahminical notions of propriety and respectability. Soon, who knows, the Dalit priest might also be replaced with an orthodox Hindu pundit, and the Bawariyas could be promoted to the status of 'high' caste Rajput heroes.

Where traditions could be so easily moulded to suit personal and caste interests, and respect for historical truth was a completely foreign notion, it was as easy to manufacture a purana to back a claim to privilege as it was to conjure a completely new god out of thin air.

As the bus to Ganganagar chugged ahead and I sat sandwiched between two quarrelling Jat peasants, both drunk out of their minds, I pondered over a verse from a Brahminical text that Ambedkar, arguably the greatest scholar of Hinduism and one of its harshest critics, quotes in one of his books, a well-argued diatribe against Brahminism. The actual words failed me, but the verse went roughly like this: 'The gods control the sacrifice and, in turn, the Brahmins control the gods.'

Images of bearded Muslim maulvis and pot-bellied Brahmin pujaris welled up in my mind, forcibly resisting my efforts to expel them. The two peasant men sitting on either side of me, now coming close to blows, menacingly rolled up their sleeves and hurled the choicest of Haryanvi abuses at each other. A band of sadhus clicked their tongues and sang a hymn to the Mata, then walked down the aisle of the bus collecting donations, ostensibly for a temple they said they were building. A corpulent Bania hurled his handbag at the conductor, protesting at having been cheated out of a rupee, or so he claimed. A woman behind me, munching on a bunch of sticky, over-ripe bananas, suddenly vomited into her dupatta. An army of flies descended on the puddle of pale yellow liquid that landed at my feet, and an overpowering stench invaded the entire bus.

Roundly cursing the evil merchants of religion and my ill-mannered co-passengers, I shuffled in my seat, hoping to catch some sleep.

10

Sarmad Shahid
The 'Martyr for Love'

Sufis see themselves as true Muslims, faithfully following in the footsteps of the Prophet, claiming access to the secret wisdom or batini 'ilm that he is said to have passed on to only a few of his chosen disciples. For most Sufis, the shari'at or the law is inseparable from the tarqiah, the 'mystical quest', that leads to mari'fa or 'divine wisdom', finally culminating in the haqiqah or the 'Truth', at which stage the individual ego is dissolved and God's will becomes one's own. This is the station of fana or 'dissolution of the self', after which the individual permanently resides in God, the station of eternal repose or baqa. Other Sufis, condemned by the upholders of the shari'at, believe that the strictures of Islamic law are meant for ordinary believers, the awam, but the spiritually elect, the khas, are believed to be free from its fetters. These be-shar'iat or 'shari'at-free' Sufis have been throughout the history of Islam some of the most radical critics of empty ritualism and bigotry, for which they have often had to pay a heavy price. Some, known as the Malamatiya, the 'blameworthy', deliberately sought to court the anger of the 'ulama by publicly flouting the strictures of the shari'at by guzzling alcohol, consuming intoxicating drugs, eating during the fasting hours of the month of Ramadan, neglecting the daily prayers and showering the choicest invectives on priests and kings. It is said that they willingly courted 'blame' (malamat), so that, shunned by the world, they could devote all their attention to the worship of God in their own way. Not surprisingly, many be-shari'at Sufis found themselves being sent to the gallows for daring to defy the upholders of the shari'at.

Love for God is a defining feature of Sufism. Many be-shari'at Sufis believed that divine love was inseparable from love for all of God's creatures—animals and humans, Muslims and non-Muslims. It was, they insisted, only through 'physical love', ishq-e-majazi, that 'true love' or ishq-e-haqiqi could be attained. The breadth of vision of these Sufis can best be appreciated when seen against the unremitting hatred for the 'unbelievers' that the venom-spewing radicals among the 'ulama nursed. Many be-shari'at Sufis, as well as of course, several of their shari'at-abiding counterparts, were known for their roaring love affairs that were the stuff local lore and scandalous bazaar gossip.

Although homosexuality is sternly prohibited in the Qur'an, the Hadith and the traditions ascribed to the Prophet, several be-shari'at Sufis were known for their amorous entanglements with other men. Many Iranian Sufis were notorious for their love for 'beardless youths', and spent hours meditating on the beauty of the faces of young boys. They believed that a young man's beauty far exceeded that of a woman and could inspire them better to describe and praise the attributes of God, one of which was jamal or beauty. C.E Bosworth, (1976) whose book on mediaeval Arab society remains a classic, writes that, 'Pederasty was a recognized vice of the antinomian Sufis'. Male homosexuality seems to have been widespread enough among the shari'at-defying Sufis for the mediaeval Mamluk poet 'Abdul Fath ibn Sayyed an Nas (1273–1334), no friend of the Sufis himself, to bitterly lament, with obvious exaggeration, that,

'The characteristics of a Sufi in our times comprise six only, no more: copulating with pretty boys, drinking wine, eating hashish, dancing, singing and pimping' (C.E. Bosworth, 1976). A leading Malamatiya Sufi of his times, the thirteenth-century Shaikh Abu Muhammad 'Ali al-Hariri, founder of the Haririya order, is said to have been 'often found in the hamam in the company of naked boys'. The venerable Shaikh, pre-dating Freud by six centuries or more, had this to advise his disciples: 'Do not deny your nafs (sexual appetite) of any of its desires or enjoyments, for whatever your nafs seeks is what is good for it; so urge it on to that' (C.E. Bosworth, 1976).

Homoerotic Sufis seem to have flourished in India, too, and Indian history is littered with examples of Muslim mystics and their male lovers. Such love need not have been sexual, but the way in which it was expressed often clearly indicated much more than simple platonic friendship. Interestingly, many of these Sufis had Hindu lovers, this double defiance—of gender norms, and acceptable relations between Hindus and Muslims— raising the hackles of the established 'ulama, and, presumably, of their Hindu counterparts as well. One of these was Shah Hussain, among the finest poets of the Punjab. Born into a weaver family in 1539, he became a disciple of the Qadri Sufi, Shaikh Bahlol Darya'i. At the age of thirty-six, while studying a commentary on the Qur'an with his teacher, Shaikh Sa'dullah, he came across a verse in the holy book: 'The life of the world is nothing but play and pleasurable distraction.' Meant as a reminder to the faithful that the world was just a sport and that true life only began after death, Hussain took it to be a licence for throwing off all constraints of piety. He rushed out of the madrasa, into the streets, singing and dancing with gay abandon (Lajwanti Ramakrishna, 1973).

Hussain established his own spiritual lineage. Novices aspiring to become his disciples were made to shave off their

beards and drink a cup of wine, both of which were anathema
to the orthodox 'ulama. Indeed, Hussain seems to have delighted
in deliberately provoking the orthodoxy. When a certain learned
Maulana once approached him to be accepted as his disciple,
he is said to have burst out laughing, saying, 'You are from
among those who strictly follow the shari'at. So then, why do
you wish to give me a bad name?' (Shafi Aqil).

For the 'ulama, perhaps the most scandalous thing about
Hussain was his passionate love affair with another man, the
Hindu Brahmin Madho Lal. Once, so the story goes, while
riding through the main market in Lahore, Hussain spotted
the young man, and, a mediaeval chronicler records, so
wonderstruck was he by his beauty that 'he tried in vain to
possess the lad for sixteen years, at the end of which he
succeeded'. Rizvi, a leading scholar of Indian Sufism, writes
that at this first chance encounter, Hussain, on seeing the man,
fell instantly 'under the intoxication of a mystical trance'.
Thereafter, he shifted to the locality where Madho lived and
'began following him like a household slave' (Saiyed Atthar
Abbas Rizvi, 1992).

'The love of Hussain for Madho,' writes one of his
biographers, 'was unique, and he did all that lay in his power
to please [him]' (Ramakrishna, 1973). Subhan, whose book on
Indian Sufism, published almost half a century ago, still remains
something of a classic, comments that their contemporaries
saw the relationship between Hussain and Madho, who had
now started living together, as 'a disgrace', although he himself
views it as an 'irresistible attraction' based on 'fervent love'
(John A. Subhan, 1960). Nur Ahmad Chishti, author of the
Sufi chronicle *Tahqiqat-e-Chishti* ['Researches on the Chishtis'],
suggests that their relationship was frowned on by the
'respectable' Lahori society, and notes that Madho's relatives,
'seeing him sleeping in the same bed as Hussain, came to
murder them both'. However, as their luck would have it, he
adds, Hussain's miraculous powers struck them blind, and as

they could not find the door to their room, they returned (Ramakrishna, 1973). Ramakrishna, a recognized authority on the Punjabi Sufis, refers to a possible homosexual bond between the two, commenting that many people 'had become suspicious of their unnatural [sic] relationship' (Ramakrishna, 1973).

Inseparable in life, they remain united in death, and the Sufi, who now rests in a simple mausoleum in Lahore, is commonly referred to as 'Madho Lal Hussain', two souls in one body.

Another such Sufi was the sixteenth-century Ibrahim Khan, better known as Ras Khan, who was born in a Pathan family at Hardoi in present-day Uttar Pradesh. Ras Khan was one of several, Vaishnavite Sufis, still remembered for the soul-stirring mystical verses he composed in praise of Krishna and his love for his gopis. Stories abound of how this Pathan warrior became a worshipper of Krishna. The most acceptable version is found in the *Bhavaprakash* of the seventeenth-century Hari Rai. Ibrahim Khan, writes Rai, was posted in Delhi as an officer in the imperial army. There, he fell madly in love with the son of a Hindu merchant. 'He watched him day and night and even ate his leftovers.' This is said to have angered his fellow Muslims, some of whom branded him as a heretic. But Ibrahim Khan, Rai says, did not care or relent, saying, 'I am as I am.'

One day, the story goes, he overheard one Vaishnavite telling another, 'One should have attachment to the Lord just as this Ibrahim Khan has for the merchant's son. He roams around after him without fear of public slander or caste displeasure!' The other Vaishnavite turned up his nose in disgust. When Ibrahim saw this he drew his sword out in anger. Trembling before him, the Vaishnavite said: 'If you loved God just as you do that boy, you would find salvation.'

Ibrahim's curiosity having been aroused, began discussing spiritual matters with him. The Vaishnavite advised Ibrahim to travel to Brindavan, and he did as he was told. When he got there, he was refused entry into the temple because he was a Muslim. He sat on the banks of the lake near the temple for three days without eating anything. At this time Krishna, the story goes, appeared before him, addressing him as Ras Khan or 'The Mine of Aesthetic Essence', and, pleased with his devotion, accepted him as a disciple. From that day on, Ras Khan began living near the temple, composing and singing soul-stirring verses in praise of the playful cowherd of Brindavan.

Ras Khan's mystical poetry deals basically with the beauty of Krishna, and the love between Krishna and his gopis. Ras Khan's Brij Bhasha writings are numerous, the five most important ones being the *Sujana Raskhana*, the *Premavatika*, the *Danalila*, the *Astayama* and a collection of padas (couplets). Of these the most well known is the *Premavatika* (The Forest of Love').

The *Premavatika* consists of fifty-three verses, most of which deal with the nature of true spiritual love, taking the love between Radha and Krishna to be a model. Ras Khan begins the work by saying, 'The dwelling of Love is Shri Radhika; the son of Nanda [i.e. Krishna] is Love's colour.' But the path of Love is not easy, he tells us. 'Everybody says: "Love! Love!" but nobody knows Love,' he notes, because 'if a person knows Love, why would the world weep?'

He then launches into a long discussion about the nature of divine love:

Love is inaccessible, incomparable, immeasurable.
It is like the ocean—He who comes to its shore will not go back.
When he drank the wine of Love, Varuna became the Lord of the Waters.
Because he drank poison out of Love, the Lord of the Mountain [Shiva] is worshipped.

When the traveller on the mystical path begins to understand the nature of true love, then external rituals and bonds begin to lose their meaning for him. Thus, says Ras Khan:

The rules of the world, the Veda and the world, shame, work and
doubt,
All these you give up once you practise love.
For what are regulations and negations when compared to Love?

'Without Love everything is useless,' Ras Khan insists,
then adds:

Of Shruti, Puranas, Agamas and Smritis, Love is the essence of all.
Without the knowledge of Love there is no experience of bliss.
Knowledge, acting and worship, all of these are the root of pride.
Reading the Shastras you become a pundit, reciting the Qur'an,
a maulvi.
But if you have not known Love in that, what is the use, asks Ras
Khan?*

Here Ras Khan embarks on an intricate description of the
path of love and surrender to God, questioning in the process
all orthodoxies, all formalisms and all man-made divisions.
This, in a sense, is the essence of his message. He ends his
work with the following lines:

Tearing his heart away from a haughty woman [i.e. the snares of
the world]
He turned into Ras Khan once he saw the beauty of Premadeva,
the God of Love.

If Shah Hussain and Ras Khan had to suffer the virulent
opposition of the 'ulama and threats of eternal damnation by
other defenders of the shari'at, they were at least fortunate enough
to have been spared their lives. A more tragic fate befell the
seventeenth-century antinomian Sufi, Sarmad, now remembered
as a shahid or martyr for his defiance of the strictures of the law.
That earned him the executioner's sword. Sarmad lies buried,
forgotten and unloved, in an unassuming grave at the foot of the
great Jami'a Masjid in Delhi, the imposing Friday mosque built
by the Mughal Emperor Shah Jahan. A gay activist group

As recited to the author by an informant at Mathura.

was planning to resurrect him as their patron saint, but I cautioned them against such misplaced enthusiasm. Sarmad's homoeroticism, his passionate love for a Hindu man, may not necessarily mean that he had been a homosexual, I warned.

I pushed my way out of the mini-bus, which barely stopped to disgorge a stream of passengers before dashing off again. Meanwhile a corpulent middle-aged man, clutching the tail of his dhoti in one hand, and a black, menacing umbrella in the other, blocked the entrance, demanding to know if the bus was heading for Mongolpuri. Before I could realize what was happening the umbrella had jabbed me in the stomach, and the man was running after the bus, his dhoti billowing out behind him like a balloon. As I gathered myself, I lunged into a heap of cow-dung decorated with a string of fresh marigold and a boiled egg sliced into two. An apparition—matted locks descending from above a dirt-caked face—fixed a pair of flaming red eyes on me and grinned, revealing a set of decaying, toothless gums. 'Baba Mohan Mahan Tantrik' announced a piece of cardboard set in front of him.

'You've stepped on the evil eye,' he laughed, a stream of saliva trickling down his chin.

He demanded to be paid, unleashing threats of a deadly disease or worse. I scowled and walked on, as the call to prayer drifted from a mosque ahead.

At the foot of the Jami'a Masjid, emaciated infants in rags chased a hairless dog through an overflowing rubbish heap. Lepers with open sores, flies feasting on pools of pus on their rotting legs, stretched their half-eaten hands for alms. A skeleton draped in a torn cloth banner with 'Vote for Congress-I' written in fading letters, slept in the shade of a mosque. Three tribal women squatted on a plastic sheet, selling porcupine quills and herbs stuffed in empty whisky bottles. A giant monitor lizard boiling in a tin on an ancient kerosene stove sent up poisonous vapours. An old cow slurped water from an open drain clogged with waste. A row of pedlars hawked velvet-padded bras and frilly sequined panties for Rs 10 a piece.

'Take one for your begum,' said one.

'For your girlfriend, then,' he quipped when I said I was unmarried.

He refused to believe that I had neither wife nor girlfriend. 'At your age, you could have been well on your way to becoming a grandfather,' he shouted out playfully.

I stood against a wall, taking in the misery that seemed to pervade the area. A limbless dwarf lay on a reed mat, dangling the stump of what should have been a foot, singing, 'Give to the poor in the name of Allah.' A crowd gathered around a herd of goats, inspecting their teeth to gauge their age. 'A two-toothed goat gives the best mutton,' explained a lungi-clad, paan-chewing butcher. The festival of the Eid of Goats was just a week away, and the animals were being fattened on a special diet of leaves and grass.

A young man walked up to me and smiled. Soon we settled down to a conversation.

'All Muslim areas are like this,' he said, waving his hands all around him.

'What can we do? It's you pundits who rule now and you want to convert us into the new untouchables,' he rued, mistaking me to be a Brahmin.

Like many other Muslims in the area, he was out of work and managed to eke out a living selling old newspapers and bottles. He was a recent arrival in Delhi, having fled here from his town in the wake of a deadly anti-Muslim pogrom. His mother had been raped in front of him, then her head had been sliced off by a horde of Hindus armed with daggers. He said they were members of the dreaded Bajrang Dal, the army of the monkey-god Hanuman.

'Allah alone knows what's going to happen to us,' he murmured grimly. 'Between Muslim and Hindu terrorists the country shall be torn to shreds.'

Ahead, a handsome, hefty Pathan perched imperiously on a stool. Wooden crates laden with boxes of dried fruit were stacked near his feet. Two wiry old men with patches of white hair clinging to their bald heads like moss, bent low and whispered a request for 'Khan Saheb's Special Medicine'.

The Pathan handed them two plastic bottles containing a black paste.

'Afghan men's secret potion,' he proudly announced, plucking his penis as if it were some strange stringed musical instrument.

'Eat it at night after dinner,' he said with a wink, 'and you'll be roaring like a tiger.'

'Don't believe a word of what he says,' joked a middle-aged man with a cauldron of a belly. 'I've tried the medicine and it doesn't work. I landed up with an upset stomach that lasted a whole week. And my wife is now on strike.'

I snaked my way through the crowd descending from the steps of the grand mosque ahead. Sarmad Sahib's dargah was situated at the foot of the mosque, a blood-red box-like structure abutting the bright green shrine of his preceptor, Harey Bharey ('The Evergreen One'). A knotted neem tree escaped from its roof, and on its wall a rusted tin board broadcasted, referring to the martyred saint who lay at rest within, a verse from the Qur'an: 'Think not those who are slain in the path of God as "dead". Nay, they are alive, but you perceive not.'

Inside, the walls were painted a pale red, the colour of martyrdom. Red ceramic tiles lined the floors. A net of red beads hung over a raised grave, draped in a red sheet, and a pale red bulb hung from a wire above. Three veiled women knelt in a corner, resting on a low, folding wooden table and reading from the Qur'an. An old man with an enormous turban sat cross-legged in front of the flower-decked grave, counting a string of plastic beads. Two Hindu women entered the shrine, and prostrated themselves on the floor. One of them scribbled a note on a piece of cardboard and tied it on to the railing that skirted the grave. Her companion fixed a little lock on the railing to remind the Pir of their visit. Once they had left, and I was sure no one was looking, I opened the note and read it:

Blessings of Ishvar be upon you, oh great saint, Sarmad the Martyr. My child, Sunila, aged six, has been suffering from a strange disease, which no doctor has been able to cure. I beg you, in humble submission, to help cure my daughter. In return I promise to visit your dargah every Thursday evening and to offer Rs 1000 worth of food to the mendicants and the poor who sit outside your grave.

Raj Lakshmi
W/o Lal Kishan
R/o Pritampura

A board proclaiming 'The Great Guru, King of Kings of the Masters of Spiritual Knowledge' pointed to a little cabin along the short shaded corridor leading out of the shrine. Pir Sayyed Muhammad Ahmad Sarmadi, the custodian of the shrine, sat reclining against a bolster, running his fat fingers over his ponderous belly. A steady stream of visitors, Hindu and Muslim, waited at the entrance for their turn. One by one they went in, bowed to the man, and poured out their hearts. A range of bottles stood on a ledge, containing various potions and powders. A distressed woman in a tattered sari sat in front of the Pir, sobbing uncontrollably. Her son had had an accident and there seemed to be little hope of survival. As she related the story, the Pir scribbled a diagram on a sheet of paper—knots and crosses filled in with Arabic letters and numerals. 'Here, take this *ta'wiz*,' he said. 'It will keep your son out of harm's way.'

I stepped out of the Pir's chambers back into the bustle of the market outside. A eunuch dressed in a tight-fitting salwar kameez, her hair neatly oiled and set back, grinned at me suggestively. Thaap, thaap, she clapped, and wiggled her tongue out of her paan-stained lips.

'You've been to see the Pir, have you? All these Pirs are charlatans, I assure you,' she laughed, her fake breasts shaking like jelly.

She drew out a visiting card from her blouse and handed it to me. 'Ms Nisha, Hijra, Expert Masseur,' it read. 'Meet for pleasure and childbirth. Attending also marriage parties for blessing.'

We walked over to a stall for a glass of sticky-sweet sherbet. Nisha tossed her hair about and cast knowing glances at the shopkeepers who grinned at her derisively. She had been born a male and named Nishit, and hailed from a Hindu family in Bihar. 'But I always felt I was a woman,' she said. At the age of sixteen she had joined the hijras, after going through a painful operation. She had been castrated with a knife by the guru or head of the hijra lineage she had joined, and a cupful of hot oil had been applied on the wound for it to heal. A neem twig had been inserted in the place her penis once occupied. She had converted to Islam following the sex change.

'Most hijras become Muslim, although they may continue to venerate Hindu deities such as the great hijra goddess Bahuchara Mata in Gujarat,' she explained.

Hijras had occupied important posts in the courts of Muslim kings: guards of imperial harems, spies and advisors, ministers and, occasionally, army generals.

'Perhaps that is why when a Hindu becomes a hijra she generally converts to the Muslim faith,' she said. 'But,' she winked at me and whispered, displaying a row of yellow lipstick-stained teeth, 'when it comes to going to bed with men, there's no Hindu-Muslim difference for me!'

The dargah of Sarmad is one of the innumerable Sufi shrines of Delhi, most of them long since forgotten. From the thirteenth century onwards, Delhi grew into one of the major centres of Sufism in the Muslim world, with scores of accomplished

Sufis flocking here from Iran and Central Asia. After setting up base for themselves in the imperial capital, they sent out their disciples to other parts of India. From Gujarat in the west to Bengal and beyond in the east, and deep down into the Deccan, these disciples set up their centres, preaching their doctrines and serving the poor. Most of these Sufis were orthodox Muslims who faithfully abided by the Islamic law. Others, such as the Malamatis, probably influenced by the Hindu environment, were lax in matters of the shari'at.

Sarmad Shahid was one of the most popular Malamati Sufis of all times, but little is known about his early life. Extant Persian chronicles are divided about his origins. Some say that he was from the 'Country of the Franks', others, from Armenia, and yet others insist that he was a Jew from the town of Kashan, in present-day Iran, and that later he converted to Islam. He is said to have set off in 1632 on a trading expedition to India and landed at the port of Thatta in Sind, then an important centre for commerce and trade between Iran, Arabia and India. Besides being home to numerous accomplished Sufi masters the port was also a great centre for music and culture and the arts.

It was at a musical concert at Thatta that Sarmad first met Abhay Chand, a young Hindu lad. The boy's beauty and his mellifluous voice are said to have so enraptured Sarmad that immediately he fell madly in love with him. As Sarmad's biographer, the present custodian of his shrine, puts it:

The boy's voice was so melodious and his beauty so captivating and the *ghazal* that he sang so full of meaning that a grievous wound was inflicted on Sarmad's tender heart and his whole being was fiercely shaken (Pir Sayyed Muhammad Ahmad Sarmadi).

Driven by wild, unstoppable passion, Sarmad now began to visit the concert hall every night to listen to the boy sing. His ship had, meanwhile, sailed away, and he had lost all care for the world. Abhay Chand responded to Sarmad's overtures with equal devotion, and the two lovers began living together in Sarmad's house.

Rumours about the couple now did the rounds of Thatta. Abhay Chand's father, variously described in the available accounts as a rich Hindu trader or a Hindu prince, appealed to the governor of the town, Mirza Muhammad Beg, to intervene. On the governor's orders, Abhay Chand was forcibly taken away from Sarmad, and locked up in his father's home.

His anguish at being separated from his lover, the chronicles tell us, drove Sarmad into a state of such frenzy that he tore off all his clothes. From that day on, he was to live completely in the nude. When Mirza Muhammad Beg learnt of this, he dispatched an emissary to him, demanding that Sarmad abide by the shari'at and cover his naked body, in return for which he promised to give him whatever he asked for. In reply, Sarmad sent a message to him saying:

I know of your great power and wealth, your jewels and your gold, but I have no need for them. All I want is my beloved (Sarmadi).

Meanwhile, Abhay Chand's distress was no less painful, and, unable to see their son suffer so, his parents finally relented and let him go back to his lover. Harried by the hostile denizens of Thatta, the couple fled to Lahore. There they stayed for thirteen years, adopting the austere path of 'those who sit on ashes'. Together, the two lovers translated the five books of Moses into Persian. It was at this time that Sarmad began to compose the stirring mystical poetry for which he is still remembered today. Abhay Chand would sing these verses in his clear, flowing voice, causing Sarmad to break into a dance. For, it is said, 'Sarmad had been pierced with the arrow of love, for which Abhay Chand's beauty and his rich voice alone were the balm' (Sarmadi n.d.).

Following in the footsteps of certain Sufis before him, Sarmad believed his love for the young Abhay Chand was a means to discover God. 'Physical love' was his way to 'divine love', for God's presence was manifest in all His creatures, and He could not be separated from them. As Sarmad put it, 'I know not whether under the heavens my God is Abhay Chand or someone else'. (M.G. Gupta, 1991). Traversing the path of love, Sarmad sang, the seeker realizes that God is present in every particle of the universe. Here, differences of caste and creed all fade away into meaninglessness:

Who is the lover, beloved, idol and idol-maker but You?
Who is the beloved of the Ka'aba, the temple and the mosque?
Come to the garden and see the unity in the array of colours.
In all this, who is the lover, the beloved, the flower and the thorn?

From Lahore, Sarmad and Abhay Chand left for Golkunda, in the south, and after a few years headed up north, first to Agra, then, in 1657, to Delhi, the imperial capital of the Mughals. There they settled down at the monastery of the Chishti Sufi, Hazrat Khwaja Abul Qasim Sabzwari, more popularly known as Harey Bharey. This Sufi is said to have had a large number of disciples, Hindu as well as Muslim. Among them was the Emperor Shah Jahan himself. By this time, Sarmad had grown into a renowned mystic, commanding a vast following. 'In piety,' writes Maulana Abul Kalam Azad, 'he had reached [such] a point that all of Shahjahanabad [Delhi] had become his mureed [devotees]' (Abul Kalam Azad, 1991). Among his closest followers was the Mughal crown prince, Dara Shikoh, the eldest son of Shah Jahan.

Dara was an accomplished Sufi in his own right. He had been initiated into the Qadri Sufi order by Hazrat Miyan Mir, whose piety had so impressed Guru Arjan Dev, the fifth guru of the Sikhs, that he gave him the honour of laying the foundation stone of the Golden Temple at Amritsar. From Hazrat Miyan Mir, Dara had inherited a sympathetic understanding of other faiths, and was one of the first Muslims to take an interest in the religious books of the Hindus, translating the Upanishads into Persian. Among his numerous works was the *Majm'a al-Bahra'in* or the 'Union of the Two Oceans', a treatise on Vedantic Hinduism and Islamic Sufism, that sought to explore the commonality between these two mystical traditions. Sarmad's universal vision, based on the love of God and all His creatures, as opposed to a mechanical adherence to religious law, was one with which Dara could readily identify. As Azad put it, Sarmad was 'far above the pedantic discussion of kufr [disbelief] and faith', characteristic of the 'ulama, the 'godly men of worldly ways'. Sarmad, he says, had 'reached the pinnacle of love from where the walls of the mosque and the temple are seen standing face to face' (translated by Syeda Saiyidain Hameed, 1996). Dara would spend hours in Sarmad's company, discussing the finer points of mysticism and metaphysics.

When Aurangzeb, Shah Jahan's younger son, usurped the throne of Delhi after imprisoning his father and killing Dara, he unleashed a bloody campaign against all of Dara's close associates and sympathizers. As Dara's spiritual teacher, Sarmad, too, was to become a hapless victim of Aurangzeb's wrath. Envious of his popularity among the denizens of Delhi, both Hindu and Muslim, Aurangzeb now set about plotting to do away with him.

One Friday, as Aurangzeb walked down from the Red Fort to offer his prayers at the Jami'a Masjid, he spotted Sarmad sitting in the nude in the street. He went up to him and sharply rebuked him for violating the shari'at by not covering his body. To the emperor Sarmad cryptically replied:

To those with sins to hide, God gave clothes to wear. And upon the pure He bestowed the robe of nakedness (Azad, 1991).

Then, pointing to a blanket lying next to him, Sarmad said to Aurangzeb, 'Pick it up and cover me with it.' No sooner had Aurangzeb lifted the blanket than, it is said, the blood-soaked heads of the men he had killed in his ruthless ascent to the throne, rolled out of it. 'Now tell me,' said Sarmad, turning to him, 'should I hide your sins or my own nakedness?'

Sarmad's fearlessness proved too much for the emperor to bear. Fearing that Sarmad would now seek to push the people of Delhi to revolt, Aurangzeb hurriedly called his chief Qazi, Mullah Qawi, and commissioned him with the task of accusing Sarmad of apostasy, the punishment for which was death. Sarmad was dragged to the court, where the Qazi brought formal charges against him. He was accused of deliberately defying the shari'at by living naked. To this charge Sarmad retorted, in a delightful play on the Qazi's name, 'What can I do? Satan is Qawi [powerful].' Then, he recited a verse:

That Exalted One has driven me mad.
He has stolen my heart and left me abandoned.
I search for him, but in vain.
It is He who has forced me to roam the streets naked.*

The angered Mullah Qawi then had Abhay Chand paraded before Sarmad and mercilessly flogged, hoping that this might make Sarmad relent. The whip lashed Abhay Chand's body, but miraculously, the pain was inflicted on Sarmad.

'You go by mere appearances and reality eludes you,' he told the Qazi. 'You did not flog Abhay Chand, but you flogged me,' he said, showing the Qazi the weals on his back.

'The God who does not let me see my beloved,' he cried out, 'is like an iron cage that smothers the spirit and bruises the heart.'

To the Qazi, Islam was a bundle of stern, inflexible laws, but for Sarmad it was, above all, a message of love. Sarmad made so bold as to declare, much to the horror of the Qazi, 'There is no fault with a mad man. The fault lies with you, for love has not maddened you yet.'

---

*As told to the author by a pilgrim at the shrine of Sarmad.

The Qazi refused to relent, and demanded, instead, that Sarmad recite the kalima shahada, the Islamic creed of confession of the faith—la ilaha il allah, muhammad-ur rasul allah ('There is no God but Allah, and Muhammad is the Messenger of Allah')—in order to prove that he was indeed a Muslim. Sarmad refused to go beyond the call of la ilaha ('There is no God'), for he had not yet reached the end of his frenzied search for God. Following Sarmad's refusal to pronounce the entire creed, the Qazi passed a death sentence against him.

Sarmad was then dragged through the streets of Delhi to the gallows and promptly beheaded. But even in his death, so legend has it, Sarmad emerged victorious. He picked his severed head in his hand and calmly ascended the stairs of the Jami'a Masjid, mocking at the emperor and his priest, loudly affirming the kalima shahada in its entirety. In death, he had found his God, testifying to the truth of his own understanding of Islam. Just as he was about to enter the mosque, so it is said, a voice called out to him from Harey Bharey's grave, pleading with him to relent, for he had now reached the end of his search, having been united with God at last. He then turned around with his head in his hand and walked down to Harey Bharey's dargah.

And there, at the foot of the great mosque, his body was buried in a little chamber next to the shrine of his master.

As for the wrathful Aurangzeb, it is said that after Sarmad's martyrdom he did not enjoy a day's rest. The Mughal Empire, the greatest in the world, collapsed shortly after.

11

THE BABA OF BHATINDA

The holocaust of 1947 in Punjab brought in its wake terrible destruction, uprooting millions of people from their homes. Several hundred thousands of others who found themselves, almost overnight, on the wrong side of a line drawn by a British imperial officer, were killed. The entire Hindu and Sikh population of western Punjab was forced to flee to India. Likewise, nearly all the Muslims in eastern Punjab were driven across the border to the newly created state of Pakistan. Thousands of women—Sikh, Hindu, Dalit and Muslim—were either raped or abducted, and property worth millions destroyed. The wounds of the Partition have yet to heal, and communal prejudices remain deeply etched in the collective Punjabi psyche, more than half a century later.

Prior to the Partition, more than a third of the inhabitants of eastern Punjab were Muslims. As elsewhere in South Asia, Islam spread in this part of the subcontinent due to the peaceful missionary endeavours of wandering Sufi saints. Scores of shrines or dargahs, built over the graves of the Sufis, dotted the eastern Punjabi landscape, attracting not just Muslim devotees, but also a large number of Hindus, Sikhs and Dalits. Following the mass expulsion and slaughter of Muslims in eastern Punjab, hundreds of mosques and Sufi shrines in the region were taken over by local Hindus and Sikhs and their co-religionists who had fled to India. Some of these were converted into houses and temples, others into cattle-sheds and godowns. Several others were tended to by local non-Muslim communities and preserved as before. Thus, despite the almost complete absence of Muslims in the area, these continued to function as Sufi shrines, for people of all caste and creed believed the 'Pir Babas' possessed mystical powers that could make their wishes come true.

One of the most popular surviving Sufi shrines in eastern Punjab today is the dargah of Haji Baba Rattan at Bhatinda. Hindus, Sikhs and Muslims all claim the Baba as their own, although there is no doubt about his Muslim Sufi connections. Little is known about the Baba, but all versions of his story credit him with a long life—over 700 years.

It appears that the cult of Baba Rattan dates back to the Mughal era and possibly even earlier, to the period of the Delhi Sultanate. The noted Indian Muslim scholar, Maulana Manazir Ahsan Gilani, (1987) observes that the first reference to Baba Rattan dates back to the twelfth century of the Christian era, when stories of an Indian companion or sahabi of the Prophet, still being alive, some 600 years after the Prophet's death, began circulating. For Muslims brought up to believe that the last of the Prophet's many companions, Hazrat Abu Tufail, had died not long after the Prophet himself, this proved to be a major revelation. Several Muslim scholars and traders from Central and West Asia, and from even as far as Andalusia in Spain, travelled all the way to the little town of Bhatinda to visit Baba Rattan al-Hindi (Baba Rattan The Indian), as they called him, to listen to his story and collect from him traditions (hadith) of or stories about the Prophet.

As Baba Rattan's fame as the only surviving companion of the Prophet spread, not only over North India but also across much of the Muslim world, several Muslim scholars began penning tracts about him. Some, such as the mediaeval Muslim historian Allama Shamsuddin Zahbi, declared him to be a liar and an imposter, while others, such as his contemporary Allama Safdi, insisted that his claim was genuine. The sixteenth-century Arab scholar, Hafiz Ibn Hajar, devoted a large section in his tome, the *Asab*, to various traditions dealing with Baba Rattan. He claimed that the Baba's grandfather was a Hindu, a certain Janak Dev Sarraf, from Bhatinda, and that he belonged to the Vaishya caste of traders. His father's name was, according to some accounts, Nusr, and, according to others, Sahu.

Ibn Hajar presented somewhat different accounts provided by a dozen Muslim scholars of how Baba Rattan, hailing from the then small village of Bhatinda, managed to meet the Prophet and become his disciple.

According to the twelfth-century Spanish Muslim chronicler, Abu Marwan Andalusi, he first heard about Baba Rattan on a journey to Basra in Iraq. Curious to learn more about him, he undertook a long journey to Bhatinda. When he arrived at the Baba's monastery, he was taken aback to see an ancient, wrinkled man, his cheeks covered with hair 'as white as cotton'. The Baba addressed him in a language he could not understand, claiming, as was later translated for him, that he was present in Medina during the famed Battle of the Trench, when the Prophet Muhammad and his followers built a ditch around the town to protect it from the marauding Quraish of Mecca. At that time, he said, he was just fourteen years old. When the Prophet saw him labouring at the trenches, he blessed him with a long life.

Ibn Hajar also referred to the Khurasani scholar Sayyed 'Ali bin Muhammad who, like Abu Marwan Andalusi, claimed to have travelled to Bhatinda to meet Baba Rattan. The Baba is said to have told him that he had actually played with the Prophet when the latter was still a child. Apparently, or so he claimed, when Muhammad was born, he heard about the arrival of the 'Seal of the Prophets', and set off on a long and dangerous journey to Arabia. When he finally got to Mecca, a fierce storm set in. On the outskirts of the town he spotted a young child herding a pack of camels. One of the camels had strayed ahead, and a deep channel of rainwater which the child could not cross now separated the child from the camel. The Baba then lifted the child in his arms and took him across the channel to rescue his camel. Touched by his kindness, the boy blessed him with a long life. The Baba then proceeded to Mecca. There he searched for the Prophet whom he had heard about, but in vain, for Muhammad was still a child and had not yet declared his divine mission. Dejected, the Baba returned to Bhatinda.

Some thirty-odd years later, he heard that the much-awaited Prophet was now in Medina. So he set off on his second journey to Arabia. When he arrived at Medina, he went straight to the mosque. There, the Prophet recognized him at once as the man who had helped him ford the channel in his childhood, and again blessed him with a long life. Thereupon, the Baba embraced Islam at the Prophet's hands and stayed with him for twelve days, after which he returned to Bhatinda.

Another mediaeval Muslim writer from Khurasan whom Ibn Hajar quoted in his chronicle was a certain Hussain bin Muhammad, who also claimed to have travelled as a youth to Bhatinda to meet the Baba. When he arrived at the town, he was taken to an old, gnarled tree, around which a large crowd of devotees had gathered. Perched high up on the tree was a little box in which the Baba lived. After offering his salaams to the Baba, he entreated him to tell the story of his meeting with the Prophet. The Baba told him, much to his astonishment, that as a young man he had accompanied his own father on a trading mission to Arabia, where he had helped the child Muhammad to cross a channel to rescue his camel. After that he and his father had proceeded to Mecca to sell their wares, before returning to India. One night, some years later, he saw the moon suddenly split into two. One part fell to the east and the other to the west, far beyond the horizon, turning the sky completely dark. After a while, the two halves of the moon were joined together once again. The Baba took this to be a divine signal. Shortly after, a caravan passed by, and the Baba asked the leader of the caravan if he had any knowledge of the incident. He was told that a certain man of the Hashmi clan in Mecca had declared himself to be the Prophet of God. His opponents had challenged him to prove his claims, and he had done so by performing the miracle of the 'splitting of the moon'.

Eager to meet the Prophet, the Baba then journeyed to Mecca, and, on being told where Muhammad lived, went inside his house. The Prophet immediately recognized him as the one who had helped him in his childhood, and offered him six dates to eat. Eating each date caused his life to increase by a hundred years. So impressed was he with the Prophet that he immediately converted to Islam.

Ibn Hajar also referred to Abul Hasan 'Ali bin Shabib who recounted a slightly different story of the Baba. He wrote that when in Egypt, he met with a certain Daud bin Saeed who revealed to him that he had personally met Baba Rattan in Bhatinda. According to him, the Baba had told him that one night a strange person had appeared to him in a dream, ordering him to abandon the worship of idols, and advising him to travel to Syria in search of the 'True Faith'. Accordingly, he set off on a long and arduous journey to Syria. When he arrived there he discovered that the inhabitants of the country were all Christians, so he himself embraced Christianity. Some years later, he heard that Muhammad had declared his prophethood and was now in Medina. He then travelled to Medina, where, after meeting the Prophet, he converted to Islam, and was blessed by the Prophet with a long life. He stayed with the Prophet in Medina for some time, taking part in a battle against the Jews. After this, he finally returned to Bhatinda.

Several other Muslim scholars left behind little anecdotes about the legendary Baba Rattan. Musa bin Majli, a Sufi dervish, claimed to have recorded some forty traditions of the Prophet as allegedly narrated by the Baba. Interestingly enough, other mediaeval Muslim scholars dismissed these as fabricated and fanciful. Allama Shamsuddin Zahbi went so far as to claim that

Baba Rattan was no companion of the Prophet, but, 'a liar and an imposter', 'a scheming devil' and even 'Satan in human form'. Zahbi wrote an entire booklet, *The Destruction of the Idol of Rattan,* to prove his point. He insisted that by falsely claiming to be a companion of the Prophet he had 'earned for himself a place in hell', insinuating that Baba Rattan, and those who believed his claims might actually have been members of a secret Shi'a sect.

Thus despite the absence of much factual information on the actual life of Baba Rattan, the numerous references to him in the mediaeval Muslim literature clearly suggest that he was a hugely controversial figure of his times, known either as a pious Muslim or a notorious imposter, not just in India, but in large parts of the Muslim world as well.

There can be little doubt that Baba Rattan actually did convert to Islam, although whether or not he was actually a companion of the Prophet is still hotly debated. Curiously enough, some Hindu Nath Yogis too claim him as their own. These Yogis credit 'Haji Baba Rattan Nath' with having discovered commonalities between Indian philosophy and the teachings of Islam, and following in the footsteps of reformers such as the Siddhas, the weaver-saint Kabir and other proponents of a formless God. He is said to have travelled to Mecca and met the Prophet Muhammad, from whom he is believed to have received divine wisdom. He is said to have spent his long life of 700 years striving to 'explain the culture and philosophy of Islam in terms that the Indian mind would find intelligible'. Through his great yogic powers, he is said to have won over many disciples, and even 'completely astonished' warrior-kings such as Muhammad of Ghazni and Muhammad Ghori. While recognizing his obvious Islamic affiliations, the Yogis believe that the Baba had also played a leading role in the spread of

Nath doctrines outside India, in lands as far as Arabia, Kabul and Kandahar. (Ramlal Srivastava, 1984).

Regarding the details of the Baba's life, the Nath version differs considerably from the legends narrated by the mediaeval Muslim hagiographers. The former refers to an oral tradition which claims that the Baba was born either in the fifth or the sixth century AD in the town of Dang in Nepal, somewhere on the present-day Indo-Nepalese border, and claims that he was actually the son of the local Raja Mankiya Parikshak.

One day, so the story goes, he set off on a hunting expedition. In a dense forest he chanced upon a 'great yogi', with heavy matted locks, ashes smeared on his body and large rings in his ears. Rattan got off his horse and touched the yogi's feet. The yogi blessed him and said, 'Non-violence is the highest form of religion. You should think of every living being as your own self. Everything is made by God, because the atma and the paramatma, the Self and the Great Soul, are one. If you want to hunt, then hunt the deer in the form of your own ego. By destroying the ego you shall become powerful and attain the ultimate goal, the vision of God.'

This 'great yogi' was none other than the great Guru Gorakhnath, the head of the Yogis. Rattan implored him to accept him as a disciple. Gorakhnath then initiated him into the Nath order, giving him the Gayatri Mantra to recite.

Shortly after, the Baba commissioned the construction of a large temple at Ratanpura, where Gorakhnath and the Baba worshipped the Devi. Later, the temple grew into the famous Shaktipeeth Devipatan is now a major centre for the Naths, and historically linked with the Gorakhnath Mandir at Gorakhpur. In the town of Dang, a large fair in which thousands of people participate, is still held every year in the memory of 'Yogi Rattan Nath'. Several Nath *gaddi*s in Nepal are also associated with the Rattan Nath monastery at Dang.

After the Baba had mastered the yogic sciences, or so the Nath legend goes, Gorakhnath instructed him to travel to the west to spread the Nath religion. In Kabul, it is claimed, he performed several miracles, including bringing a dead tree back to life. The ruler of Kabul is said to have been so impressed that he granted him a large plot of land to build a temple, and invited him to stay with him in his palace, even allowing him to set up a dhuna, the holy fire of the Naths, inside it.

From Kabul the Baba travelled to Attock, now on the frontier between Pakistan and Afghanistan. He did not have any money with him and the boatmen refused to take him across the river. Thereupon, he flew into a rage and cursed the boatmen, turning them into stones. He then spread his mat on the river and miraculously sped across it.

The Nath version refers to another oral tradition according to which Rattan, through his great yogic powers and knowledge of astrology, received the news that 'a great prophet of Ishwar who would soon be born in Arabia would spread the dharma'. Shortly after Muhammad had declared his prophethood, the Baba travelled to Mecca, where he 'received darshan' of the Prophet, spending three years with him, according to one Nath version, and ten times that number, according to another. He then came back to Bhatinda, and from here, after many years of 'great penance and yogic austerities', he set off to western India to spread the teachings of yoga.

According to another Nath version, on his return from Arabia, he spent the rest of his life at Bhatinda itself, dying at the ripe old age of 700.

Like many Sufis and yogis, the Baba is also said to have played a key role in the politics of his time. Surprisingly, the Nath version speaks of the Baba as having helped the Muslim Shihabuddin Muhammad Ghori in his campaign against Prithviraj Chauhan, one of the many icons of today's furiously anti-Muslim Hindu 'nationalists'. It says that in 1189, in order to win the battle of Bhatinda against Prithviraj, Muhammad Ghori appeared before the Baba and sought his blessings. The Baba distributed water from his vessel to the Turkish soldiers, and prophesied that the sultan would be able to conquer Bhatinda because of two of his brave Sayyed soldiers who, however, would be martyred fighting. As predicted, Muhammad Ghori captured the Bhatinda fort after heavy fighting with the Rajputs, in course of which the two Sayyeds, along with many others, were slain.

The details of the Baba's secret political dealings, however, are not clear. The Nath version refers to another oral tradition according to which the victorious general was Mahmud Ghaznavi, not Muhammad Ghori, but notes that whoever it might have been, it was through the Baba's 'extraordinary yogic powers' that he was able to 'quench the thirst of a massive army'. It is interesting to note that a similar story was narrated by H.B.W. Garrick, the British orientalist and assistant of the Archaeological Surveyor of India in the late nineteenth century. In his *Report of a Tour in the Punjab and Rajputana in 1883-84* he referred to the widespread belief that Hajji Rattan, also known as Chankar, a noble in the court of Raja Venu Pal, 'connived' with Sultan Mu'izzuddin Muhammad ibn Sam and helped him conquer Bhatinda in 1191–92. He then converted to Islam and made the pilgrimage to Mecca.

The Nath tradition credits Baba Rattan with numerous philosophical and religious treatises, among which are the *Awwal-i-Suluk* ('The First Sufi Path') and *Kafir Bodh* ('The Wisdom of the Unbeliever'), both believed to contain esoteric explanations of yoga in the light of Islamic teachings. These two books are said to contain a trenchant critique of 'empty ritualism'. In the *Kafir Bodh*, Baba Rattan is said to have declared:

I roam the world barefoot.
In peace, contentment and mercy.
I have devoted myself to the welfare of all.
I harm no soul, big or small.
I am a Fakir [Yogi], and not a Kafir.
A Kafir is he who walks on the path of sin
And does not fear the justice of Allah Param Atma.

In addition, the Nath sources tell us, two *shabad*s penned by Baba Rattan, on the importance of the guru, the master on the spiritual path, are to be found in the *Gorakhbani*, a compendium of verses ascribed to the mysterious Gorakhnath.

The remarkably fluid identity of Rattan who was credited with being both a yogi and a Muslim at the same time, is hardly surprising. Several noted Indian Sufis were revered by yogis for their miraculous powers, and some of the former were included among the latter. At a higher level, the worship of the one formless God and a fierce opposition to empty ritualism brought antinomian Sufis and yogis into a shared universe of discourse, allowing for multiple identities and challenging the logic of sharply defined boundaries between Hindus and Muslims.

At one end of Bhatinda town, adjacent to the wholesale grain market, a newly built concrete welcome arch announced the dargah of Haji Baba Rattan. A narrow winding lane, lined on either side with open drains clogged with plastic bags and human excrement, led to an open square. A group of young men, skullcaps on their heads, dressed in long kurtas and checked lungis, walked in a single file towards a recently renovated mosque, one of the only places of Muslim worship left in a town which once had many others. Adjacent to the mosque, at the foot of a gnarled tree, lay neatly stacked bags of salt and dozens of brooms—humble offerings of unknown pilgrims flocking here for cures to a variety of ailments. A wooden door painted bright green opened into a box-like structure topped with an onion-shaped dome. Inside, in a cold, perfumed chamber, a raised grave stretched out on the floor, draped in a sheet of green silk. This is the resting place of the legendary Haji Baba Rattan, and is said to be the earliest surviving monument from the Sultanate period in eastern Punjab.

A middle-aged man, dressed in a long sky-blue kameez and a pair of baggy salwars, his shawl tightly wrapped around his chest to keep out the cold, sat at a low wooden table near the entrance. Let me call him Hussain.

'Asalaam Aleikum,' Hussain said, as he grinned from inside his shawl, wrapping his legs around a charcoal stove.

He introduced himself as a member of the recently established Muslim Human Welfare Society in charge of running the affairs of the dargah.

'I was told that the dargah is under the Punjab Waqf Board,' I remarked, referring to the government-constituted body that administered all Muslim endowed properties in the state.

'Well, in theory that might be so. But, you know, the Waqf Board is notoriously corrupt, so some of us local Muslims have set up our own committee here.'

It was not, however, just stories of inefficiency and embezzlement that had prompted the setting up of a rival organization to administer the shrine.

'The Waqf Board people are mostly Deobandis, who have no faith in the Baba,' said Hussain with visible disgust. 'And Allah says that he who wages war against his friends shall earn His wrath.'

While the Deobandis were not opposed to Sufism as such, they perceived popular piety and local customs at the shrines as 'wrongful', Hinduistic 'innovations' not sanctioned by Islam, akin to polytheism. That is why, Hussain said, the Waqf Board authorities displayed little interest in the proper running of the Baba's shrine.

I begged Hussain to tell me the story of Baba Rattan.

'First eat, then listen,' he insisted, in an Urdu liberally peppered with Punjabi, thumping me heartily on the back.

'Oye Sultana!' he cried out into a hole in the wall that opened out into a dark, smoke-filled kitchen. 'Make a crisp aloo paratha with an extra blob of ghee for our brother here. Imagine! He's come all the way from Delhi to meet the Baba!'

He made it sound as if the Baba were still alive, having been granted a fresh lease of another 700 years. Then, curling his legs under his shawl to keep them snug, he began to tell his story.

Baba Rattan's actual name was Pandit Rattan Lal. He was born in a Brahmin family and rose to become a master astrologer and one of the nine jewels in the court of the legendary Raja Bhoj of Ujjain.

One night, the Raja witnessed the moon suddenly splitting into two. Realizing that this was no ordinary event, he asked Rattan to explain the phenomenon to him.

The Pandit answered, 'I have read in the Vedas that when the guru of the whole world will announce his arrival, the moon shall be split into two.'

Shortly after, eager to meet the much-awaited messiah, the Prophet Muhammad, who had performed this great miracle, the Pandit set off for Mecca, bearing with him a pyjama and a paan leaf carefully wrapped up in a cloth as presents. When he finally got to Mecca he met the Prophet and offered him the gifts.

The Prophet, without even opening the cloth said, 'Oh, you have brought a pyjama for me, but you have forgotten the nara, the string to tie it with. And you have also brought a paan leaf, but where is the *supari* to go with it?'

The Pandit was taken aback, and realized that Muhammad was indeed the 'Guru of the World', or how else would he have known what the parcel contained without having opened it? Rattan was now convinced of Muhammad's claims to prophethood. At once he recited the Islamic creed of confession and became a Muslim. He later performed the Haj, and earned the title of Haji.

After staying with the Prophet for many months, Rattan decided to return to India. At the time of his departure, the Prophet gave him more than a hundred presents. The Prophet asked him what else he wanted, and the Baba answered, 'By God's grace I have everything I need. I have enough riches, and, above all, the wealth of faith, so I don't need anything else.' Thereupon, suitably impressed with his piety and devotion, the Prophet blessed him with a long life of 700 years. At that time, Rattan was just a century old.

On seeing the many gifts that the Prophet had given Rattan, Abu Bakr, one of the favourite disciples of the Prophet and the father of Ayesha, the last of the Prophet's wives, requested the Prophet that he, too, be allowed to give Rattan a present. He provided him with a sturdy she-camel, on which Rattan rode back from Mecca to India.

All through the journey Rattan remained deeply immersed in meditation, his eyes tightly shut. When the camel stopped abruptly and refused to go any further Rattan opened his eyes and found himself in the town of Bhatinda. Taking this to be a divine sign, he decided to settle on the outskirts of the town, spending some 600 years here till he died and was buried here some time in the early thirteenth century.

'I've considerably summarized his story,' Hussain reminded me.

'As you can imagine,' he said, 'since he lived 700 years his story must indeed be much, much longer than this.'

Hussain took me on a tour of the dargah, pointing out old, faded inscriptions on the walls, the bare, unassuming mosque built by Razia, the only woman ruler of Delhi, and the lock-shaped grave of a fierce jinn at its foot, whom the Baba had vanquished in a great spiritual battle at the Bhatinda Fort. A long, flat slab of red stone carved as a slumbering dromedary stretched under a wrinkled tree.

'The grave of the Baba's faithful camel,' Hussain explained.

It was Thursday afternoon, a special day at all Sufi shrines. A large crowd, mainly Sikhs and Hindus, trailed through the entrance, bowing with folded hands at the Baba's grave and dropping coins into a tin offering box. A pasty gruel of rice and dal bubbled in an enormous black-bottomed cauldron on a clay oven, sending up jets of steam that threatened to throw off the metal plate that covered it. On the floor of the *langar khana*, devotees—Hindus, Muslims and Sikhs—squatted on their knees in one long row, and bent over piles of the holy substance. At the Baba's shrine notions of purity and pollution, and, for orthodox Hindus, the abhorrent Muslim touch, were momentarily laid aside.

A sturdy middle-aged man, with sparkling light-brown eyes, a long, slender nose and a deep cleft splitting his well-carved chin stepped out of the community kitchen, flicking off the remains of his meal with a cloth that had been slung on his shoulder. He wore a Sikh-style turban wound tightly around his head, and a striped cotton lungi. A heavy woollen blanket took care of the cold. A friendly enough face, I thought, and smiled at him as he walked past.

'Asalaam Aleikum,' I said to him and introduced myself.

'Waleikum Salaam,' he replied cheerfully, and sat down on a chair next to me.

He gave me a firm handshake, introducing himself as Muhammad Zaman.

I stared at him in open-mouthed amazement. I had taken him to be a Sikh trying to pass off for a Muslim.

'Yes, I know what you are thinking,' he said gravely, somewhat embarrassed. 'My father was a Muslim. In 1947, the Muslims in our village were either killed or forced to flee to Pakistan. My father and a few others survived though, agreeing to convert to Sikhism.'

There were many more such secret Muslims left in the Indian Punjab, he said. Muslims who owned land were slaughtered or driven across the border, while people like his father who were landless but rendered valuable services to the 'higher' castes as iron-smiths, water-carriers, horse-carriage drivers or bangle-makers were spared their lives, provided they changed their faith. Hundreds, if not thousands, of Muslim women were abducted by Sikh and Hindu men, and forcibly married off. Some of these Muslims had, five decades after the

Partition, completely forgotten their ancestral religion. Others, like him, he said, concealed their belief in Islam, their Muslim identity being a carefully guarded secret.

In their villages they were known by Sikh names and observed Sikh practices. But here in the 'Baba's court', as he put it, and among their co-religionists, they could drop the suffocating mask for a while.

Akbar, as I shall call him, was clearly not pleased with me. He sat on a wicker chair, at the entrance of the Waqf Board office, browsing through an Urdu newspaper, his spectacles delicately balanced on the tip of his nose. As I approached him, he put down the newspaper, and took off his grey woollen monkey-cap to scratch his hairless head.

'Tell me, what did those grave-worshipping Barelwis say to you about us? he asked with ill-concealed curiosity.

'They told me their version of the story,' I replied, not wanting to reveal more.

'Very well,' he said with an air of nonchalance, 'if you won't tell me, I shall tell you what I think of them.'

Baba Rattan, he proclaimed, like a judge giving his verdict, was a scheming imposter and a pathetic liar who had falsely claimed to be a companion of the Prophet.

'It was a cheap trick,' he snarled, 'to win instant popularity and money.'

'If he was really a companion of the Prophet, how is it that no Muslim badshah or nawab came to visit him? Why are the reliable historical accounts of the times silent about him?' he demanded to know.

'These people are incorrigible,' he said, violently clearing his throat and shooting out a blob of rubbery green phlegm into a tin spittoon.

'They worship graves and collect money in the name of the Sufis. Why, some days ago my own uncle, who was notorious for not saying his prayers, died, and now these illiterate fools have started worshipping at his grave, begging for wishes and making offerings!' he exclaimed, chewing his paan like cud, a trail of red juice slithering down his chin.

'Money is a bad, bad thing, my son,' he rued, shaking his head and twirling the end of his beard. 'All the religious strife that you see in the world today is only because of the love for money.'

Across the brick wall that encircled the diminutive dargah, the gleaming white marble domes of the newly renovated Haji Rattan gurdwara loomed like a skyscraper. Wading through puddles of slush, passing by old, neglected Muslim graves— this was till 1947 a large Muslim colony—I made my way to the Sikh temple, set in a sprawling complex built on the banks of a large pond. Inside, a bearded *granthi*, dressed in starched, tight breeches and a white kurta, a short kirpan slung around his waist, was seated under a canopy reciting from the Granth Sahib. I joined a group of Sikh men on the thickly carpeted floor, listening for a while to the shabad of the Sufi Baba Farid about the pathos of the lover looking for his beloved, sung in a deep, mellifluous voice to the accompaniment of a dholak and the plaintive wail of the harmonium.

I asked the officious manager of the shrine to tell me about the history of the gurdwara. Did the name of the Sikh temple, I asked, suggest any connection with the Muslim Baba next door?

'All that you want to know is written there,' he answered, pointing to a freshly painted board that hung on a pole in the courtyard.

A young Sikh pilgrim translated the Gurmukhi inscription for me. The Sikh version of the legend of the Baba of Bhatinda gave it a twist to inflate Sikh pride and denigrate the Muslims.

Guru Gobind Singh, the last of the Sikh gurus, it claimed, had travelled to Bhatinda to meet Baba Rattan and deliver him from the cycle of death and rebirth. When a pack of local holy men learnt of the arrival of the Guru, they flocked to him, begging him to relieve them of an evil spirit, the one-eyed Kana Dev, whose insatiable hunger had driven him to murder, mayhem and destruction. The Guru, in his 'mind's eye' spied a fierce buffalo in the distance. He sent some of his followers to slay the animal, and sent the carcass to Kana Dev as a meal. The great hunk of raw meat finally satiated the devil's irrepressible appetite. The Guru then dispatched the demon-turned-believer to Sirhind to fight along with Banda Bahadur, his lieutenant, against the Muslim Mughals.

However, I was to soon discover that the Sikh association with Baba Rattan, neither ended nor, in fact, started there. Harvinder, a young Sikh, volunteered to take me around the gurdwara and tell me what he claimed was 'the real story' of the Baba.

'Baba-ji,' he said, as we settled on the banks of the holy pool at the rear end of the gurdwara, sipping tea and drinking in great quantities of pale sunshine, 'was actually a Brahmin, who went to Mecca and became a Muslim there'.

'He was a very pious man,' he said, raising his bushy eyebrows to indicate the Baba's great spiritual stature, and so the Prophet Muhammad gave him many costly parting gifts when he finally returned to India, and also blessed him with a long, long life.'

'But,' he said, lowering his voice and clearing his throat for a lengthy discourse, 'all this honour and wealth soon went to the Baba's head. Now, Shri Guru Nanak Dev-ji Maharaj was in the habit of visiting men, both Hindu and Muslim, who claimed to be religious, to admonish them for their evil ways. When he heard of the Baba, he came to Bhatinda to meet him. Rattan, being a Muslim, knew the art of black magic, and commanded two stones shaped like horses to rush at Guru

Nanak-ji to scare him away. The Guru-ji, however, was protected by God. As he lifted his palm in benediction, the horses suddenly stopped in their tracks and bowed before him. Then, the Guru-ji went to meet Rattan, and gently admonished him for not having conquered his ego. Rattan repented and mended his ways, leading the rest of his life as a good Muslim. Many years later, Shri Guru Gobind Singh-ji Maharaj, hearing of the Baba, also came to meet him and finally delivered him from the cycle of rebirth.'

I trailed behind Harvinder as he guided me around the gurdwara, pointing to places of local historical interest.

'Here,' he said, indicating an ancient neem tree, 'is where Shri Guru Gobind Singh-ji Maharaj tied his horse when he came to meet Baba Rattan.'

The tree was considered particularly holy, he told me, although the worship of relics is strictly prohibited in the Sikh religion.

Nearby, an immense stone shaped like a ball lay in a pile of dust, neglected and lonely.

'Baba Rattan flung this stone at Shri Guru Gobind Singh-ji Maharaj when he approached him,' Harvinder explained, his dark face lighting up with pride, 'but the Guru Sahib stopped it in mid-air with the tip of his finger.'

'Arrey, no!' interrupted an elderly Sikh man who had been eagerly following our conversation. 'That's not true. Guru Nanak and Baba Rattan once played marbles together with the stone.'

He wagged his head to and fro as if he had himself seen them play.

'Who knows, Babaji?' answered Harvinder reverentially, 'We weren't around that time. And that was so many centuries ago!'

The conducted tour proceeded along an extended pillared corridor that ran along one side of the gurdwara, and ended at the main entrance. Large oil paintings graced the spotless walls, depicting scenes from the lives of various Sikh gurus. All of them told tales of bloodshed, war and martyrdom: Sikh gurus being sawed apart by blood-thirsty, evil-looking Muslims; modestly clad women with halos around their heads being abducted by wild, bearded Pathans; little children being thrown up in the air and speared with menacing lances wielded by turbaned Mughal warriors.

'Our history,' said Harvinder gravely as he painstakingly explained each painting to me, 'is a ceaseless strife between Muslims and us.'

An hour later, we finally finished with the last painting and arrived, much to my relief, at the entrance gate. The never-ending display of gore had driven Harvinder into a sullen silence.

'So, what do you think of the paintings?' he asked, perhaps expecting me to burst into a volley of fiery imprecations against 'Muslim monsters'.

'All this may indeed be part of your history,' I said sympathetically. 'But, tell me, brother,' I asked out of genuine concern, 'why is there not a single picture of Guru Nanak himself here?'

Why, I went on, was Mardana the Muslim, Nanak's favourite disciple, absent from this graphic display of Sikh lore? And the Muslim divine Miya Mir, whom the fifth guru, Arjan Dev, had, in a spirit of brotherhood, chosen to lay the foundation of the Golden Temple? And what of Baba Farid, the Muslim Sufi whose verses abound in the Granth Sahib, some of which I had heard being sung at the gurdwara a short while ago? And what, indeed, of Baba Rattan himself, playing marbles with Guru Nanak or discoursing with Guru Gobind? Were these also not part of the rich Sikh tradition?

'Oh yes, that's true,' Harvinder readily admitted. Then, pondering for a while, he said slowly, 'To be honest with you, no one has ever thought of putting up pictures of these saints as well. Perhaps we should, some day.'

12

THE SUFIS OF JAMMU

A black blanket draped the sky like a shroud that had fallen over the town as the bus finally pulled into a parking lot outside Jammu's main bus-station. A sleeping mass of humanity, like corpses impatiently awaiting an undertaker, lay at the entrance, while street dogs sniffed piles of rotting garbage. A man dressed in a tattered election banner munched hungrily on a half-eaten cob of roasted corn that had been tossed aside in a drain clogged with dirt. A bare bulb glowed a jaundiced weak yellow from a string that trailed from a pillar, casting a pale pool of light on an old woman, who was asleep cradling a cur. On a concrete electric pole hung a rusty tin board announcing, 'Welcome to the City of Temples'. Below it, a cardboard banner preached, 'Clean City, Happy City,' in bold letters in English which few people could actually read, and even fewer understand. Perhaps it was not meant to be understood at all.

'See, a Donkey Is Urinating Here!' exclaimed a slogan painted on the white-washed wall of Rajnee Vaishno hotel. Little ceramic tiles with the Hindu sacred syllable, Om, a cross impaling a bleeding heart, and the Muslim holy number of 786 were set together on the wall in a rare display of inter-faith camaraderie, to indicate that this was holy ground and not a free public toilet. A malarial puddle of fermenting urine had formed at the base of the wall. Inter-faith dialogue, it seemed, had made little headway in Jammu.

A week before my arrival, a grenade had been lobbed by 'unidentified militants' into a crowded bazaar near one of Jammu's main temples, killing more than a dozen people, and injuring numerous others. Tension between Hindus and the minority Muslims in the town had come to a head. Helmeted policemen, armed with stout batons, had been posted outside places of religious worship, and metal gates had been set up at the entrance to the little Muslim island around the town's Friday mosque, to stave off angry Hindu mobs. Posters screaming for revenge and extolling Hindu pride had mysteriously covered the city walls. The local newspapers were abuzz with fears of further attacks from 'Islamic terrorists' and warned of more bloodshed to come. People in the streets talked in hushed tones of a possible civil war, of mass massacres of Muslims and Hindus. But in the dargah of Pir Raushan 'Ali Shah, Jammu's oldest Muslim mystic, the brutal killings seemed to have had almost no impact on the Hindus and Muslims gathered there that evening. They went about their quiet, humble devotions, seemingly unconcerned about, or, more likely, benumbed by the gory events unfolding around them. Such was also the ambience at the other Sufi shrines dotting the City of Temples that I had come to explore.

Till 1947, a majority of the inhabitants of Jammu, as in neighbouring Kashmir, the two wings of the largest princely state of India, were Muslim. Here, as elsewhere in India, Islam attracted a large number of followers principally through the missionary endeavours of Sufi mystics. Scores of 'low' castes, victims of an inhuman caste system, sought to escape Brahminical tyranny by embracing Islam. Numerous warrior-caste Rajputs, too, converted to Islam, establishing close relations with powerful Muslim families. A smaller number of Muslims made their way to this region from Iran and Central

Asia, some claiming descent from the Prophet himself, although the authenticity of such a claim was often debatable.

The Islam of the masses differed greatly from the scripturalist, hide-bound Islam of the clerics, of the pen-wielding and fatwa-hurling 'ulama. It was an earthy, lively and colourful religion, with a fair share of festivals and melas, feisty folk songs and syrupy love poetry, and ballads, epics, lore on the cults of the Sufi saints—intermediaries between ordinary men and a distant God. For the hard-working peasant, popular religious cults promised deliverance from worldly woes through simple acts of charity and devotion.

Believed to be in close communion with God, Sufi saints had a large following, not only among Muslims, but other communities as well. As divine beings and repositories of enormous shakti or miraculous power, they were accommodated into the expansive pantheon of Hindu folk deities, and feared, propitiated, beseeched and adored like the latter. In many cases, Hindus, Sikhs and Dalits outnumbered Muslims as regular worshippers at the shrines of these saints. Caste and religious differences remained—they were too deeply embedded to be set aside by devotion to a common god—but collective participation in worship at Sufi dargahs helped to foster a culture of limited tolerance. While orthodox Hindus balked at the thought of consuming food cooked by a Muslim or even touched by his 'polluting' shadow, Hindu worshippers at dargahs happily accepted sweets and holy water from Muslim sajjada nashins—'keepers of the prayer carpets' and descendants of the buried saints. Bonds between Hindus and Muslims were cemented at nightly vigils at Sufi shrines. Hindu devotees willingly accepted Muslim mystics as spiritual guides. Likewise, courting the wrath of their conservative co-religionists, some Sufis readily accepted Hindu meditational practices, hanging upside down in a well by a rope for forty days or sleeping on a bed of thorns, or going so far as to compose mystical poetry glorying Hindu religious figures.

By the turn of the twentieth century, however, this shared religious tradition that had once flourished at Sufi shrines could no longer withstand the mounting tide of Hindu-Muslim antagonism that now threatened to pit communities, who, for centuries, had lived together as peaceful neighbours, against each other. Aggressive Hindu organizations established a strong foothold in Jammu town, and found favour with middle-class Hindus and the nobility attached to the ruling Dogra house. Their agenda was to crush the Muslims, either by converting them en masse to Hinduism, or by stripping them of their rights and forcing them into submission. The Muslim Conference held under the fiery Chaudhri Ghulam Abbas, who split from the National Conference led by the Kashmiri Shaikh Abdullah after the latter opened the party to Hindus in the late 1930s, was hailed by the Muslims of Jammu, particularly by those in the hilly tracts of Poonch and Rajouri. It allied itself with the Muslim League, and as the date for the withdrawal of the British from India drew closer, it demanded that Muslim-majority Jammu and Kashmir join Muslim Pakistan. Muslims, it insisted, were a nation by themselves, distinct from and at war with their Hindu neighbours.

In mid-1947, the maharaja of Kashmir, notorious for his extreme Hindu right-wing leanings, along with fiercely anti-Muslim Hindu organizations, unleashed a wave of terror on the Muslims of Jammu. Scores of Muslims were slaughtered in cold blood, and entire Muslim villages destroyed. This prompted the Muslims of Poonch, a war-hardened race of fighters who had recently been stripped of their weapons by the maharaja, to rise in revolt, taking into control a vast chunk of land along the western tracts of the state, and declaring what they called the state of Azad or 'Free' Kashmir. The genocide of Muslims in Jammu continued unabated thereafter. According to rough estimates, more than 200,000 Muslims were killed in the region by the maharaja's troops and militant Hindu groups. A further 500,000 Muslims fled across the border as refugees to the newly created state of Pakistan. As the revolt in Poonch gathered momentum and fierce Pathan warriors, abetted by the Pakistan army, came down the mountains in hordes to the Kashmir Valley, ostensibly to the rescue of their beleaguered co-religionists, the maharaja hurriedly signed a controversial Instrument of Accession with India. Indian forces flew into Srinagar airport the next day, and the war between India and Pakistan over Kashmir began, a war that, more than half a century later, threatens to plunge the region into a nuclear nightmare.

The pogrom of 1947 almost decimated the entire Muslim population of Jammu town. A few Muslims stayed behind in the smouldering ruins of what, for centuries, had been their homes. It was only after a semblance of peace was gradually restored that Muslims began settling down, once again, in the town, huddled together in little pockets to ensure safety in a hostile environment. Later, migratory Muslim cattle-grazing Gujjars and goat-herding Bakkarwals from Poonch and Rajouri, smaller groups of co-religionists from the mountain fastnesses of Doda and Kishtwar, itinerant peddlers and government servants from the Kashmir Valley, settled down in these pockets as well. As a result, the Sufi shrines of Jammu that had been neglected for years, slowly crept back to life.

Little historical evidence is available on the Sufis of Jammu. All we have are legends, passed on from one generation to the next, constantly being retold and refurbished in the process. While sifting fact from fiction in stories of flying fakirs and dervishes drunk on divine love is a folklorist's delight, it is a historian's nightmare. For their followers, however, no story is too fanciful to be disbelieved, for the Sufis are denizens of a world beyond cold logic and bland reason.

The earliest known Sufi to have settled in Jammu was a certain Pir Raushan 'Ali Shah. Popularly known as Nau Gazi

Pir, he is said to have been a full nine *gaz* tall. According to the *Gulab Namah*, a late mediaeval text on the history of Jammu, he was a companion of the Prophet Muhammad, suggesting, therefore, that he was born in the sixth century AD. A more convincing date of his birth, however, is sometime in the thirteenth century, when he is said to have arrived in Jammu around the time of the Mongol invasion led by the notorious Timur the Lame, of the flourishing Muslim cities of Iran and West Asia. At the base of an old crumbling wall, Raushan 'Ali now rests under a stone platform, a raised exclamation mark fifteen feet long.

'He was a giant indeed,' said Ram Lal, drawing his arms as wide as he could while beads of perspiration dribbled into the cone of spiced puffed rice he was making for me at his stall outside the unassuming entrance of the shrine.

'In those days, people ate nuts and consumed pure milk and ghee, not like the adulterated stuff that you get nowadays, so they grew to great heights!' He shook his head furiously, lamenting the rapidly declining standards of Indian food products.

Legends about the giant Pir abound. He is said to have performed many great miracles, and to have won the heart of the then king of Jammu, the Hindu ruler Raja Sarpala Dharma, by presenting the latter with a fine Arabian steed. The raja is said to have insisted that the Pir settle down in his town to protect it with his prayers from being attacked by the marauding Turks. After the Pir died, the raja constructed the imposing domeless Dargah Naugazi Pir for him. To date, Hindus and Muslims worship together at his grave.

I met Inayat—a rugged Punjabi-Muslim lad with a finely chiselled nose, a pair of chocolate-coloured eyes like liquid lozenges, with the face of a mediaeval saint—when worshippers trailed out of the mosque after the evening prayers had given over. A well-trimmed moustache crawled over his upper lip and a faint stubble covered his firmly carved jaw. Altogether, a very attractive face, I decided, and I took to him at once.

He drew up to me, his salwar kameez flapping in the gentle breeze like a bird in flight.

'You wouldn't mind if I asked you something, would you?' he asked, lowering his eyes like a bashful maiden.

Apparently, so he suggested, word had spread that although not a Muslim, I seemed, as he put it, 'to know more about Islam than the Muslims themselves', and he wanted to confirm the rumour for himself.

At first, my story did not convince him at all. He curled up his nose, and knitted his eyebrows together suspiciously. 'You may well be a government spy, or, who knows, an agent of the RSS,' he said gravely, referring to the dreaded anti-Muslim Hindu organization.

I had earlier heard similar stories before, of my being in the employ of a dreaded Muslim outfit or being an unofficial employee of the Mossad, so I smiled to myself and took the accusation in my stride.

We headed for a smoke in the shade of a tarpaulin stretched between two electric poles, sat on inverted oil cans, and slurped syrupy tea from stained cups. After three rounds of tea and twice the number of cigarettes, Inayat's initial apprehensions seemed to have been put to rest.

'All right, I believe you,' he said reluctantly, but added firmly, 'if you know so much about Islam, why don't you become a Muslim?'

I evaded the question by asking for another round of tea.

By the time we parted, we had agreed to spend the next few days together combing the town for its many hidden Sufi shrines. I assured him, however, as we parted later that evening, that I had no plans of putting myself through the painful ritual of circumcision.

The sun shone in all its fierce glory the next morning, while little slivers of cloud carelessly stretched their arms out across the sky. The rickshaw crawled up the narrow street packed with early morning shoppers and office-goers; cows lazily munched on banana skins and sturdy Gujjar women gingerly balanced pails on their heads, driving their bleary-eyed buffaloes from door to door to supply fresh milk.

I followed Inayat down a side lane, negotiating my way through piles of human and animal refuse. A mountain of rubble, pyramid-like, stood at the far end of the lane leading to the eternal resting place of Pir Lakhdata, the 'Giver of Hundreds of Thousands', who now rested ingloriously under a pile of humble rocks. At the entrance to the grave a little clay lamp, blackened with years of soot, sent up a curl of smoke. A man, visibly a Hindu, his neatly-ironed dhoti tucked between his thighs, lowered his head and folded his hands as he passed by. A burly matron, her thunderous bosom shivering like a blob of jelly, bent down with difficulty to scoop out some soot from the lamp and smeared it on her forehead.

We walked over to a tea-stall: a little kettle hissing on a kerosene stove, with empty wooden crates for stools. The forlorn Giver of Hundreds of Thousands, Inayat lamented as he slurped his tea, no longer had a sajjada nashin to take care of his grave.

'No one even cares to remember who he was,' he whined pitifully.

The owner of the stall, a Brahmin, his holy thread wound round his hairy chest, lifted up a dozen jalebis with a perforated ladle from the frying pan. 'Oh no!' he protested, 'He's the saint of this bazaar, and even if others have forgotten him, I certainly haven't.' He placed two plates of the sticky sweets on a box before us and began his story.

Pir Lakhdata's real name was Sultan. He was a poor and pious Muslim from a village called Nigahia near Multan. One day, Guru Nanak, along with his two favourite disciples, the Hindu Bala and the Muslim Mardana, passed through the village. Knowing Nanak to be a great fakir, Sultan offered him a cupful of parched gram. Nanak accepted the gift but gave it

to Mardana to eat. Thinking that perhaps Nanak did not accept
solid food, Sultan offered him a bowl of milk. Once again,
Nanak took the gift and handed it, this time, to his other
companion, Bala, to drink. Sultan was greatly distressed at the
thought that perhaps Nanak had refused to eat anything touched
by him because he was a Muslim. Being a true Sufi, Nanak
could discern his thoughts in his mind's eye. 'There is no
difference between a Hindu and a Muslim,' the fakir announced,
setting at rest Sultan's unfounded fears. Touched by his simple
devotion and faith, Nanak blessed him, saying, 'Because of
your generosity you shall become famous as the giver of
hundreds of thousands, as Lakhdata.'

Few seemed to remember the story today, however.

'He was some sort of sadhu, but who knows, that was a long
time ago,' said a chirpy schoolboy labouring under an overloaded
satchel.

'A powerful Pir, they say, but I don't know,' said a corpulent
Bania from behind his cash-box in a cloth shop, shrugging his
shoulders to confess his ignorance.

The Lakhdata bazaar was flooded with provocative saffron
flags, its walls splattered with shrill appeals to 'restore Hindu
pride' by helping to construct a temple in distant Ayodhya.
Meanwhile, the little shrine of the 'Giver of Hundreds of
Thousands', once the patron saint of the locality, was fast
disappearing under a growing pile of rubble.

The crowded mini-bus dropped us off at a crossing outside the
forbidding walls of the airport at Satwari. At a distance, the
tarmac glimmered like a lake in the searing mid-day sun. We
waded through the mirage for a third of an hour, till the green
dome and the welcome arch of the dargah came into view. A
party of Sikh men rode out of the arch on cycles, while a group
of soldiers marched in carrying their shoes in their hands. A
stone plaque erected by an armed regiment on a pillar at the

entrance commemorated the holy spot. A bleating goat, proudly displaying a necklace of marigold flowers, was tethered to the pillar. A clump of peasants, mostly Sikhs, stretched out on the cool marble floor under a gently purring fan. An elderly Sikh man bent to touch the steps leading inside the shrine with his hand, then lifted it to his forehead. Trellised screens shaded the shrine from the relentless glare of the sun. Inside, under a bed of roses lay the grave of one of the most popular Sufis of Jammu, the enigmatic Baba Budhan Ali. A young lad with a crocheted skullcap, striped saffron, white and green like the Indian flag, pressed the length of the grave with his bony hands, massaging the tired body of the slumbering saint.

Inayat scouted around for the custodian of the shrine, but he was nowhere to be seen. A distraught woman sitting in the courtyard on a strawberry-pink straw mat in the shade of an expansive tree, removing lice from her hair with a comb, announced that he had gone to the market to buy a chicken. Lice crackled like popping corn between the painted tips of her thumbnails.

A middle-aged Sikh man, his sword drawn provocatively across his waist, his limpid beard turning yellow at the edges, beckoned us into a corner.

'Myself Tejinder Singh,' he announced for all to hear, squeezing my limp wrist in his powerful sweaty grip.

'Come, come,' he said, dusting the ground with his handkerchief. 'Sit with me and I shall tell you all you want to know about Baba-ji.'

Baba Budhan 'Ali Shah, or so we were told, christened Sayyed 'Ali Shamsuddin at birth, was the son of an illustrious family of Sayyeds of the village of Talwandi, near Lahore. At a young age Sayyed 'Ali abandoned all worldly pleasures, and became a disciple of the great master of the Qadri order, Hazrat Pir Jama'at 'Ali Shah. Thereafter, he survived on a frugal diet of a cupful of milk a day. Talwandi, where he was born and had grown up, was Guru Nanak's ancestral village. As seekers with a similar quest, the young Sayyed 'Ali and Nanak became close friends. They also spent much time together meditating and discussing spiritual matters. Legend has it that Nanak blessed the young Sayyed with a long life, which is how the latter earned the title of the 'Old Baba'. Popular lore has it that he lived for over 200 years, and was visited even by the last of the Sikh gurus, Gobind Singh.

Given the Baba's association with the Sikh Gurus, it is hardly surprising that Sikh devotees outnumber Muslims at the shrine. Tejinder Singh, like many other Sikhs who were present at the dargah, was a regular visitor. That day he had come with his entire family—his elderly father, bent over a stick, his left eye covered with a green cloth patch, like a pirate gone to seed; his frail mother with her embroidered dupatta modestly wrapped around her head; and his wife, dressed in a shimmering silk salwar kameez, imitation gold rings dripping like giant globes from her ears, rocking a squealing infant to sleep in her arms.

Tejinder Singh beamed with pride, slapping his sides with his hairy hands in uncontrollable excitement.

'You see here,' he cried out, grabbing the child from its protesting mother, 'this is my son, my very own *puttar*. And he's going to be called Budhan Singh, because Baba Budhan has gifted him to us.'

'Many many years we tried and waited,' he said, rivulets of perspiration flowing down his face, 'but now my wife has given birth to this boy, all thanks to the Baba.'

Mrs Singh Jr tugged at the dupatta over her head, stuffing its corner into her mouth in suitable embarrassment, while her husband burst out laughing in child-like glee.

The next morning I met Inayat at the Tawi bridge. A wizened priest, his face lined like a crumpled parchment, clanged a metal plate at the entrance of a roadside shrine. A group of women circumambulated the shrine with folded hands and closed eyes, bowing low before a tulsi bush. Below the shrine's hillock, the Tawi, a scrawl of a river, little more than a sewage drain, seemed eerily still, like a snake in deep slumber. Huge copper-coloured boulders on the banks jutted out like camels' humps. A solitary *dhobi* pounded away at a pile of clothes on the rocks, while his donkey, tied to a tree, looked on bemused. Two trucks stood somberly mid-stream, spouting clouds of black smoke. A sadhu in saffron busied himself with his early morning ablutions.

We scrambled down the boulders leading to the edge of the river, and waded through little cakes of fresh human waste on which a swarm of flies and silver-green beetles were feeding. Thorny cacti jutted out from crevices in weathered rocks, and brambles twisted themselves in knots like a sadhu's matted hair. A lone frowning eagle flew overhead in circles, inspecting us like a stern border guard—Pakistan was only a few miles down the Tawi. On a clear summer night the lights of Sialkot, the nearest town across the frontier, were visible from the Jammu Fort that perched precariously on a promontory on the other side of the river. Snatches of sound drifted from above: the roaring of an auto-rickshaw straining up the slope; the shrill horns of mini-buses; a pack of dogs fighting over a bitch; and the garbled rumblings of an early morning drunkard roundly cursing the world.

The sun shone brightly when we finally got to the shrine of Pir Mittha, the 'Sweet Saint', with thorns invading our sandals, our faces caked with a fine layer of dust and grime. We sat in the shade of an enormous banyan tree and unpacked our soggy sandwiches. Soon, we were joined by a middle-aged man, dressed in a peppermint green salwar kameez, and a white prayer cap. Muhammad Rashid was the sajjada nashin of the shrine. His family, descendants of the Pir, had been custodians of the dargah for as long as he could remember. An inviting, comforting calm seemed to envelop his face. I imagined a halo dancing gently behind his head, the wings of cherubic angels shading it from the sun. The whiff of *ittar* from his robes beat off the overpowering stench of excreta rising from the wastes below.

A pimply teenager brought us a tray laden with iced sherbet and ginger biscuits. Rashid introduced him as Rajesh, a very good boy indeed, he said with an approving nod. Then, taking me by the hand, he led me into the shrine.

Fresh rose petals were strewn along the length of a raised grave draped in a green silk sheet. Carved marble stoppers stood at the four corners, under a marble screen. Knots of red thread tied on the gaps in the screen reminded the Pir of the prayers of a long queue of supplicants. In one corner a framed picture of the grand mosque at Medina, flooded with pilgrims, hung on the wall. Rashid lifted his hands in prayer, reciting a lengthy Arabic litany.

'Ameen,' he said gravely, wiping his face with his cupped hands. Inayat and Rajesh repeated solemnly after him.

He dropped a rose petal and a ball of sugar in my hand. We walked backwards out of the shrine, bowing slightly as we left through the low door, and settled down in the warm shade of the banyan tree. Over another round of sticky, sweet sherbet Rashid now began to tell us the story of the 'Sweet Pir'.

Pir Mittha, also known as Sayyed Qutb-e-'Alam, 'The Pole of the World', was born in the town of Sabzvar in Iran sometime in the late fifteenth century. Like other great Sufis, he was an intrepid traveller, wandering from city to city, and from one country to another, in search of God and other God-fearing men like himself. He is said to have reached Jammu during the reign of Raja Ajaeb Dev, and taken up residence in a cave on the banks of the Tawi. Meanwhile, the raja's wife had been afflicted by a dreaded disease which no doctor or pundit could cure. One morning, Baba Chiddhi the Bhishti, the royal water-carrier, went down to the Tawi to fill a pitcher for the raja's kitchen. On his way back, he passed by Pir Mittha, sitting outside his cave and sunning himself. The Pir made so bold as to touch the royal pitcher with his hand. Baba Chiddhi, a good orthodox Hindu himself, flew into a frenzy and flung the pot on the ground—the 'polluting' touch of a Muslim mleccha having made the water unfit to be consumed by a Hindu. Baba Chiddhi picked up another pot, walked down to the river and filled it with water. Pir Mittha played the same prank once again. And once again, the Baba reacted angrily. Several broken pitchers later, when the Baba's legs began to ache with the effort, he reluctantly walked back to the palace bearing a pot of water 'polluted' by the touch of a Muslim. He was, however, careful to conceal the fact from the raja.

No sooner had the queen drunk the water that Baba Chiddhi gave her, Rashid went on, as if he were a personal witness to the miraculous event, than she was cured of her illness. The raja had Baba Chiddhi hauled to his court, suspecting the latter of having cast a powerful spell on his wife. Fearing for his life, the hapless Bhishti finally confessed about the 'polluting' touch of the Muslim whom he had encountered.

To his utter amazement, the raja, instead of dispatching him promptly to the gallows, rewarded him with a bag of gold. Convinced that the Muslim was a true man of God, the raja rushed to his cave and fell at his feet. He begged for his blessings and pleaded with him to make Jammu his home. Pir Mittha willingly conceded to the raja's desperate entreaties.

Attracted by the force of the Pir's personality and stories of his miraculous powers, many Hindus of the town, probably the low-caste Bhishtis led by Baba Chiddhi himself, converted to Islam at his hands. Predictably, this stirred the wrath and envy of the Hindu priests, dismayed at the thinning number of their flocks. A certain Gorakhnathi sadhu, Gharib Nath, led the Hindu opposition to the Muslim fakir, demanding that he put a firm halt to his missionary endeavours. A contest of miracles ensued between the two. Sadhu and Pir both flew in the air, and sought to outwit each other in a series of spectacular airborne acrobatic displays. The fierce war in the firmaments remained inconclusive, however, the sadhu and the Sufi being equally powerful. By the time they were back on earth, the two foes had turned into friends. They set up home together in Pir Mittha's cave, where they lived together for many years.

Then, one day, or so it seems, the sadhu decided to renounce the world. He left through a tunnel in his cave-house, never to return again. On hearing the news of the disappearance of their guru, his distraught disciples appeared before the Pir, and pleaded with him to accept them as his followers. Fiercely loyal as he was to his friend, the Pir declined. They were to remain devoted to their guru, he insisted, but the disconsolate followers of the sadhu pressed on. At last, the Pir relented somewhat, granting them the right to fashion themselves as Pirs, after him, although they were, he said firmly, to continue owing allegiance to their original master. Thus, the sprawling Shaivite Nath monastery that now occupies the grotto of the Pir and the sadhu is still referred to as Pir Khoh or the 'Cave of the Pir', and in memory of Pir Mittha, its abbot is called a Pir as well.

Till recently, said Rashid, nearing the end of his story and wiping sweat from his forehead, there was much give-and-take between the dargah of Pir Mittha and the temple at Pir Khoh. On festive occasions, the dargah authorities would send uncooked food to the monastery. The late Pir Sindhia Nath, head priest of the monastery, had once even volunteered to pay for Rashid's father's pilgrimage to the holy cities of Arabia.

'Things are fast changing now, however,' he said gravely. 'Hindus and Muslims see each other as enemies. All signs of the impending Day of Doom.'

Yet, despite the growing Hindu-Muslim chasm, and Rashid's lamentations, Hindus continue to flock to the shrine. Rajesh, who had been listening attentively to our conversation, while shooing away annoying flies and plying us with plates of sweets, was one of them, a member of the Kashp caste, a Hindu community that had had a special bond with the Pir since time immemorial. A family of Kashps stood before the shrine with folded hands. A middle-aged Kashp stirred a great vat with an iron ladle, serving generous blobs of steaming rice cooked in sugar syrup, on paper plates, a humble offering to the Pir reputed for his fondness for sweetmeats. Hindu and Muslim mendicants and devotees sat together on the floor in the scorching heat, partaking of the holy offering.

Like many residents of Jammu town, the Kashps are recent arrivals. Their ancestral home is across the border—the villages around the town of Sialkot, now in Pakistan. Pir Mittha is the patron saint of the Kashps, a status that he has enjoyed for several centuries. It is rumoured that they are children of Baba Chiddhi the Bhishti, one of Pir Mittha's first disciples. For their part, the Kashps, perhaps seeking to bestow their caste with a loftier lineage, insist that they are Rajputs, descended from the sun and the moon.

In 1947, when terror struck Punjab, the Kashps, like the other non-Muslims of the area, were forced to flee across the border to India. Thousands of people were slaughtered by blood-thirsty mobs. But, said Himmat Singh, labouring at the cauldron of sweet rice, not a single Kashp was killed or injured in the mayhem that uprooted the entire community from its ancestral homeland.

'It was all by the grace of the Pir,' he insisted, humbly bowing in the direction of the grave.

If the Pir had been unable to prevent them from being hounded out of their homes, he had at least saved their lives and ensured them a safe passage to their new land. And for that blessing they remained grateful.

The cult of the Panj Pirs, the 'Five Pious Elders', has millions of followers in north India. In hundreds of villages and towns, little stone platforms with five raised box-like compartments commemorate the five saints, whose identities are as obscure as the origins of the cult. Some historians believe that the origin of the cult lies in the worship of the five Pandavas of the epic Mahabharata. Others argue that it grew out of the popular veneration of the Panjatan Pak, the 'Holy Family of Five,' Muhammad, his daughter Fatima and her husband Imam 'Ali, and their two sons, Hassan and Hussain. In some places the five holies consist of Hindu heroes, in others of Muslim saints, and in yet others, of a curious mélange of the two.

The dargah of the Panj Pirs in Jammu is built on a cliff behind the stately Edwardian Hari Niwas—the royal Dogra palace now converted into a hotel—off the main highway leading to Srinagar. Vehicles travelling on the highway generally stop at the dargah, and passengers drop coins into a tin fastened to a tree trunk, before embarking on the perilous journey ahead.

Kuldip Singh Charak, a burly Dogra Rajput Hindu, the custodian of this shrine of the five Muslim saints, peeked through a hole in the wall, and then welcomed us in. We sat on a sagging charpoy in a room adjacent to the dargah, its walls decorated with pictures of Mecca and Medina and a turbaned Sufi saint playfully perched atop a giant fish.

'You must be surprised seeing a Hindu caretaker of a Muslim shrine,' he said smilingly, reading my thoughts as he poured tea from a round-bottomed kettle in a steel tumbler.

Indeed I was, I said, and pleasantly surprised at that.

'Oh, Hindu, Muslim, these things really mean nothing, you know,' he said, swatting an army of flies that threatened to invade the pile of cakes he had spread out on a low-lying table.

He had married a Muslim woman, the daughter of the first custodian of the shrine, who had been appointed to that position by the raja, no less. Their marriage had, predictably, created a scandal, but frayed tempers cooled down after a while, and after his father-in-law's death, he had inherited the post of custodian of the shrine.

Kuldip confessed that he knew little about the holy men whom he tended to with such devotion. It is said, 'but only

God knows really', he added, that the five Pirs were actually five brothers who, having fled the snares of the world, had settled here to perform great austerities. Then, they went different ways, the first to Basohli, the second to Paramandal, the third to the mountains of Rajouri, the fourth to Punjab, and the last to faraway Calcutta.

One day, long after they were dead and gone, the five brethren appeared in a dream before the raja of Jammu and scolded him for sleeping with his feet in the direction of the *chillah* where they had spent years in deep meditation. When he awoke the next morning, the penitent raja ordered the spot the brothers had indicated to him to be dug up. An embroidered umbrella and five large kettledrums, announcing the presence of the five brothers, appeared at the same spot, much to the consternation of the rag-tag archaeological team. The raja, suitably impressed, arranged for a shrine to be constructed at the spot, appointing his Muslim royal charioteer as its custodian.

A group of Hindu pilgrims on their way to the temple of Vaishno Devi up the hills beyond Katra spilled out of a jeep that screeched to a sudden halt. Bowing their heads at the entrance of the dargah, they folded their hands in humble supplication. Kuldip dipped his hand into a plastic bowl full of little sugar flakes blessed by the five saints to distribute the prasad to them. A woman, bent with age, probably a Hindu from the red felt dot that she sported on her forehead, approached us. Taking out a ten-rupee note tucked away safely in the warmth of her blouse, she stuffed it into the tin donation box.

She said she lived in a village in distant Doda, and had come to plead with the Pirs to bless her daughter with a son. Seven years ago her daughter had got married, taking with her more than Rs 1 lakh as dowry. That was nearly half of what her now deceased husband had saved up working all his life as a mason. Having failed to produce what she had been primarily intended for—a son to carry on her husband's name—her daughter was constantly being harassed by her in-laws. They beat her up every day, and demanded more dowry. To the latest demand of Rs 50,000 had been added a scooter, a fridge and a camera. If these demands were not met, her daughter would be promptly sent back to her mother's home, suitably disgraced.

Tears rolled down the old woman's wrinkled cheeks, and she burst out sobbing into the folds of her dupatta. Her journey of woe had taken her far and wide—to the temple of the Mother at Katra, to the sprawling temple of Ram in Jammu, even to a gurdwara and a church. She had fasted long days, and spent much money on earning the goodwill of a motley crew of priests. All these ardent exercises, it seemed, had failed to move the hard-hearted gods to pity. She was now in the court of the Pirs, having heard that they were powerful beings capable of granting her wishes. Her own sons had scolded her for setting off to the dargah to plead her case. A Hindu widow visiting a Muslim shrine, they told her in no uncertain terms, was a disgrace to proud Hinduhood. They were, she confirmed my suspicions, active members of a certain all-India Hindu militant group that dressed in khaki shorts and black caps, wielded batons, and on occasions daggers, and specialized in dispatching Muslims to their graves. Clearly she had a low opinion of her sons.

'We are all creatures of God, no? The same red blood runs in our veins,' she mused philosophically.

She had desperately sought to explain these elementary facts of biology to her sons, but they had simply refused to listen.

'In any case,' she said, heaving a deep sigh, 'I told them that if a Muslim can help me out, why should I refuse? Would you turn away a doctor on your deathbed just because you didn't like his face?'

The vision of their harried mother hurtling to the grave is said to have melted the hearts of her cruel sons, and they finally relented, allowing her to travel to Jammu—a journey of some ten hours down the mountains—for her tryst with the five Muslim holy men.

Inayat remained curiously silent on our way back as we trudged down the highway. The sun, now a giant orange ball of fire, was slipping below the flat plain which stretched beyond the Tawi into Pakistan that lay somewhere in the distance.

'How can an ordinary mortal, dead and lying below layers of mud and stone, be expected to hear the poor woman?' he spat in disgust.

'All this is a load of mumbo-jumbo,' he said with an air of finality, 'an easy way for charlatans to make a fast buck. If I were that woman I would have given her son-in-law a sound thrashing instead of kowtowing before an imaginary saint.'

I could hardly have agreed more.

Baba Jiwan Shah's shrine, off the main road leading into a crowded bazaar from the Raghunath temple, was a hub of activity that morning. Giant shamianas were being fixed on to tall bamboo poles, and an army of workmen lolled around, drinking tea and smoking their beedis. The grand annual 'urs, the 'marriage' ceremony of the Pir, was to be held the next week, and several thousand people were expected to arrive. The Pir was long dead, of course, or so the rest of the world believed, but for his followers he continued to be an invisible guardian angel around his grave. His death anniversary was celebrated each year with great joy and jubilation, for in passing from this world to the next he had entered into holy 'matrimony' with God, and was now in closer proximity to Him than he had ever been while on earth. And because of this, it was said, he had even greater powers to intercede with God than when he was in his mortal garb.

One of the more recent of Jammu's many Sufis, Jiwan Shah was born in a village near Sialkot in 1852, as a scion of a Sayyed family that claimed direct descent from Muhammad. At the age of twenty-three he abandoned the world. On the instructions of his Sufi mentor, the venerable Chishti Pir Sain

Baqir 'Ali Shah, he spent the next twelve years meditating in a cave on the banks of the river Ravi near Akhnoor. Thereafter, he shifted to Jammu, where he spent a similar length of time in the precincts of a desolate graveyard.

Legend has it that one day, a Hindu peasant called Bicchu came down to the Tawi to hew logs of wood to sell in the market. As he looked ahead he saw to his horror the Baba immersed in the river, the water reaching up to his chin, muttering to himself in a strange, incomprehensible tongue. Taking him to be an evil sprite Bicchu ran to the town, hollering for help. Hearing him, a group of young men armed with sticks rushed down to the river. When they got there, on closer inspection they discovered that the strange creature was actually a very holy man. They fled from the scene, and made their way to the palace to inform the raja, Ranbir Singh, of the arrival of the drowning Baba in his dominion. The king, a great patron of holy men, rushed down to the river and pleaded with him to emerge on terra firma. He requested him with folded hands to grace his city with his presence, and when the Baba consented, he was borne in a royal palanquin by a bevy of servants to a house not far from the royal palace. There he was to live till he breathed his last in 1919, and the locality that grew around his house, where he is now buried, is today named in his honour.

Muhammad Aslam, the middle-aged sajjada nashin of the Baba's shrine, was bent over a basin shaving himself when I entered the shrine compound. He waved to me to sit on a cane chair and wait. Meanwhile, he grimacing as he sliced his chin with his clumsily wielded razor, complained of how the workers he had expected would paint the shrine before the festival had yet to arrive.

'People here have no sense of time or commitment,' he moaned.

The singing party, whom he had booked well in advance, had suddenly called off their visit. He had sent desperate messages to the halwai for sweets but had heard nothing from him in a week. The bulbs needed to be replaced, but the electrician was nowhere to be seen. All in all, the situation was spearheading towards a disaster.

More Hindus were expected at the festival than Muslims, Aslam said, as he slipped into a cool salwar kameez and planted himself on a bed next to me. The Baba had numerous Hindu disciples, and most of their descendants still revere the Baba. Impressed with the Baba's great powers, the maharaja of Kashmir, himself an orthodox Hindu, had gifted him a hukkah and a shawl, and had granted him a royal monthly stipend of Rs 15 and 8 annas to meet his expenses, a sum that is still duly paid to his successors from the public exchequer. The Baba, boasted Aslam, bursting with pride at his ancestor's royal connections, was also regularly invited to the palace to meet with the maharaja and his brother.

Jiwan Shah's Hindu following, however, was not limited to the aristocracy. Sona Shah, a humble trader, was another of the Baba's many Hindu admirers.

Munching on a samosa, Aslam blew out a curl of steam as he recounted the story of Sona Shah's first meeting with the Baba as if it had happened just the other day.

One day, Sona Shah was riding through the streets on a horse, harassing his debtors and forcing them to pay him their long-standing dues. Just then, the Baba, on his way home from the market, happened to pass by. The shouting and jostling, and the crowd of curious by-standers attracted his attention, and he made his way to the scene of the brawl.

Scolding the trader for his greed, he admonished him saying, 'Shame on you! Why are you wasting your life collecting money? Instead, you should spend it collecting spiritual merit. Don't sit on your mare like a princely bridegroom. You should be carrying ashes on your head!'

Suddenly, the stone-hearted Sona Shah fell off from his horse and floundered at the Baba's feet, begging for mercy. That day, he gave up all his wealth, and from then on remained in the Baba's service till the latter's death.

The story of Sona Shah was now becoming even more curious, and I was all ears as Aslam went on, his eyes aglow.

One day, Sona Shah began screaming in a frenzy, 'I see walls around me! Where should I go?'

The house shook with his ranting, and everyone trembled in fear. The Baba, however, simply ordered him to be silent. And, in compliance with his master's order, Sona Shah remained silent for the next twenty years. Hence he is more popularly known today as Sain Chup, the 'Silent Saint'.

Following Aslam's directions I went down the lane that led from the main road to the dargah. Off the corner, a stone arch topped with a mushroom-like dome stood over a short metal gate that led into a little structure built into the wall of the house of a wealthy mahajan, the caretaker of this modest roadside shrine. The gate squeaked as I entered, the powerful odour of incense filling the air like a cloud. A stone platform in a corner, marking the grave of Sain Chup, was suitably shrouded in silence. The Silent Saint had been entrusted with the onerous task of shooing away jinns and other such noisome creatures from his master's grave further ahead. He was assisted in his duties by the 'low' caste leather-worker Muluk Shah, and his female disciple, the Hindu Bania woman, Basanti Devi, who, after years of faithful service, were buried next to him labouring under little stretches of stone under the floor at the foot of the Silent Saint's grave.

I first heard about the dargah at Chamaliyal from Rajesh, at the shrine of Pir Mittha. His rich harvest of pimples simply refused to wilt under the careful ministration of numerous bottles of fairness cream and anti-acne lotion. Nor, it seems, did his earnest pleas at Pir Mittha's seem to have any effect. Despairing of the idea of being permanently saddled with a spotted face, he decided to pay a visit to the shrine at Chamaliyal in the hope of a miraculous cure. The Baba of Chamaliyal, he had heard, had special powers for curing various skin ailments. Different Sufi saints, it seemed, specialized in different cures. There was even a Baba to whom lovers in distress flocked. His special skill lay in uniting young men and women in holy matrimony by eventually winning over their distraught parents and clansmen.

I had almost given up hope of curing my facial scars, so an appointment with a divinely assisted folk skin specialist was, therefore, accepted with alacrity. Added to that was the lure of travelling to a village that nestled uncomfortably right on the bloodstained Line of Actual Control that divided India from Pakistan.

The rickety bus from Jammu to Ramgarh, a distance of some forty kilometres, took more than two hours to reach its destination, stopping every twenty minutes to pick up large crowds heading for the Baba's shrine. Lunch at Ramgarh was a simple fare— hot dal, *sarso ka saag* swimming in oil, and thick, crispy rotis, washed down with a glass of sweet, frothy lassi.

News had spread of a heavy exchange of fire the night before in the vicinity, between the Indian Border Security Force and the Pakistan Rangers. Luckily, Chamaliyal had been spared the fury of the gunshots, though it was said that some neighbouring villages on both sides of the Line of Actual Control had been hit.

'This happens almost every day,' said a burly, mustachioed Muslim Gujjar herdsman who sat facing me, seeking to put my mounting apprehensions at rest. 'It is actually news when the guns fall silent for a day or more,' he said, giving the recalcitrant goat kid that he cradled in his arms a playful spank.

Vans and buses were no longer plying to the border villages for fear of coming within the range of the continuous shelling. Our hopes of visiting the Baba's dargah-cum-beauty parlour seemed dim when an amiable Sikh rode up to us in his tonga. He offered to take us to the dargah for Rs 100. I readily agreed, and hopping on to the tonga, we set off for Chamaliyal, some five kilometres away.

As the tonga wobbled along the potholed road, we passed by lush green wheat fields, alternating with stretches of bright yellow mustard flowers, like a patchwork frock. Robust Sikh women carried bales of hay on their heads while herds of buffaloes lazed around in little muddy pools. A family of Gujjars moved ahead of us, their animals sending up large clouds of dust in the air. A tractor growled its way through an empty field, readying it for the next crop.

All along, the garrulous tonga-driver pointed out the local sights of importance.

'Here,' he said, indicating a field bursting with a rich harvest of carrots and onions, 'was where more than a hundred Muslim villagers were slaughtered overnight during the violence of 1947.'

He had not witnessed the event himself, and hardly any of those who had lived through those tumultuous times now remained. Prodding the tired horse, and downing a swig from a bottle containing a pale-yellow, foul-smelling liquid, he related a horrific tale of the bloody massacres of that eventful year, in which he and his family, along with several thousand other Sikhs and Hindus, had fled across to Jammu from Sialkot, and of how an equally large number of Muslims in Jammu had forcibly been pushed across into the newly formed state of Pakistan.

Several thousands had been slaughtered in the violence in the area, and villages that were home to Muslims, Hindus, Sikhs and Dalits were put through one of the most brutal experiments in ethnic cleansing the world had ever seen.

Almost an hour later, we passed by the village of Dagh, the last settlement on the Indian side of the Line of Actual Control. Fording the empty bed of a stream, the tonga strained up a narrow mud path, to emerge into a clearing. The Sikh tugged at the reins, and the tonga drew to an abrupt halt. With a dismissive wave of the hand he pointed out to a clump of eucalyptus trees hardly a stone's throw away.

'That's Pakistan,' he said rather matter-of-factly, as if one passed by Pakistan every other day.

A sudden wave of excitement welled up inside me sending shivers down my spine. Pakistan! So close, and yet so far!

The tonga trudged down the path in the direction of the trees as streams of sweat trickled down the horse's hairy black coat. Gradually, the low mud huts of Chamaliyal nestled together on a knoll came into view, faintly visible behind a thin film of dust. A deep sigh of relief escaped the horse's chained mouth and it trotted into the village, coming to an abrupt halt outside a gaudily painted welcome arch. We clambered off the tonga as a smart, uniformed Border Security Force guard barked at us, demanding to know what we were doing in the area.

'Casually visiting,' I said to him, too embarrassed to tell him of the appointment that we had at the Baba's beauty clinic. That did not seem to fully satisfy him, for no causal visitors, we were told, had ever come to the village before. Nevertheless he let us in.

A great green dome hovered over the box-like shrine under which the Baba lay in eternal rest. In the open courtyard, stretched in the shade of a large, gnarled peepul tree, the two Muslim-style graves of the Baba's closest disciples stood in silence. I walked towards the entrance with measured steps, half expecting a sudden cost-free facelift the moment I stepped in. Inside, a Muslim-style grave was draped in a green and ochre silk sheet with a heavy gold border. On the tiled walls were posters, not of Mecca and Medina as I had expected, but, and much to my surprise, of various Hindu gods and goddesses astride an assortment of beasts, armed with a range of fearsome weapons. A little pot of red powder and a conch lay at the foot of the grave. A soldier rang a little brass bell and invoked the name of the Baba, while a pack of pilgrims murmured their prayers.

'Victory to the Baba of Chamaliyal,' the crowd burst out, throwing their arms about and falling prostrate to the ground.

The dargah of the Pir had undergone a facelift even if I had not. It was now, for all practical purposes, a Hindu temple.

No one was quite sure, as I asked around, who the Baba of Chamaliyal actually was. Some said that they had heard rumours about him being a certain Hindu Rajput named Dalip Singh Minhas. A fading board hanging by a string outside the shrine revealed that the last custodians of the shrine had shifted to Pakistan in the wake of the holocaust following the Partition. Why would the descendants of a Hindu warrior flee to Muslim Pakistan, I wondered, but, again, nobody seemed to have even the faintest idea. Some others, whom I was more inclined to believe, suggested that the Baba might actually have been a Muslim Sufi, a wandering dervish.

I put together the pieces of the puzzle and formed a hazy picture. Chamaliyal, like almost the entire belt along the border, had been cleared of Muslims in 1947. The Baba's Hindu followers, who had comfortably fitted him into their elastic pantheon of deities, now tended to his little shrine. For the Hindus of the area, a Muslim saint, believed to be a powerful source of worldly benefit and divine succour, was hardly a novelty. Abandoned by its Muslim custodians, the shrine was now in the watchful care of the Border Security Force. With few or no Muslims visiting the shrine now, it was gradually being converted into a Hindu temple.

In any case, whether Muslim or Hindu, the Baba had clearly been a charismatic local hero. He is said to have been particularly popular among the peasant castes, and had led them in a bloody revolt against an oppressive landlord. In the great battle that ensued, the Baba was brutally martyred. Even after his head had been severed from his body he had kept up the fight. Holding his head in the palm of one hand, and brandishing his sword in the other, he finally fell on the spot where his grave is now located, but not before having dispatched scores of his enemies to their gory end.

Of the Baba's two closest disciples, one is said to have been martyred along with him, while the other fled the battlefield in fright. That night the Baba appeared to the traitor in a dream, cursing him with leprosy. The next morning the man awoke to discover his body covered with festering sores, and his limbs rotting away. He ran to the Baba's grave and begged him for mercy. The next night, the Baba visited him again, and, taking pity on him, instructed him to smear himself with the mud and water from a pond near his grave. The man did as he was told and, suddenly, the sores and rashes vanished. Soon, stories of the curative powers of the Baba's shrine spread far and wide. Large crowds began flocking to the shrine in the hope of finding a cure for various skin ailments.

Till today, patients arrive in Chamaliyal in droves from as far as Bihar in the east and Mumbai in the west, in the hope of an instant cure, making the Baba's shrine by far the most popular dermatological clinic in the whole of Jammu and Kashmir.

From a pit some ten-feet deep, a pack of pilgrims, some with their bodies festering with open, pus-filled sores, others with large purple blobs on their backs or shedding flakes of skin like dandruff, scooped up oodles of rich, loamy mud in tins, mugs and little plastic buckets, like a battalion of coolies in a Chinese coal mine.

'*Shakkar*,' explained a dark spindle of a man with a series of enormous boils on his thigh.

'The Baba's sugar,' he said excitedly, and invited me to jump into the pit to give him a helping hand.

From a row of taps on a cement tank nearby, water trickled into a row of copper pots. A long queue of sick men and women patiently waited for their share of the Baba's sherbet, the holy nectar. Armed with their packets of shakkar and bottles of sherbet, the patients made their way to the bathrooms—low-lying, unadorned concrete walls—where they lathered themselves with a rich chocolate-brown paste prepared from the holy substances. Five or more men bathed together at a time, furiously massaging the magic lotion on to their wounds. I could not think of a more effective way of promoting a free exchange of ailments, and hurriedly abandoned all hopes of a magic facelift.

A dozen pilgrim-patients sat on stools and on patches of grass, looking like a pack of angry ghouls, with the furious sun drying up the paste of mud and water on their faces and bodies into shrouds. Mahesh Kumar strode about in the pitiless sun like a neglected caged lion, caked, from head to toe, in the Baba's magic potion. Clearly, he had seen better days. He hailed from a town in eastern Bihar, where he ran a series of tea-stalls and the town's only gas station.

'I was great handsome man and all womens in town looking only at me alone,' he boasted, running his hairy hands over his cauldron-shaped belly, sighing heavily as he recalled his two mistresses and, less enthusiastically I noted, his wife.

Then, suddenly one day, he noticed a rash of boils on his groin, sprouting like little yellow mushrooms, that were excrutiangly painful and oozing pus. He consulted all the doctors in his town and in the neighbouring big city, but they had all thrown up their hands in despair. They jabbed needles into his arms and buttocks, prescribed costly pills and powders, suggested various diets and fasts, but the hardy mushrooms only grew more luxuriant.

'Doctor saying it is secret illness not possible for cure,' he noted somewhat embarrassedly.

Someone suggested to him to try out Chamaliyal Baba's magic lotion of shakkar and sherbet, and that was why he had travelled 1000 miles to this little outpost on the wilderness of the India-Pakistan border. His wife's desperate pleas and reminders of fierce fighting on the frontier had failed to deter his iron-willed determination to rid himself of his boils. His mistresses had flatly refused to entertain him till his groin was cleansed, he said, with a naughty gleam in his eye. The Baba's ministrations were working wonders, he claimed, adding that he would be going back to his waiting mistresses sooner than he had hoped.

The Baba's curative skills are in great international demand, it seems. Across the imaginary line that separates India from Pakistan, he is said to be even more sought after than on the Indian side of the blood-drenched border. Till the late 1980s,

I was told, pilgrims from Pakistan would cross the frontier in droves to attend the annual festival held at the shrine each June. Together, Hindus and Muslims, Indians and Pakistanis, would worship at the Baba's door, sing his praises, and feast and dance in merriment in a rare display of transnational bonhomie. Then, two days later, the Pakistani devotees would be herded back across the border, carrying with them bucketfuls of shakkar and sherbet to distribute to their ailing friends back home.

The violence raging in Kashmir, however, has now put a firm halt to the steady stream of the Baba's international clients. Despite this hopefully temporary business hitch, his cross-border trade still continues to flourish, albeit in a less spectacular way. While Pakistani citizens may no longer cross the border, the gallant Border Security Force arranges for buckets of mud and tankers of holy water from the dargah to be transported to the frontier, from where the Pakistan Rangers, sworn enemies of the Indian frontier guards for the rest of the year, collect the holy parcels to distribute among hordes of anxiously waiting devotees on the other side.

Dusk was falling like a dark curtain, turning the sky into a vast purple lake. The last remaining band of patients, having spent the entire day in the sun nursing their sores, wound their way back to the hall, rolling out their mattresses on the bare floor. Rajesh went into the shrine to tie a red string on the grill fencing the grave, just in case the Baba, weighed down by the heavy rush of his flood of devotees, forgot about his case.

'Not very likely,' he said, half-amused, 'but why take any chances?'

I strolled over to the Border Security Force bunker just behind the shrine and looked beyond. A hundred metres ahead, all was quiet in the humble huts of the Pakistani village of Sayyedan Wali. A tall border watchtower, its green and white flag drooping in the still air, stood sternly to attention. A bus gently rolled down a road puffing out clouds of smoke.

'Arrey! You there!' boomed a loud voice tearing me away from my short-lived reverie.

A hard, cold hand gripped my shoulder, forcing me to turn around.

'It is not allowed to look into Pakistan for more than five minutes,' growled the grim-faced border guard, his thin black lips curling into an angry pout.

What would the Baba have to say to that, I wondered, as I scrambled into the waiting tonga and headed back to Ramgarh.

13

NUND RISHI
THE 'FLAG-BEARER OF KASHMIR'

The call to prayer drifted from a mosque somewhere beyond the lake, piercing the deafening silence. A thousand stars littered the black, cloudless sky like little sequins on a dark veil. Through a blanket of mist the crags of thickly forested hills jutted out like death-defying whirling monsters. The water softly lapped the houseboat, rocking it gently, swaying the oil lamp that hung from a nail on a wooden post, casting eerie shadows on the veranda. Hamid pulled furiously at his hukkah, puffing out his cheeks and letting loose a whorl of sweet-smelling smoke. His intense eyes, his carved beak-like nose, his full, pink lips and his clear, cream-coloured complexion made him altogether a handsome man, and quintessentially Kashmiri. The deep furrows in his forehead, his weary, leathery eyelids and the dark pouches below his eyes made him look at least two decades older than his actual thirty.

'There's no hope for us,' he said, matter-of-factly, as he stoked the coals in the little clay bowl of the hukkah. 'I've had no customer for the last two months. Tourists have stopped coming to Srinagar, and I still have to pay the Rs 2 lakh the bank had loaned me for this houseboat.'

I settled on a cushion in the veranda overlooking the lake. Rows upon rows of houseboats stood in a line, their shutters drawn together and locked up, abandoned by their owners for want of customers. Somewhere ahead a police patrol on a motorboat sliced through the still lake, sending up enormous waves that shook our houseboat furiously. The crackle of gunshots could be heard from the town on the other side of the lake.

'Don't worry,' said Hamid, 'nothing will happen here. Or, if anything has to happen it will, and there's nothing that you can do about it.'

Gunshots rent the air for almost five minutes. Hamid shrugged his shoulders and lifted his eyes towards heaven. Sulaiman, Hamid's brother, ran his fingers through his beard and said, 'Whatever Allah wills, will happen. Who knows who has been killed there now? It must be another innocent child or woman. Seventy thousand already killed. We've even stopped counting.'

I took a deep drag from Hamid's hukkah. The smoke shot straight down my throat, and I broke out into a cough, forgetting for a while the furious battle that was raging in the town. Hamid's wife appeared at the door with a samovar of *kahwa* tea flavoured with spices and nuts. Hamid poured the tea into little glass cups and passed them around. He had been blessed with a son a week ago, and he had invited his relatives and friends to a party.

The Pir Saheb arrived in a shikara, a slim boat covered with a frilly cloth dome, accompanied by two of his disciples. He was the head of a Sufi shrine in Srinagar, famous for his piety and scholarship. He had been on pilgrimage to the holy cities of Arabia, and earned for himself the well-deserved title of Haji. Dressed in a long, coarse woollen *firan*, a cloak that reached down to the ankles, and worn-out leather shoes, he looked like any ordinary Kashmiri peasant. His large, watery eyes exuded warmth and he seemed as gentle as a woman as he lifted up the end of his firan to climb up the steps leading to the veranda of our houseboat.

Hamid and his relatives stood at attention as the Pir came aboard, taking his hand in their own and bowing down to kiss it. The Pir hesitantly withdrew his hand and drew them into the warmth of his bosom, gently patting their backs and planting his lips on their foreheads. Tears trickled down the hollows of his cheeks. He had been away on a long journey to visit some of his other disciples, and had only just returned.

'He's come from India,' said Hamid to the Pir, as he introduced me to him. For most Kashmiris I had met, Kashmir was not a part of India, and by now, after almost two weeks in Srinagar, this no longer surprised me. The Pir took me by the hand, and led me inside. The others in the houseboat came in after us.

'Allah bless you,' he said, as he blew a draught of air on to my face after muttering an incantation in Arabic.

'What brings you to Kashmir?' he asked, as he seated himself on a finely woven carpet that had been spread out in the main hall of the houseboat.

I told him I was working on a project on Sufism and that I was in Kashmir to visit various Sufi shrines.

'Oh, then you must come to visit me at Chrar-e-Sharif tomorrow,' he said excitedly, breaking into a child-like smile. 'I'm going there for a few days to the dargah of Hazrat Nund Rishi and I'm sure you would love to see it.'

The party lasted late into the night. Hamid had arranged for cooks from a popular restaurant to come over to prepare an elaborate *wazwan* dinner—a variety of meats cooked in spices and herbs, mounds of rice and platters of nuts and fresh fruits, washed down with several rounds of sherbet and kahwa. The musicians arrived just before dinner, carrying their instruments with them—mud-pot drums, a stringed contraption like a zither and an enormous local version of a violin. For three hours they sang, plaintive Sufi dirges and odes to the Prophet and walis, the friends of Allah, while the men and the women swayed from side to side in rapture, clicking their tongues at a particularly moving verse, and sometimes throwing up their hands in uncontrollable passion.

The party finally gave over at midnight. The Pir recited a long prayer that the men and women repeated after him. Then, the women went indoors, while the men spread their blankets out on the carpet and curled off to sleep. It was too late for them to go back to their homes in the curfew-bound city.

Hamid woke me up early next morning. 'You're meant to be going to Chrar-e-Sharif today,' he chided me gently as I threatened to go back to bed. There was no time for a bath, and, in any case, it was much too cold. I packed my bags in a hurry and asked Hamid to settle the accounts. He refused to take any money for the two days I had spent on his houseboat.

'You're studying the Sufis, and that is payment enough for me,' he insisted.

We quarrelled over that for a good ten minutes, but he remained adamant.

'All right,' he finally relented. 'If you want to repay me, get me some tabarruk—blessed sugar balls—from Hazrat Nund Rishi's dargah.'

I waited on the other side of the lake for an auto-rickshaw to take me to the bus-stand. An hour had passed, but few vehicles plied on the street. A long convoy of army trucks, packed with grim-faced, dark-skinned soldiers menacingly brandishing their weapons lumbered down the road. A young man passed by and, seeing me, stopped.

'No autos on the road today,' he said. 'They've called a strike against the killing of a young man in the town by the army last night.'

The gunshots that we had heard the night before, as I learnt in the newspapers that morning, had taken the life of a newly-wed man, whom, the papers insisted, was perfectly innocent.

In Kashmir, it seemed, anyone could be killed at any time, and for any reason, and the killers could be anyone as well—

soldiers, militants, hired mercenaries or simply common criminals.

The bus to Chrar-e-Sharif was half-empty. Only a few people had dared to step out of their houses that day. Large parts of Srinagar had been placed under curfew and there were rumours of possible violent confrontation between the police and the protestors who were to take the body of the slain man to the 'Martyr's Cemetery', a large, rolling plain dotted with endless rows of graves, including a separate section of empty tombs waiting to be filled up by the seemingly never-ending stream of corpses. The bus rattled through the town, over the bridge across the Jhelum, here reduced to a stinking sewer, and past what were once neat-looking cottages of the Pundits, but were now boarded up with planks of wood, their occupants having long since fled to Jammu and Delhi.

We passed through vast stretches of paddy fields, bordered with tall, slender white-barked safeda trees, and small villages with their thatched cottages and pagoda-shaped mosques. Outside almost every village, sombre-looking soldiers stood guard, totting their guns and waving us past.

Every half an hour or so the bus screeched to a halt at an army check-post. We tumbled down from the bus, raising our hands like prisoners of war, while soldiers ran their grubby fingers roughly over our bodies to check for possible weapons.

We left the flat valley behind as we gently chugged up the narrow road snaking into the mountains. The towering peaks of the Pir Panjal ahead were covered with an early blanket of snow, and the sunlight bounced lightly off them, turning them into large sheets of gold. The branches of apple trees were weighed down with fruits, while the majestic chinars were turning a blood red in the early autumn cold. A flock of migratory geese flew overhead, and red-crested woodpeckers hobbled up the thick trunks of furry pine trees. Gujjar herdsmen, their turbans wound like bandages on their heads, drove packs of shaggy sheep down the mountains, in search of pasture and warmer climes—a picture of an idyllic paradise straight out of an India Tourism Bureau propaganda pamphlet. But the worried, fear-stricken faces of my co-passengers and their conversations, which inevitably veered round to the number of people killed or raped that day, told a very different story.

The bus finally arrived at Chrar-e-Sharif late that afternoon, after a puncture, a short lunch-break and three long halts at army check-posts. At the third check-post, a young man was dragged away by a grim-faced soldier, while the rest of us stood silently watching, dreading to imagine what would become of him.

'Shut your mouth and don't ask. Do you want to be taken away, too?' said a thunderous Jat soldier when I asked him what the matter was.

'You should be very careful with what you say to anyone,' said the elderly woman sitting next to me after we got into the bus once again. 'Who knows what they can do?'

It was Thursday evening, and throngs of pilgrims, mainly from nearby villages, had descended to Chrar-e-Sharif, the resting place of Hazrat Nuruddin Nurani, better known as Nund Rishi, the patron saint of Kashmir. Peasants, hook-nosed and firan-clad, like some forgotten Old Testament prophets, huddled together over a hukkah. Women carrying green vegetables and apples in wicker baskets hurriedly made their way from the market to the shrine. Children dressed in rags played with a punctured football, their faces smeared with dust. A group of Sufis seated on a fading *namda* rug spread out on the dusty floor of the bus-stand sipped salty tea poured into china cups from a copper samovar. Seated on a bench carved out of the roots of a giant chinar tree the Pir Saheb I had met at Hamid's house the night before was waiting for me.

'Welcome, welcome,' he grinned infectiously, the first smile I had seen that day.

As evening fell, the call to prayer, floated from the makeshift mosque. The courtyard was filled with worshippers, spilling out into the streets, their heads covered with white skullcaps, bobbing up and down as they genuflected, their faces turned towards Arabia. I stood outside, waiting for the Pir to emerge. An old man bent over a stick, walked up to me.

'Aren't you going to pray, son?' he asked, wondering what I was doing sitting on a rock while the rest of the men were immersed in prayer.

'I'm not a Muslim myself, Baba,' I replied hesitatingly.

'Oh, well, I guess it does not matter,' he mused, as he parked himself next to me on the rock and placed his hand around my shoulder. 'In Baba's *darbar*, all are welcome. Did you know that before the onset of militancy, Pundits would come here in large numbers? They used to call the Baba Sahazanad or the Beautiful One. But all that is almost finished now. The Wahhabis are taking over.' He cleared his throat and spat out in disgust.

The prayer gave over half an hour later, and the Pir emerged from the mosque followed by a crowd of supplicants. Someone wanted him to come to his house to bless his newborn child. A woman begged him for a talisman to cure her daughter who had been driven half-insane after being raped by a militant, or an army man, she wasn't sure. A young man, hobbling on a pair of bamboo poles, asked him to pray for him so that he could get his feet back.

'I can't do anything myself,' the Pir confessed, looking flustered. 'It's all in Allah's hands.'

The crowd seemed disappointed.

'If he were a true Pir he would be able to do whatever he wanted. He could even fly in the sky or walk on water,' murmured a disgruntled woman who had hoped for a miraculous cure to an unknown ailment.

'Mother, you seem to think that the Sufis are magicians,' the Pir turned to her and said gently. 'We are just ordinary human beings—we live, we suffer and we die, just like all of you.'

'These people have turned the Sufis into miracle-mongers,' he said to me, shaking his head in annoyance, as we walked down to the dargah. 'They seem to have completely forgotten that the Sufis were, above all, great social reformers. They came to change society, not to impress people with fanciful tales of miraculous powers.'

I followed the Pir down the narrow lane, and joined a band of pilgrims headed in the direction of the dargah. We climbed down a slope, passing through the remains of burnt-down houses—charred shells, broken pots and shattered, fire-stained roofs.

Memories of that fateful day in April 1995, when the shrine, along with scores of houses in the town, went up in flames, filled my mind. I shuddered at the thought of all those who perished in the flames that had engulfed the town as the Indian army and Islamist militants fought each other in a grim battle that lasted many days. The thought that I had probably been walking over the ashes of scores of little red-cheeked children transformed in a flash to mangled corpses, filled me with horror and guilt.

At the foot of the slope stood the remains of the dargah of Nund Rishi. I had seen pictures of it taken before the deadly encounter that had turned it to rubble—a towering green structure shaped curiously like a Buddhist temple, with carved wooden arches. Its inner walls of walnut wood had been painted over with flowers in little vases, and verses from the Qur'an in intricate Arabic calligraphy. Thick hand-woven carpets had graced its hallowed floors. Now, as I gazed upon it, this finest specimen of Kashmiri architecture had been transformed to a roofless box-like structure, shaded from the elements with plastic sheets. Stains from the devastating fire that had engulfed it were still visible on what remained of its walls. Piles of bricks, wood and cement bags lay strewn carelessly all around.

I followed the pilgrims, and bent down to touch the stone step at the entrance. Inside the dark tomb-chamber lay several large graves. At the centre stood the largest of the graves, that of Nund Rishi himself, draped in an embroidered silk sheet, covered with rose petals. Women wailed as they stood quivering before the grave, their open palms raised to their faces in supplication, while a group of men knelt in a corner reciting verses from the Qur'an in soft, sonorous voices. A Kashmiri Pundit, who had fled Srinagar and settled with his family in Jammu, knelt before the grave, rubbing his flaming red tilak on the ground. Tears welled up in his eyes as he choked with emotion.

'I've come to visit my Baba after ten long years,' he said, when I met him outside.

The Baba of Chrar, I thought to myself as I stood in silence, seemed unmoved by this tragic display of sorrow and solemnity, indifferent to the mayhem that had engulfed the land of which he was considered the patron saint.

I spent that night with the Pir, at the house of one of his many disciples. We stayed awake till the early hours of the morning, sipping kahwa and puffing away at our hukkahs, keeping sleep at bay till the muezzin's call to the early morning prayer floated in. I asked the Pir to tell me what he knew about Nund Rishi and the Muslim Rishis of Kashmir. This is what he told me:

Kashmir is a land of Sufis and Rishis, or Peer-vaer and Rishi-vaer as the Kashmiris call it. Legend has it that a great saint, Kashp Rishi, was the first denizen of this land. He drained the vast Satisar lake that formerly occupied the territory of Kashmir, and settled people in the country from the plains below. Numerous Rishis followed after him. Most of them retired to unknown caves in the mountains, where they spent their lives in austerities, meditating on God.

Over time, however, a rigid caste system took root in Kashmir. The Brahmins conspired to subjugate the vast majority of the people, whom they condemned as 'lower' castes, reducing them to slaves or worse. And that is why, by the third century BC, enthused by the Buddha's crusade against caste and his belief in the fundamental equality of all human beings almost all of Kashmir, barring the Brahmins, converted en masse to Buddhism.

From the seventh century, however, there was a remarkable revival of Brahminism in Kashmir. Scores of Buddhist shrines were transformed, often by force or fraud, into Brahminical temples. Hundreds of Buddhist monks were put to the sword, and the peasants and the artisans were once again turned into slaves. Soon, Buddhism was almost completely wiped out in Kashmir.

Through these tumultuous times, the 'lower' castes sought to protest against the oppression of the kings, and the Brahmins who legitimized their rule. The eighth century AD witnessed, in the form of the Traika Shaivites, the emergence of a new protest movement against the hegemony of the Brahmins. Kashmiri Shaivism preached the oneness of humankind and bitterly opposed the empty ritualism and idolatry of the Brahminical religion. But then, over time, it, too, was tamed, drained of its radical potential and absorbed into the Brahminical system.

Although the first contacts between Islam and Kashmir date back to much earlier times—unconfirmed legend has it that the Prophet Muhammad had dispatched a follower to the court of a Kashmiri prince—the first major Muslim presence in Kashmir dates from the conversion of Rinchen, the fourteenth-century Ladakhi Buddhist ruler of Kashmir. He, along with his family and some of his ministers, converted to Islam at the hands of a wandering Iranian Sufi, Bulbul Shah, after the Brahmins refused to accept him as a Hindu.

Following Bulbul Shah, many more Sufis began settling in Kashmir, travelling from as far as Iran and Central Asia. Sometime in the middle of the fourteenth century, Mir Sayyed

'Ali Hamdani, a famous Kubrawi Sufi, arrived in Kashmir. He won the favour of the then king of Kashmir, Sultan Qutbuddin, and settled in Srinagar at a hospice—the Khanqah-i-Mu'alla—that he constructed on the banks of the Jhelum. He was accompanied by 700 disciples, many of whom were expert craftsmen and artisans. It is said that they introduced several new crafts to the Kashmiris, for which they are now so well known, including papier mâché, calligraphy, and carpet- and shawl-weaving. Gradually, owing to the influence of these Sufis, a unique Kashmiri culture—an amalgam of Iranian, Arabic, Tibetan, Indic and indigenous traditions—began to evolve.

These foreign Sufis, however, did not make many converts. Most of them settled in Srinagar and other big towns, and were closer to the rulers than to the masses. They spoke and wrote in Persian and Arabic, which ordinary Kashmiris could not understand. They taught a form of Islam that stressed the importance of the law, the shari'at, and found many customs of the Kashmiris to be un-Islamic.

Spreading the teachings of Islam among the Kashmiri masses was left to Nund Rishi and the Muslim Rishi order that he established. With the Rishis, conversion to Islam now assumed the form of a mass movement. It was under their influence that almost all of Kashmir voluntarily accepted Islam. The Islam that Nund Rishi preached focused on the purification of the soul, bitterly critiquing the oppression of the Brahmins, the Mullahs and the rulers. This is why Nund Rishi is regarded by the Kashmiris as the Shaikh-ul 'Alam or 'The Teacher of the World', and as the 'Alamdar-i-Kashmir or 'The Flag-Bearer of Kashmir'.

Nuruddin Nurani, the founder of Kashmir's only indigenous Sufi order, was born in 1377, to Shaikh Salaruddin and Sadra Mauj, Rajputs recently converted to Islam, who traced their descent to the rajas of Kangra. Legend has it that soon after his birth, a woman mystic, Lal Ded or Lalleshwari, came to his parents' house to visit him. The child had refused to drink his mother's milk, and Lal Ded scolded him, saying, 'You were not ashamed to come into this world, then why do you hesitate to drink milk?' She thrust her breast into his mouth, and immediately the child began to suck at it hungrily. It is said that in this way in which Lal Ded transmitted the secrets of the inner world to him.

Little is known about Lal Ded although she occupies such an important place in the Kashmiri imagination. She is also one of the many figures revered equally by local Muslims and Pundits. She is said to have been born in a Brahmin family at the village of Sampora, near Srinagar in 1335. Like most other women of her times, she was forcibly married against her will. Her husband was an ill-tempered temple priest. Envious of her spiritual attainments, her in-laws and husband made her life miserable. In protest, she fled from their house. Living completely in the nude, she travelled from village to village, crusading against caste discrimination, and preaching the oneness of God and humankind. She is said to have resumed wearing clothes after seeing Mir Sayyed 'Ali Hamdani. When asked why, she answered, 'All this while I had not seen a true man, but now I have, so I must cover myself.'

There is little doubt that Lal Ded came under the influence of the Sufis, although her mystical verses have a distinctly local Shaivite form. Today, both Hindus and Muslims claim her as their own. Fortunately, no one knows where she is buried; otherwise Hindus and Muslims would probably have been slaughtering each other over her grave.

Tradition has it that Lal Ded died in 1400 just outside the Jami'a mosque in the town of Bijbehara. Instead of her body, her followers found a heap of flowers. Her Hindu disciples consigned them to flames, while her Muslim followers buried their share, in accordance with their own religious custom. No one can really say whether Lal Ded was a Hindu or a Muslim— it is probably best that no one knows. All, however, admit that she believed in a universal God, known by various names by Hindus and Muslims. As she herself put it:

Shiva is All-Pervading
Do not differentiate between a Hindu and a Muslim
If you have the understanding, then realize your own self
In truth, this alone is the means to realize God.

Till Lal Ded's death in 1400 when Nund Rishi was twenty-two, the two would meet regularly. It is then hardly surprising that she was a seminal influence on Nund Rishi's own understanding of religion and the world around him. So closely intertwined are their thoughts that one can easily mistake Lal Ded's *vakh*s for Nund Rishi's *shruk*s. In fact, many mediaeval chroniclers did just that, indiscriminately mixing them together. As a modern-day Kashmiri Pundit scholar notes, 'Even today it is not possible to separate the verses of the two from each other' (Nand Lal Talib, 1996).

Lal Ded employed imagery borrowed from the monotheistic Kashmiri Shaivite tradition in her poetry while Nund Rishi's compositions are set within a largely, although not exclusively, Islamic Sufi worldview. A Kashmiri-Muslim writer observes, 'As far as their statement of the love for God is concerned they both shared the same goal.' That is why, he says, 'Till this day, both the Hindus and the Muslims of Kashmir hold both of them in great esteem' (G.M. Ansari Nishat, 1965).

Nund Rishi freely acknowledged his debt to Lal Ded thus:

That Lalla of Padmanpore
Who had drunk to her full the nectar
Oh God, grant me the same spiritual status.

Elsewhere, he earnestly pleaded with God, while acknowledging Lal Ded's greatness:

Lalla drank fully at the fountain of immortality
She has witnessed the omnipotent glory of Shiva
We treasure adoration for her in the inner recesses of our hearts
She carved for herself that exalted stature
O God, grant that very same boon to me.

As a child, Nund Rishi refused to go to school, preferring to spend his time in caves and forests meditating on God and practising austerities. Forcibly married off, he renounced the world at the age of thirty. Following in the footsteps of the ancient Rishis of Kashmir, he roamed in the mountains and survived on a frugal diet of wild fruits.

Twelve years later, he came under the influence of the charismatic Iranian Sufi, Hazrat Mir Muhammad Hamdani, son of Mir Sayyed 'Ali Hamdani, and took the oath of allegiance or ba'yt from him. This was to prove a major turning point in his life. He now came to believe that fleeing from the world was sheer escapism. Helping the poor and struggling against social injustice was the only way to win God's favour.

Under Nund Rishi, Kashmiri Rishism was radically redefined as a means for social transformation and the spread of Islam. It was through the untiring efforts of Nund Rishi and his deputies or khulafa that Muslim Rishism now took the form of a mass protest movement in Kashmir, a revolt against Brahminical tyranny, on the one hand, and the legalism of the Muslim 'ulama, on the other.

While preaching Islam to the Kashmiris, Nund Rishi did not overlook what was of value in the pre-Islamic religious traditions of the land. Just as he had eagerly accepted Lal Ded as one of his spiritual guides, he was equally willing to learn from other Hindu sources. There is an interesting story about how, stirred by the simple kindness of a humble Hindu peasant girl who could not speak, he pleaded with God to help him walk in her path.

Bhawan earned her livelihood carrying pots of water from the river below to a village perched on a hilltop, and spent all her savings feeding wild birds while she herself starved. When Nund Rishi met her on one of his travels, so moved was he by her example that he cried out to God thus:

The dumb girl in a small village
Who quenched the pangs of the thirsty

Flew in the high heavens with her pet birds.
Bestow on me, my Lord, the same grace.

Nund Rishi's expansive understanding of Islam enabled Rishism to take Islam to the Kashmiri countryside, by making the new religion intelligible to the populace. Inculturating itself to the Kashmiri milieu, Islam, as presented by the Rishis, readily appealed to the Kashmiris, for it did not appear to them as an alien and radically new religion, but as one firmly rooted in their own traditional view of the world. Thus, the Muslim Rishis followed several practices associated with pre-Islamic Rishism, adding a new dimension to them, although for this they were often condemned by the 'ulama as un-Islamic.

Nund Rishi and his disciples were strict vegetarians, so much so that they desisted from eating fresh vegetables, on the grounds that this would mean taking the life of sentient beings. Most of them survived on a frugal diet of water and dried leaves from the jungles, probably being a legacy of the centuries of the Buddhist presence in Kashmir. Many Rishis remained unmarried, and were sternly rebuked for this by the 'ulama attached to the royal court, who saw them as defying the sunnat or practice of the Prophet Muhammad.

Unlike the Iranian and Central Asian Sufis, the Rishis wrote and preached in the local language, emerging as the pioneers of Kashmiri literature as they endeared themselves to the common people. In contrast to the voluminous tomes that Pundits and Mullahs penned, often to please the rulers, the Rishis composed mystical verses that were easily memorized, set to tune and sung. The verses were suffused with metaphors reflecting the daily lives and tribulations of peasants and artisans. In fact, what seems to have particularly attracted vast masses of downtrodden Kashmiris to the Muslim Rishis was their message of social emancipation, which, along with devotion to God, seems to be the central theme of Nund Rishi's poetry. Thus, bitterly critiquing the Brahmins for their oppression of the 'lower' castes, Nund Rishi cried out:

One who prides himself in his caste is a fool.
In this world, only the good can claim noble descent.
In the Hereafter, caste has no meaning.

He reminds, the downtrodden of their true worth:

Grass of a seemingly lower stock,
Ignored even by animals,
See, it reaches the crown of the king!
How can animals recognize its true worth?

Then again, Nund Rishi says:

He who works hard and earns a livelihood,
Offering his prayers regularly,
Leads a life meaningful.
He who toils in his fields in this way
Shall reap a rich harvest
Crossing the river, he shall remain immune to the fire.

For Nund Rishi, true religiosity was inseparable from helping the poor. As he explained to one of his principal disciples, Baba Nasru:

Oh Nasruddin! He shall win the world who serves others,
Whose beard grows white in the quest for wisdom,
And who eats only after the others have eaten.

Appealing to both Hindus and Muslims, he reminded them of the finitude of the world and of how they would finally be held accountable before God:

Feed those in need and be happy.
Think of the Day of Reckoning
When an account shall be made of each little grain.
Oh Hindus and Muslims! What reply will you give then?
If you don't take good deeds with you,
Then prepare yourself for the angel who shall drag you to Hell.
Oh Hindus and Muslims! Turn to God and enter His service.

Not surprisingly, his championing the cause of the poor and downtrodden won Nund Rishi the wrath of the religious establishment, both Hindu as well as Muslim. According to one story, an envious group of priests, variously described as pundits or maulvis, conspired to defame him and sent a dazzling female dancer named Yavan Matchi to tempt him. Their plans, however, failed. The woman repented for her ways and became his disciple. Nund Rishi is also said to have angered the reigning sultan, Sikander, by protesting against his mindless destruction of temples and forcible conversion of Hindus to Islam, so much so that the sultan ordered him to be imprisoned (Muhammad Amin Shakib, 1992). Pundit Jonaraj, a contemporary of Nund Rishi, and the court historian of Sikander's son Sultan Zain-ul 'Abidin, writes in his *Zainataringini* that Nund Rishi (whom he calls 'Mulla Nuruddin' and describes as the 'most accomplished Sufi among the Muslims') was imprisoned by Sikander 'for fear that he might cause a revolt'.

Nund Rishi bitterly critiqued the Pundits and the court 'ulama for reducing religion to a set of soulless rituals, for using it as a means for self-aggrandizement and for fuelling conflict Hindus and Muslims. In one of his numerous shruks on the cupidity of the priests he boldly declared:

The Mullah in the mosque
And the Brahmin before the idol of stone
Perhaps only one of a thousand of them will be redeemed
Otherwise, Satan shall grab them all.

Elsewhere, he was equally harsh on them:

Poring over books, they have become strangers to their own selves.
Verily, like donkeys whose backs are laden with books.
The Mullah is happy with gifts and feasts
The Shaikh is driven by greed and lust.
The Sufi stops not from cheating others.
Eating three seers of mutton and a *maund* of rice.
The old Pundit searches for a young virgin wife.
Near to his funeral pyre, he refuses for a wife a widow.

Although, or perhaps because, he remained firmly rooted in the Islamic Sufi tradition, Nund Rishi insisted that, despite their external differences, Hindus and Muslims must live together in love and harmony, as fellow creatures of God. Appealing to both Hindus and Muslims to recognize their spiritual unity, Nund Rishi cried out in anguish:

Children of the same parents,
When will Hindus and Muslims cut down the tree of dualism?
When will God be pleased with them and grant them His grace?

We belong to the same parents,
Then why this difference?
Let Hindus and Muslims worship God alone.
We came into this world like partners.
We should have shared our joys and sorrows together.*

Nund Rishi breathed his last in 1438, and was buried at Chrar, where he had spent the last years of his life. Over the centuries, Chrar emerged as Kashmir's most hallowed pilgrimage centre for Muslims and Hindus alike. But when I visited it, Chrar was no more than a ghost town with its burnt-down houses, stern-looking soldiers, curfews twelve hours a day, tales of missing men and slaughtered innocents. And yet people continue to hold on to an indefatigable faith in the Rishi of Chrar that simply refuses to die.

I spent the next week in Srinagar, consulting libraries and meeting students and teachers at the university. Teaching hours had been drastically curtailed from six to two a day, and the library closed soon after lunch. Militancy had brought in its wake an almost total collapse of the university. Gun-totting

---

*As recited to the author by a pilgrim at Chrar-i-Sharif.

militants who had once stalked the campus had now been replaced by equally fierce soldiers, nervously guarding the entrance, leaning on their guns and cursing their unenviable fate for being posted in an area where death constantly hovered over them.

I heard numerous stories of teachers and students being tortured or harassed by both militants and the army. Some had even been killed for their political affiliations. Others had simply gone missing. They might have crossed over into Pakistan, braving the icy winds and heavy snow of the high mountain passes. Or, nameless, faceless armed men on the streets might have killed them.

Salman sat bundled in a corner of the ramshackle university cafeteria, where the only food available was syrupy tea and two-day old samosas. His hair fell down in soft curls over his forehead, and his eyes were a sparkling blue. A faint smile seemed to be permanently planted on his lips, and a carefully trimmed moustache curled below his nose like a giant caterpillar. There was something very intense about him, as if an unknown sorrow had driven him to irrevocable despair and hopelessness, a predicament that almost every Kashmiri seemed to share.

Salman had spent two years at the university, but was forced to abandon his studies when, a group of armed men—Indian soldiers or militants, he did not tell me—had killed his brother. On that fateful night they had raided his house on the pretext of searching for a wanted man. They ransacked the house and, not finding the man they had come to get, shot dead his brother.

He himself had had a narrow escape, by jumping out of a window in the kitchen. It was then that he had decided to join a certain militant Islamist organization advocating Kashmir's merger with Pakistan.

He remained with this organization for a year, during the course of which he read various books on the concept of jihad, the Afghans' struggle against the Russians, the revolution of the Mullahs in Iran and the works of leading Islamist ideologues and advocates of the 'holy war' such as Maulana Maududi of the Jama'at-e-Islami of Pakistan and Sayyed Qutb of the Muslim Brethren in Egypt. For these fiery writers, internal 'renegades' were as threatening as those non-Muslims whom they condemned as 'enemies of Allah'. In particular, those Sufis who were lax in matters of the shari'at, or who did not believe in the centrality of the Islamic state and the relentless struggle against 'unbelievers', were condemned as arch-heretics, as inveterate enemies of the faith.

'Islamists believe that Sufism is an anti-Islamic plot to divide and weaken the Muslims, and dilute their faith,' announced Salman. 'They insist that religion is, above all, a matter of worldly power and that is why, for them, capturing state power is of such importance. They see the Sufis as other-worldly, as having renounced this world and thereby having weakened the Muslims and allowing what they call the enemies of God to subjugate them.' He shrugged his shoulders in obvious disapproval.

'In the course of the year that I spent with the Islamists,' he went on about a past he wished to forget, 'I, too, began to see Sufism as anti-Islamic, although my own father was himself a practising Sufi. Perhaps it was some sort of inter-generational revolt. It was also a reaction to the oppression of the Indian army. We found the Sufis too meek and mild, seemingly unconcerned about the plight of our people. Thus slogans of Islamic Revolution swept us off our feet.'

But, like many other young Kashmiris I met, Salman soon grew disillusioned with the Islamists, with their illusory promises of a grand utopia. The mounting ethnic and sectarian strife, corruption and general lawlessness in Pakistan made him firmly oppose the idea of Kashmir joining that country. The bitter internecine feuds between various Islamist groups in Afghanistan once they had succeeded in ousting the Russians had shattered his hopes for a successful Islamist struggle against the Indian army. Salman was now convinced that the only hope for Kashmir lay in independence, being free from both India and Pakistan.

'Most Kashmiris feel that way,' he whispered as a group of bearded students dressed in salwar kameez walked in. 'But we also know it is almost impossible to challenge the might of the Indian army. So, we continue to hope despite knowing that what we dream of may never be possible to achieve.' He heaved a sigh, and wiped his tear-filled eyes.

Having abandoned the Islamists and turned into an ardent Kashmiri nationalist, convinced of the need for Kashmiri independence but equally sure of its impossibility, Salman had now become a disciple of a noted Sufi Pir. Out of work, surviving on a small stipend that he received from his uncle who ran a bookstall in Srinagar, Salman spent his time studying the history of the Sufis and Rishis of Kashmir. He was writing a book on the subject and had collected a number of ancient, frayed manuscripts from old, established Sufi families.

'Sufism is true Islam,' he said authoritatively, making sure the students sitting at the table across ours, obviously Islamists of some sort, did not hear him. 'The Islamists have reduced our rich faith to a dry, empty ideology. For them the shari'at is a new idol, whereas for us, it is simply a means to an end, a road to the final goal of establishing communion with God.'

'Sufism is the path of love,' he read out from a notebook that contained his scattered, unpublished writings, articles that probably no newspaper in Kashmir would publish for fear of courting the wrath of militants.

'But for militant Islamists, love is a hated word. In the place of love for all, which the Sufis have taught, they insist that we should hate all those who disagree with us. I think they are the greatest enemies of the faith. There's no difference between them and the Hindu fascists in India. They both speak the same language—of unrelenting hatred. And they both have no understanding at all of true religion despite claiming to be its greatest champions.'

We talked about the book he was writing as we strolled in the lawns by the lake adjacent to the magnificent marble mosque of Hazratbal, one of Kashmir's most hallowed shrines and the repository of the hair of the beard of the Prophet. A great army of pigeons fluttered above its gilded turrets. Peasant women squatted in rows selling spiced beans, glassy-eyed fish and stacks of fresh vegetables in wicker baskets from the lake's famed floating gardens. A shikara floated past carrying fresh roses and marigolds.

'Much has been written about Kashmiri Sufism already,' said Salman, as we nestled under the tumbling arches of a decaying Mughal monument. 'But for most of these writers and for many ordinary believers, the Sufis are seen as superhuman heroes and performers of miracles. What I want to do is show how they actually were strong crusaders for social justice and inter-communal harmony.'

It was only by showing how relevant the Sufis were to people's daily lives, to their own struggle for a better, more peaceful and just world, he insisted, that Sufism could be rescued from the hands of the Islamists, who dismissed it as crass superstition. Salman also saw his book salvaging Sufism from those who claimed to be its defenders, the custodians or sajjada nashins of the Sufi shrines.

'They've made Sufism into a business,' he lamented, 'charging exorbitant fees for spurious cures to illnesses. Most of them are simply wily charlatans, living off the credulous poor. That is why so many people have lost their faith in the Sufis themselves.'

Salman came with me that evening to the Tourist Reception Centre to see me off on the bus to Jammu. There were no tourists in sight, of course, and I seemed to be the only non-Kashmiri present. As I boarded the bus, he slipped a packet into my hand through the window. I opened it as the bus moved out of the stand, passing through the deserted, heavily barricaded street. It contained a collection of poems by Nund Rishi translated into Urdu, and an envelope with rose petals, little sugar balls, and bits of holy tabarruk from Nund Rishi's grave.

I thought of Hamid, the houseboat owner who had asked me to bring back some of these blessed sweets for him from Chrar.

On my return I had gone to his houseboat with the present, and an embroidered cloth that the Pir had given me. Hamid's wife sat in the veranda, surrounded by a crowd of wailing women, beating their breasts and tearing their hair. Unknown killers, suspecting him to be a government informer, had shot Hamid dead the night before. His body had been found in a pool of blood in a ditch by the Jhelum with his head missing. It had probably been thrown into the river. They had buried his headless corpse near the martyrs' graveyard the next morning.

As the bus lumbered down the highway, past the martyrs' graveyard, now draped in a thick shroud of fog, I nibbled at a rose petal and said a silent prayer in my heart for him.

Conclusion

AND THE JOURNEY MUST CONTINUE

The travels that I have described in this book, spanning a period of two years and undertaken in several short stretches, have been for me journeys of discovery. I had expected to find myself travelling to oases of harmony and tolerance, inhabited by people of different faiths. I was, however, to be disappointed. Many of the shrines I visited were now centres of furious contestation. Rival religious groups have locked horns over the ownership of the shrines' properties and the donations that they received from pilgrims. Today, as popular pilgrim centres, promising cures for worldly woes in return for a fee, they were controlled by a class of priests who lived off the fears of the credulous. The holy men whom these shrines commemorated were the first casualties of this gradual transformation. Their legacies were now fiercely disputed. Having spent their lives crusading against narrowly inscribed religious barriers, they had now been completely transformed out of recognition, into straitjacketed 'Hindus' or 'Muslims'. Saints who had bitterly critiqued sectarianism had been summarily appointed as founders of sects and religions that claimed to represent them. Reduced to the status of communal icons themselves, the radical thrust of their own basic message—their trenchant opposition to soulless ritualism, invidious distinctions of caste and community and the tyranny of priests—had almost been completely forgotten, or else drained of all subversive potential.

As I write these lines, a genocide of sorts has taken place in Gujarat. According to unofficial reports, well over 2000 people have been killed, many of them hapless children and women, burnt alive for no fault of their own. A hundred dargahs or more where Hindus and Muslims had, for centuries, worshipped together, have been reduced to rubble by violent mobs, encouraged by the agencies of the State.

Shared religious traditions seem to have little power to resist the growing might of organized religious fascism. And not just in Gujarat, but everywhere else in India, too, such traditions have been wiped out by religious terrorism. In Kashmir, for instance, almost every village is home to a dargah, but this has not prevented Islamist radicals, many of whom are vehemently opposed to Sufism, from carving out a large constituency for themselves.

At times such as these it is easy to despair and abandon all hope for a return to sanity. And yet, the struggle must go on, and we must eventually learn to come to terms with what is often the disconcerting predicament of religious pluralism. No longer can secularists afford to leave religion altogether in the hands of Hindu and Muslim militants, dismissing it as a false consciousness, a plebian myth, a mere epiphenomenon doomed to disappear with the irrevocable march of modernity. Imagine how a critical reading of a Nund Rishi or a Bulhe Shah could heal the wounds of millions of Muslims and Hindus, saving them from the depredations of Hindutva and Islamist terror, reconciling them to their common humanity. If India as a whole, and true spirituality itself, are to be rescued from ultimate doom, indigenous theologies of inter-faith dialogue and social liberation need to be resurrected urgently. In this, I believe, the inspiration and insights of the men of God whom I had 'met' in the course of my journey have a crucial role to play.

References

Chapter 1

Aslam, Muhammad Shafi, *Karzar-e-Shuddhi: Ya'ani Sarguzasht-e-Fitna-e-Irtidad*, Karim Press, Lahore, 1924.

Bari, Abdul, *Fitna-e-Irtidad Aur Musalmano Ka Farz*, Firanghi Mahal, Lucknow, 1923.

Ghubar-e-Ufak, Sayyed Ghulam Bhik Nairang, Almas Press, Delhi.

Habib, Mohammad and Afsar Salim Khan, *The Political Theory of the Delhi Sultanate*, Kitab Mahal, Allahabad.

Hutton, J.H., *Census of India, 1931* (vol. 1, Part 1), Government of India, Delhi, 1933.

Siddiqui, Abdul Halim, *Asbab-e-Irtidad*, Jami'at Markaziya 'Ulama-e-Hind, Delhi, 1923.

Chapter 2

Burman, J.J. Roy and Mathews, A.F., 'Shabarimala: Symbol of Inclusive Secularism', *Indian Journal of Secularism*, vol. 4, no. 1, January–March, 2001.

Srikant and Manoj, C.V., *Sabarimala: Its Timeless Message*, Integral Books Payyanur, 1998.

Thomas, P.T., *Sabarimalai and Its Sasatha*, Christian Institute for the Study of Religion and Society, Bangalore, 1973.

Chapter 4

Government of Karnataka, *Gazetteer of India: Karnataka State, Belgaum District*, Bangalore, 1987.

Menon, Parvathi, 'A Parivar Project in Karnataka,' *Frontline*, 1 January 1999.

Srikanth, B.R., 'Not Another Ayodhya,' *Outlook*, 14 December 1998.

Chapter 5

Elmore, Wilber Theodore, *Dravidian Gods in Modern Hinduism: A Study of the Local and Village Deities of Southern India*, Christian Literature Society of India, Madras, 1925.

Government of Karnataka, *Gazetteer of India: Karnataka State, Belgaum District*, Bangalore, 1987.

Chapter 7

Ajgaonkar, Chakor, *The Shining Glory of Sri Shirdi Sai Baba*, Diamond Pocket Books, New Delhi, 1998.

Anand, Swami Sai Sharan, *Shri Sai The Superman*, Shri Sai Baba Sansthan, Shirdi, 1998.

Hattiangadi, Shaila, *Sai's Story*, Sai Towers Publishing, New Delhi, 1998.

Kamath, M.V. and Kher, V.B., *Sai Baba of Shirdi: A Unique Saint*, Jaico Publishing House, Mumbai, 1998.

Narasimhaswamiji, H.H., *Devotees' Experiences of Sri Sai Baba*, Akhanda Sainama Sapthaha Samithi, Hyderabad, 1989.

Narayan, B.K., *Saint Shah Waris Ali and Sai Baba*, Vikas Publishing House, New Delhi, 1995.

Osborne, Arthur, *The Incredible Sai Baba: The Life and Miracles of a Modern-Day Saint*, Orient Longman, Hyderabad, 2000.

Ruhela, S.P., *Sri Shirdi Sai Baba: The Universal Master*, Sterling Paperbacks, New Delhi, 1998.

Warren, Marianne, *Unravelling the Enigma: Shirdi Sai Baba in the Light of Sufism*, Sterling Paperbacks, New Delhi, 1999.

Chapter 8

Mehta, Vimla, *Mahamati Prannath: Sachitra Gatha*, Shri Prannath Mission, New Delhi, 1979.

Nizami, Khwaja, *Fatimi Da'i-e-Islam*, Delhi, 1338, A.H.

Sila-khan, Dominique, *The Pranami Faith: Beyond 'Hindu' and 'Muslim'*, Bangalore, 2001.

Thomas, Padri John, *Mirat-ul-Hunud*, Methodist Publishing House, Lucknow, 1898.

Chapter 9

Government of India, *Census of India Report* (1961), vol. xiv, Rajasthan, Part vii–b: Fairs and Festivals.

Satyendra, *Lok Varta ki Pagdandiya*, Bharatiya Lok Kala Mandal, Udaipur, 1975.

Chapter 10

Aqil, Shafi, *Punjabi ke Qadim Sha'ir*, Anjuman-e-Taraqqi-e-Urdu, Karachi.

Azad, Abul Kalam, *The Rubaiyat of Sarmad*, trans. Syeda Saiyidain Hameed, Indian Council for Cultural Relations, New Delhi, 1991.

Basworth, C.E., *The Medieval Islamic Underworld: The Banu Sasan in Arabic Society and Literature* (part 1), E.J. Brill, Leiden, 1976.

Gupta, M.G., *Sarmad the Saint—Life and Works*, M.G. Publishers, Agra, 1991.

Hameed, Syeda Saiyidain, *Impact of Sufism on Indian Society*, unpublished manuscript, Centre for Contemporary Studies, Nehru Memorial Museum and Library, New Delhi, 1996.

Ramakrishna, Lajwanti, *Punjabi Sufi Saints*, Ashajanak Publications, New Delhi, 1973.

Rizvi, Saiyed Atthar Abbas, *A History of Sufism in India* (vol. 2), Munshiram Manoharlal, New Delhi, 1992.

Sarmadi Pir Sayyed Muhammad Ahmad, *Tazkira-i-Hazrat Sarmad Shaheed*, Kutubkhana Sarmadi, Delhi.

Subhan, John A., *Sufism: Its Saints and Shrines*, The Lucknow Publishing House, Lucknow, 1960.

Chapter 11

Gilani, Maulana Manazir Ahsan, *Ek Hindustani Sahabi: Baba Rattan Hindi Sahab-I-Rasul ke Halat*, Jamhur Book Depot, Deoband, 1987.

Srivastava, Ramlal (ed.), 'Haji Rattan Nath', *Yogavani*, vol. 9, no. 1 (special issue on the biography of Nath saints), Gorakhnath Mandir, Gorakhpur, 1984.

Chapter 13

Nishat, G.M. Ansari, 'Kashmiri Sha'yri Daur-i-Saltanat Main', *Hamara Adab*, 1965.

Shakib, Muhammad Amin, 'Rishiyat Aur Salatin-i-Kashmir,' *Rishiyat*, Rashid Nazki (ed.), Jammu and Kashmir Academy of Arts, Culture and Languages, Srinagar, 1992.

Talib, Nand Lal, 'Lalla 'Arifa', *Khayaban-i-Khayal*, Ghulam Nabi Khayal (ed.), Srinagar, 1996.